Asia's Educational Edge

Asia's Educational Edge

Current Achievements in Japan, Korea, Taiwan, China, and India

Yugui Guo

LEXINGTON BOOKS
Lanham • Boulder • New York • Toronto • Oxford

LEXINGTON BOOKS

Published in the United States of America
by Lexington Books
An imprint of The Rowman & Littlefield Publishing Group, Inc.
4501 Forbes Boulevard, Suite 200, Lanham, Maryland 20706

PO Box 317
Oxford
OX2 9RU, UK

British Library Cataloguing in Publication Information Available

Library of Congress Cataloging-in-Publication Data

Guo, Yugui, 1952–
    Asia's educational edge : current achievements in Japan, Korea, Taiwan, China, and
India / Yugui Guo.
        p.   cm.
    Includes bibliographical references and index.
    ISBN 0-7391-0737-2 (cloth : alk. paper)
    1. Educational evaluation—Asia—Cross-cultural studies.   2. Educational
indicators—Asia—Cross-cultural studies.   3. Educational planning—United
States.   I. Title.
    LB2822.75.G86 2005
    370'.95—dc22   2004016985

Printed in the United States of America

∞ ™ The paper used in this publication meets the minimum requirements of American
National Standard for Information Sciences—Permanence of Paper for Printed Library
Materials, ANSI/NISO Z39.48–1992.

Table of Contents

Tables

Figures

Foreword

Most Americans think America is the biggest and best in everything—or nearly everything. Over the past two decades there have been occasional stories in the news about some Asian nations doing better in international tests than Americans. But who cares about tests, for after all that is not what the American system is about, is it? Isn't it rather about nurturing thoughtful and creative children who will become smart workers in the new high-tech economy. Isn't America best at that?

This book by Yugui Guo, a talented scholar from China, agrees that America has indeed developed an education system that nurtures smart workers. But an astoundingly high proportion of these smart workers are actually foreign-born individuals that joined the American system for graduate or postgraduate studies. And an additional important group are the American-born children of these foreign-born individuals. In other words, America's high-tech success has depended in surprising degree on a bountiful supply of "guest" students and workers rather than on the successes of the native-born Americans.

All might be well if America could continue to borrow talent from the education systems of other nations, especially Asian nations. But there are signs that the days of the American brain gain are dated. America, thanks to September 11th, is imposing new barriers on the inflow of foreign students to the U.S. Thus Asian students are flocking to other destinations for their advanced studies. And among these destinations, a remarkable new development is the increasing number of Asian students who decide there is no place like home. Asian higher education systems have rapidly expanded in recent years and are thus offering more opportunities to their best and brightest. By 1991, more Korean students received doctoral degrees from Korean universities than from the universities in the United States, and by 1998 the same was true for Taiwan. The year 2001 marked the first year that more students graduated from Chinese universities and colleges than from American universities and colleges.

The year 2000 marked the beginning of the era when the number of Asian students seeking education outside of their home countries began to level off. Dr. Guo predicts that this leveling-off trend will be followed by a time when increasing numbers of Asian students decide to stay home rather than to study in America and then to serve as guest workers to advance the interests of corporate America. As Asians begin to stay home, America will begin to experience a shortage of smart workers. And this shortage may lead to a collapse of American leadership in global high-tech competition. One possible salvation for America might be that careers in science and engineering would become more attractive for native-born Americans. But Dr. Guo finds that native-born Americans generally perform poorly in basic courses in math and science; so relatively few are likely to become effective as smart high-tech workers.

In other words, this book tells us, based on fact after fact after fact, that the U.S. is in deep trouble unless it can find a way to reengineer American education so that it is truly the biggest and best. The book provides a number of good suggestions for this reengineering project. But mainly it warns that five Asian settings—Japan, Korea, Taiwan, China, and India—are moving very fast towards surpassing America in educational excellence. And that should not be acceptable to the American public. In the conclusion, Dr. Guo offers several sensible recommendations.

This is a well-documented argument that anyone interested in the future of American education and especially in the future of the educational underpinnings of the American high-tech economy should read. Additionally, this book will become a valuable resource for those involved in teaching courses that compare U.S. education with the accomplishments of other education systems.

—William K. Cummings
Professor of International Education and Policy,
George Washington University

Preface

This book is the product of a research project funded by Building Engineering and Science Talent (BEST) and its findings have already been used to illuminate BEST's report submitted to the United States Congress. BEST was launched as a public-private partnership by the Council on Competitiveness in September 2001 to follow through on the September 2000 recommendations made by the Congressional Commission on the Advancement of Women and Minorities in Science, Engineering, and Technology Development. The Commission issued a national call to action to redress the demographic imbalance of the U.S. technical workforce, which threatens the economic future of all Americans.

My research was requested to focus on the following questions by introducing an international perspective:

1. Quantity Issues: Given the fact that the United States clearly has been losing momentum in the production of talent in the physical sciences and engineering, does this trend reflect a global downturn of interest in these fields or does it reflect factors that are specific to the United States? Are certain economies in Asia gaining momentum?

2. Quality Issues: Given the fact that the quality of U.S. elementary and secondary education is poor in mathematics and science in comparison with education in major Asian societies, is it a matter of K–12 superior math and science preparation in these societies? Is it a matter of cultural values or education systems?

3. International Mobility: Given the fact that other nations, especially Asian countries, are increasing their capacity to provide world-class science and engineering education and R&D infrastructure, will this affect

the flow of foreign-born talent to the United States as well as the retention of such talent?

In response to the questions, this book presents to American educators the approaching challenges posed by the major Asian societies: Japan, Korea, Taiwan, Mainland China, and India.[1] These are the five leading nations and regions of Asia in terms of size and developmental level of their economies, quality of their education, and strengths of their S&T. This book also provides, from different perspectives and backed up by the most up-to-date statistics, a comprehensive picture of these Asian economies' current achievements and recent education reforms in K–12 education, higher education, and international education.

This book is based on a critical review of various research that has been published to date in English and other languages. The author has incorporated his own past research in various fields of education. The author, extensively and deliberately, conducted quantitative research with the intent to lead American policy makers and educators to the center stage so that they can make their own judgments and conclusions.

This study, which began in mid-2002 and was completed by the end of 2003, focuses mainly on the current educational practices and achievements in the five Asian nations and economies. Nevertheless, considerable attention is also devoted to tracing their historical backgrounds since World War II and to predicting their future trends. Not only will educators and researchers benefit from a review and comparative discussion of current development in the five nations and economies, so will policy makers and entrepreneurs. The United States cannot afford the price of further ignoring the positive experience and practice of other nations. Looking across cultures is one of the best ways to see beyond the blinders and sharpen our view of ourselves. The author is sure that the findings in this book will also be of great benefit to those nations, whether in Europe, Africa, Asia, or Oceania, who attempt to solve educational issues similar to those faced by the United States.

The author would like to draw readers' attention to the fact that no education system is flawless. Every system has its merits and demerits. While the author is presenting a favorable picture of these five Asian education systems, he acknowledges that these systems may be rightly criticized. In Japan, Korea, Taiwan, and China, there are, in varying degrees, too rigid administrations controlled by centralized systems, rigorous college entrance examinations, over-standardized nationwide curricula, students' passive participation in class activities, too great stress on academic courses relative to creativity training, and the relatively weak level of higher and especially graduate education. India and China continue to experience high dropout rates, relatively low literacy, and low college enrollment rates although giant strides have been made in the past half-century.

However, the purpose and task of this book is to explore the positive experience and practices in these foreign education systems in an attempt to convince the American people of the challenges posed by other nations and to provide implications for the United States in its reforms. Accordingly, the book focuses mainly on the merits, rather than the demerits, of the education systems in Japan, Korea, Taiwan, Mainland China, and India. No doubt, the American education system possesses great strengths that are well recognized worldwide.

The author hopes that this book will contribute to the existing knowledge of international and comparative education and serve as useful reference material for those who are majoring in this field.

The author plans to extend this research to comparisons of S&T (R&D) and S&T workforce between the United States and the five major Asian economies. He thinks these topics will be of equal importance and value to both educational policy-makers and comparativists.

This book, as mentioned above, focuses a special attention on two critical issues: quantity and quality of American education. Given the fact that America's high tech success has largely depended on a bountiful supply of "guest" students and workers, a question to raise is: who will fill the gap left by them if more and more "guest" workers flow back home in the future for various reasons? Even if the American educational system is able to generate adequate workers, are they of high enough quality to meet the ever-growing needs of a global economy? Assuming that the United States takes action today, and will be able to solve both the aforementioned quantity and quality issues within the next ten to twenty years as the NSB has recently declared, the most recent phenomenon—offshore outsourcing—will lead to another issue. In the future, the limited number of S&E jobs available to recent college graduates will discourage upcoming students to study in this field.

Shortly after the author completed this book, he started to work on a new project, namely, "The Potential Long-Term Impact of Offshore Out-sourcing on American Education." This topic, largely unstudied so far, will have a significant impact on the U.S. high-tech workforce, and presents a long-term challenge to the nation's leadership role in technology, military, and homeland security. He thinks this will be another hot topic for society and will present valuable implications for the country with regard to its future education and S&T policymaking. Given the fact that this issue could be a logical extension and continuation of the quantity and quality issues described in this book, he is in a better position to pioneer this research.

The author sincerely welcomes and invites anyone with the same interests to join in this research project. His contact information is as follows:

Yugui Guo
2 Prairie Landing Court
North Potomac, MD 20878
United States
E-mail: gillguo@msn.com
Or gillguo2003@yahoo.com

---

[1] Throughout this book the author will use Korea to refer to South Korea and treat Taiwan as a regional economy.

Acknowledgments

This book could not have been completed without the help of many people. First and foremost, I would like to express my sincere appreciation and heartfelt gratitude to my former advisor, Professor William Cummings, for spending so many hours copyediting the entire book and writing a nice foreword. I am much obliged to John Yochelson, President of the Building Engineering and Science Talent (BEST), who assisted with the initial outline for this research and provided thoughtful guidance.

I am deeply indebted to Alfred Berkeley, Chairman of the Community of Science, Inc. and former President and then Vice Chair of the Nasdaq Stock Market, Inc., whose strong recommendation and encouragement have led to my involvement in this important and successful research project.

I am particularly grateful to Rebekka Brooks, my editor at Lexington Books, for her valuable and professional comments. Her editing work goes far beyond the bounds of her duty.

I would like to extend my special thanks to Jean Johnson and her colleagues at the National Science Foundation (NSF) for providing bulky up-to-date data without which this book would have never been as substantial in content.

Many people read drafts of the book at various stages, and their suggestions and comments have greatly improved the book. These readers include Stephen Dunnett, Jean Johnson, Jing Lin, Jimil Salmi, Susan Fallon, Colette Chabbott, and David Baker.

I wish to extend my deep appreciation to all the other people who provided invaluable information and data, which were the key to the completion of the book. Special thanks go to Larry MacDonald, Hiroshi Kamiyo, and Kyewon Ryuk.

I must acknowledge the funding I received from Building Engineering and Science Talent (BEST), which made it possible for me to complete the first draft of the book.

My most profound thanks go, of course, to my wife, Jilan Chen, and son, Gill Guo, who have supported and kept me sane throughout the course of my research. They showed their understanding and patience and shared with me the hardships of a scholar's life. To them this book is dedicated.

Chapter One

Introduction

The United States has been greatly enjoying global leadership in economic affairs and research and development (R&D) over the past half century. It has the world's strongest national economy with the largest per-capita income and its R&D expenditures equal the combined total expenditures of Japan, the United Kingdom, Canada, France, Germany, and Italy. U.S. scientists and engineers produce nearly one-third of the articles published in the world's most influential technical journals. U.S. researchers participate in a wide range of international collaborative research efforts, and the results of these efforts are widely cited by scientists in other nations, attesting to their quality and usefulness.[1]

As the world enters the twenty-first century, the United States is reluctant to be confronted with the reality that its leading position in the world is challenged by economic globalization, which is characterized by the international flow of capital, technology and knowledge, and the S&T workforce. The United States' lengthy economic boom has hidden the fact that it does not provide enough skilled labor to support the country's prosperity.[2] It is no secret that the United States has long relied heavily on foreign-born scientists and engineers and increasingly so in the closing years of the twentieth century. In April 1999, 27 percent of doctorate-holders in S&E in the U.S. labor force were foreign born. The lowest percentage of foreign-born S&E doctorate-holders was in psychology (7.6 percent), and the highest percentage was in civil engineering (51.5 percent). Almost one-fifth (19.9 percent) of those with master's degrees in S&E were foreign-born. Even at the bachelor's degree level, 9.9 percent of those with S&E degrees were foreign-born. The largest percentages of foreign-born S&E bachelor's

1

degree holders were in electrical engineering (18.3 percent), chemistry (16.1 percent), and computer sciences (15.2 percent).[3]

By the year 2008, according to projections by the U.S. Department of Labor, jobs requiring technical degrees are projected to grow at three times the rate of occupations in general. An estimated 6 million job openings are projected for technically trained workers between 1998 and 2008, the majority of them in computer, mathematics, and operations research; medical and health technology; and engineering. Before the end of this decade, the United States is expected to create about 2 million new jobs in science and engineering. There are currently 600,000 job openings in information technology alone.[4] The structural imbalance between America's need for, and production of, scientists and engineers, together with the risks and uncertainties of relying on imported talent, should give real urgency to questions such as: Who will do science in the new millennium given the low enrollment of U.S. undergraduate and graduate students in science and engineering? Will the U.S. K–12 education system produce enough quality S&T workforce to fill the gap left by the foreign-born talents should they become less available? The weak performance of American K–12 students in a number of international science and mathematics assessments held over the past years offers little basis for optimism in the future.

As we live in a rapidly changing world where all nations interact with each other through economic globalization and information technology, events that occur in one place inevitably affect other parts of the world. This truth leads to several questions: Does the trend away from S&E in the U.S. reflect a global downturn of interest in S&E fields? Or does it reflect factors specific to the United States? Will certain economies in Asia gain momentum and why? To answer these questions, I have selected the five major Asian economies—Japan, Korea, Taiwan, Mainland China, and India—to be our research objects. Hopefully, this research will have some value for U.S. policy makers, industrial leaders, and educators.

RATIONALE FOR SELECTING FIVE MAJOR ASIAN ECONOMIES AS THE RESEARCH SAMPLE

Why, instead of economies located closer to the U.S., such as Mexico or Brazil, have I selected nations and economies located on the other side of the earth? The following are five reasons.

First, the United States has relied more on Asian-born scientists and engineers than on those from other parts of the world: Asian students comprised 56.7 percent of all foreign students enrolled in American universities in the 2002–2003 academic year and India, China, Korea, Japan, and Taiwan are the five leading home nations and economies, whose students combined accounted for 45.1 percent of the whole foreign student population in the United States (see table 1.1).

Secondly, these five nations and economies are the most important economies in Asia in terms of their developmental level, rate of growth, and scale. Japan stands alone as the most advanced industrialized nation in the region and the world's second largest economy next to the United States. Korea and Taiwan—often referred to as two of the "four tigers" or as newly industrialized economies (NIEs)—have made dramatic leaps forward in the global economy over the past two decades. The remaining twin giants, China and India, lag far behind Japan and the two NIEs in terms of economic and technological development. Yet each of these two

Table 1.1. Leading Countries of Origin, 2002–2003

Rank	Place of Origin	2002–2003	% of U.S. Foreign Student Total
	WORLD TOTAL	586,323	100
1	India	74,603	12.7
2	China	64,757	11
3	Korea	51,519	8.8
4	Japan	45,960	7.8
5	Taiwan	28,017	4.8
6	Canada	26,513	4.5
7	Mexico	12,801	2.2
8	Turkey	11,601	2
9	Indonesia	10,432	1.8
10	Thailand	9,982	1.7
11	Germany	9,302	1.6
12	Brazil	8,388	1.4
13	United Kingdom	8,326	1.4
14	Pakistan	8,123	1.4
15	Hong Kong	8,076	1.4
16	Kenya	7,862	1.3
17	Colombia	7,771	1.3
18	France	7,223	1.2
19	Malaysia	6,595	1.1
20	Russia	6,238	1.1

Source: Institute of International Education (IIE), *Open Doors,* 2003.

nations has exhibited tremendous growth on both these fronts, therefore they are here referred to as the emerging Asian economies (EAEs). Their consecutive GDP increase at more than 7 percent and 6 percent over the past years might mean that one or both of them could become the next "tiger" of Asia.[5]

Thirdly, they are backed up by the largest population in the world—these five economies represent about 77 percent of the Asian population and 42 percent of the world's population. These five economies annually produce more than two million bachelor's degrees and almost one million S&E bachelor's degrees, 1.7 times and 2.5 times as many as the United States (see table 1.2).

Fourthly, the high educational attainment of Asian Americans, the so-called model minority in the United States, is well recognized all over the nation. The data in table 1.3 provides strong evidence that, at each grade level, a larger percentage of Asian/Pacific Islander students scored at the Basic, Proficient, and Advanced levels in 2000 than their white, black, Hispanic, and American Indian/Alaskan Native counterparts. For example, while 41 percent of Asian/Pacific Islander 12th graders scored at or above the Proficient level in 2000, only 23 percent of white, 4 percent of Hispanic, 3 percent of black, and 10 percent of American Indian/Alaskan Native 12th graders scored at that level.

The data in table 1.3 does not report scores for Asian/Pacific Islanders by nation of origin. Collapsing all Asian/Pacific Islanders into a homogeneous ethnic category can conceal wide variation in outcomes by nation of origin. Data collected in the National Educational Longitudinal Study of 1988 (see table 1.4) shows mathematics and science achievement dif-

Table 1.2.   First University Degrees and S&E Degrees Granted in Five Asian Economies and the United States, 1999 or most recent years

	All first Univ. degrees		Total S&E degrees	
Location	No.	Percent	No.	Percent
Total, all world	6,781,885	100	2,649,460	100
Five Asian economies	2,015,182	30	975,359	37
United States	1,199,579	18	384,674	15

Source: Computed and compiled by the author from: National Science Board (NSB), *Science & Engineering Indicators 2002,* vol. 2, A2-66 and A2-67.

Table 1.3. Percentage of 12th-Grade Students at Each NAEP Mathematics Achievement Level, by Race/Ethnicity: 1990 and 2000

Year and characteristic	Advanced	Proficient	Basic	Below basic
Total				
2000	2	17*	65*	35*
1990	1	12	58	42
White				
2000	3	20*	74*	26*
1990	2	14	66	34
Black				
2000	#	3	31	69
1990	0	2	27	73
Hispanic				
2000	#	4	44*	56*
1990	#	4	36	64
Asian/Pacific Islander				
2000	7	34	80	20
1990	5	23	75	25
American Indian/Alaskan Native				
2000	#	10	57	43

Note: # = Percentage is between 0.0 and 0.5.
*Significantly different from 1990 at 0.5 level.
Source: National Science Board (NSB), *Science and Engineering Indicators 2002* (Volume 1), p. 1-12.

Table 1.4. Percentile Scores on Mathematics and Science Tests in 1992 and Postsecondary Enrollment Rates by 1994 of 1998 8th-Grade Class, by Race/Ethnicity

Race/ethnicity	1992 Percentile score		Postsecondary enrollment rate by 1994
	Mathematics	Science	
All students	51	51	65
White	56	56	68
Black	33	29	57
American Indian/Alaskan Native	29	29	35
Asian/Pacific Islander	60	54	83
China	76	65	94
Philippines	62	57	89
Japan	69	67	65
Korea	75	69	95
Southeast Asia	61	52	79
Pacific Islanders	39	35	50
South Asia	71	66	91
Hispanic	39	37	54

Source: National Science Board (NSB), *Science and Engineering Indicators 2002*, vol 1, 1–13.

ferences between Asian 8th graders from different nations of origin when tested in 1992. For example, students with ancestry in China (including Taiwan), Korea, Japan, and South Asia (including India) tended to have higher scores than Asian/Pacific Islanders as a whole, and Pacific Islanders had lower scores. College attendance rates among Asian/Pacific Islanders also varied by nation of origin. For example, about 9 out of 10 Chinese, Korean, and South Asian (including India) students in the eighth-grade class of 1988 had enrolled in postsecondary education by 1992, compared with only 50 percent for those with a Pacific Island heritage.

The above-displayed high educational attainment of the "model minority" in the United States, particularly of those with ancestry in Mainland China, Japan, Korea, Taiwan, and India, should make us eager to see what the education systems in their homelands look like, how much their education systems differ from ours, how rapidly their education systems have developed and are developing, and how their respective education systems produce a high quality workforce to meet their rapid economic and R&D developmental needs.

Lastly, the U.S. approach to education is not systematically informed by experience with education in the rest of the world. In the past two decades since 1984, when the United States withdrew from UNESCO, the United States has been isolated from the international community of education. Consequently, U.S. policy makers, researchers, and educators have been offered little information about differences in education systems in various nations. Most individual policy makers, practitioners, and parents in the United States know little more about education in other nations than that "we are not number one in mathematics and science."[6] So this book intends to increase the knowledge base and broaden the U.S. perspective by introducing unique Asian educational ideas, beliefs, values, and practices. Hopefully, U.S. policy makers, researchers, educators, businesspeople, and the general public will review these Asian ideas, beliefs, values, and practices and incorporate those that have the potential for improving education in the United States.

EXPLANATION OF BOOK'S STRUCTURE

Chapter 2 highlights both quantity and quality issues facing the U.S. education system by summarizing the statistics, setting the stage for the comparative studies to follow. Chapters 3 to 7 present results for the five Asian nations and economies examined—Japan, Korea, Taiwan, China, and India—covering the areas of K–12 education, higher education, and international education. These chapters provide a comprehensive picture of historical development, recent education reforms, and current achievements in the respective education systems. Chapter 8 provides both quantitative and qualitative comparisons between the education system of the United States and those of these five Asian nations and economies. The final chapter highlights implications for the United States in its education reform.

The collection of up-to-date data is very important for this research. It is, however, difficult to obtain adequate data for comparative use. I have done my best, employing numerous channels, but the results are still not satisfactory. I must make do with the data currently available.

NOTES

1. National Science Board (NSB), *Science and Engineering Indicators—2002*, vol. 1 (Arlington, VA: National Science Foundation, 2002), 2.

2. Shirley Ann Jackson, "The Quiet Crisis: Falling Short in Producing American Scientific and Technical Talent," *Building Engineering and Science Talent* 2002, http://www.bestworkforce.org/publications.htm (10 Sept. 2002), 2.

3. National Science Board (NSB), *Science and Engineering Indicators—2002*, vol. 1, 3-3.

4. Jackson, "The Quiet Crisis," 3.

5. Lawrence M. Rausch, *Asia's New High Tech Competitors*. U.S. National Science Foundation, NSF 95-309, http://www.nsf.gov/sbe/srs/s4495/report.htm (14 Nov. 2002).

6. Colette Chabbott and Emerson J. Elliott, ed. *Understanding Others, Educating Ourselves*. The National Academies Press (Washington, DC: 2003), 2.

Chapter Two

The Challenges Facing U.S. Education

Summary of findings: Historically, the United States has benefited from the contributions of foreign-born scientists, engineers, and graduate students. This foreign-born talent has helped advance the frontiers of knowledge and propel the United States to a position of global leadership in S&T. Analyses of current trends in supply and demand indicate both quantity and quality issues: Who will fill the gap left by foreign scientists and engineers should they become less available some day in the future? Can the U.S. education system adequately train high-quality students to meet the growing national needs? This chapter presents a thought-provoking picture.

The United States, a relatively young nation full of pioneering and innovative spirits, is well known for its success in assimilating and developing whatever is beneficial in S&T, culture, business, and education in particular, from other parts of the world. Throughout its history, the U.S. education system has benefited immensely from ideas borrowed and adapted from the education systems of other nations. These ideas range from methods for early childhood education (France, Germany, and Italy), research-oriented higher and graduate education (Germany), goals for mass urban education (England), to the Suzuki method of teaching music (Japan).[1]

However, the United States' interest in the ideas and practices of education in other nations has greatly waned during the postwar period, since the United States rose to its position of world leadership. In 1957 the nation was shocked by the sudden launch of the Soviet Sputnik. Later the highly influential study "A Nation at Risk" (1983) made extensive use of findings from the then-current national and international comparative studies of student achievements to highlight shortcomings in U.S. education. These two events served as a timely wake-up call for the American people, who, for the first time, faced the serious quality problems in their education system, especially in math and science education. "U.S. Seniors Near Bottom in World Test," "A World-Class Education Eludes Many in the U.S.," "Poor Scores by U.S. Students Lead to 10-State Math Efforts"—headlines like these were splashed across the pages of major newspapers and journals in the United States with increasing frequency in the following years.[2]

Since then, many calls for domestic education reform have been justified by citing large gaps between the academic performance of U.S. students and their peers in other nations. Unfortunately, although various reform efforts have been promoted in the past decades, not much progress has been made in the quality of U.S. elementary and secondary education. In many subsequent international achievement tests, U.S. students still performed poorly. The situation appears even worse as the United States enters the twenty-first century—the era of economic globalization characterized by the international flow of capital, technology, and knowledge as well as S&T workforce. In addition to the above-stated educational quality issues, the United States also encounters quantity issues: America is falling short in producing scientific and technical talent. As Jackson (2002)[3] pointed out in his influential paper, there is a quiet crisis building in the United States—a crisis that could jeopardize the nation's preeminence and well-being. The crisis stems from the gap between the nation's growing need for scientists, engineers, and other technically skilled workers, and its production of them. The structural imbalance between America's need for and production of scientists and engineers, together with the risks and uncertainties of relying on imported talents, should give real urgency to the difficult questions: Who will do scientific research in the new millennium? Will the U.S. education system adequately train high-quality students to meet the ever-growing needs? In view of the low educational quality of U.S. schools, there are no grounds for optimism. These quality issues will inevitably affect the competitiveness of U.S. industry, threatening its leading position in the world.

QUANTITY ISSUES

A key challenge for the higher education system in the United States is to remain a leader "in generating scientific and technological breakthroughs and in preparing workers to meet the evolving demands for skilled labor."[4] The United States' lengthy economic boom in the last decade of the past century hid the fact that there is not enough technical talent in the pipeline to replace the skilled labor responsible for America's prosperity.[5] This section provides readers with a true picture of the quantity issues in the U.S. higher education system. The data and statistics are drawn mainly from the U.S. NSB *Science and Engineering Indicators 2002*.

Demographic Changes in Higher Education

In the past couple of decades, the size of the college-age cohort has decreased in all major industrialized countries, although within somewhat different time frames. Figure 2.1 provides comparative data for the demographic changes in the college-age cohort of the United States and other

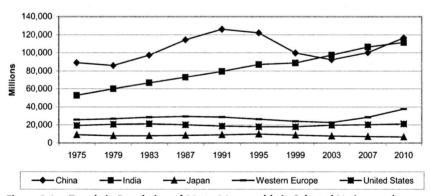

Figure 2.1.   Trends in Population of 20- to 24-year-olds in Selected Nations and Regions: 1975–2010

Source: Compiled by the author from: National Science Board (NSB), *Science and Engineering Indicators 2002* (Volume 2), p. A2-1.

selected nations and regions. The U.S. college-age population decreased from 22 million in 1980 to 17 million in 1997, a reduction of 23 percent. Western Europe's college-age population has begun an even steeper decline, from 30 million in 1985 to a projected 22 million in 2005, a reduction of 27 percent. Japan's college-age population of 10 million in 1995, which began to decline in that year, is projected to slump to a low of 7 million in 2010, representing a loss of 30 percent.

Due to these trends, the United States and other major industrialized nations have recruited foreign students to help fill their graduate S&E departments. Most of these foreign students have been drawn from developing countries with far larger populations of potential college students. For example, China and India are major countries of origin for foreign graduate students in the United States. The college-age cohorts in China and India are both at approximately 90 million and projected to reach as high as 180 million and 160 million in 2010, respectively. The large base of the college-age population in these two Asian giant nations makes it possible to maintain the momentum of producing more skilled labor.

Undergraduate and Graduate S&E Enrollment

It is of growing concern whether students in the United States are interested in studying S&E fields. Figure 2.2 reveals that the long-term trend has been for fewer students to enter engineering programs. At the undergraduate level, engineering enrollment decreased sharply from 1983 to

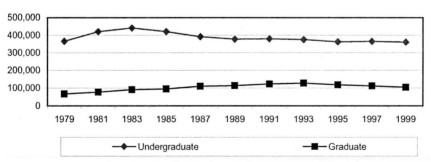

Figure 2.2.   U.S. Engineering Enrollment, by Level: 1979–1999 (full- and part-time students)

Source: Compiled by the author from: National Science Board (NSB), *Science and Engineering Indicators 2002* (Volume 2), pp. A2-9 and A2-10.

1990, followed by fluctuating and slower declines in the 1990s. At the bachelor's degree level, undergraduate enrollment declined by more than 20 percent from 441,000 students in 1983 (the peak year) to 361,000 students in 1999. At the associate degree level, enrollment in engineering technology dropped precipitously from 1981 (the peak year) to 1999. During this period, the enrollment of first-year and second-year students in such programs declined by 68 and 71 percent, from 65,893 to 21,349 and from 40,774 to 11,706, respectively. The long-term trend of increasing enrollment in graduate engineering programs persisted for a couple of decades, peaked in 1993 (at 128,081), and has continued downward since then, declining by 18 percent through 1999 (to 105,070).

Comparative Trends in U.S. White and Foreign Graduate Enrollment in Selected S&E Fields

The white student body usually constitutes a majority in graduate S&E programs in the United States, though its proportion has declined in recent decades: from 65 percent in 1975 to less than 53 percent in 1999. In contrast to the decreasing enrollment of U.S. whites in graduate S&E programs, the number of foreign students in U.S. graduate S&E programs has increased sharply. As figure 2.3 indicates, despite the four-year (between 1993 and 1996) decline, the long-term trend shows increasing enrollment of foreign graduate students in S&E fields in U.S. institutions. In 1999,

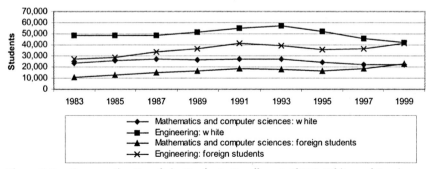

Figure 2.3.   Comparative Trends in Graduate Enrollment of U.S. White and Foreign Students in Mathematics and Computer Sciences and Engineering: 1983–1999

Source: Compiled by the author from: National Science Board (NSB), *Science and Engineering Indicators 2002* (Volume 2), pp. A2-29 and A2-30.

this increasing foreign enrollment, coupled with the declining number of U.S. white (majority) students, resulted in an approximately equal number of white and foreign students in the U.S. graduate programs in mathematics and computer sciences and in engineering.

Comparative Trends in Bachelor's Degrees Earned by All Students and Foreign Students in S&E Fields in Selected Years

When we review the long-term trend of bachelor's degrees awarded in S&E fields, we can find in table 2.1 that, from 1975 to 1998, the ratio of overall S&E degrees to total degrees remained at approximately 33 percent. But the percentages in the fields within S&E shifted during this period. From 1985 to 1998, the percentage of bachelor's degrees declined in all the fields except for biological and agricultural sciences and social and behavioral sciences. The proportion of bachelor's degrees earned in engineering declined especially steeply, from 7.8 percent in 1985 to 5.1 percent in 1998.

Foreign students usually earn a smaller percentage of S&E bachelor's degrees than of graduate degrees in the United States. However, during

Table 2.1.   Bachelor's Degrees Earned by All Students and Foreign Students in S&E Fields in Selected Years (Percentages)

Field	All students			Foreign students		
	1975	1985	1998	1977	1985	1998
All S&E*	33.7	33.5	32.6	2.5	4.1	3.6
NS&E	16.7	20.9	17.1	2.1	2.8	2.3
Physical sciences	1.7	1.6	1.3	2.5	2.7	2.7
Earth, atmospheric, and ocean sciences	0.5	0.8	0.4			
Biological and agricultural sciences	7.1	5.2	7.1	1.9	2.6	2.0
Mathematics	2.0	1.6	1.0	2.2	5.0	6.6
Computer sciences	0.5	3.9	2.3	4.1	5.4	7.9
Engineering	4.3	7.8	5.1	7.2	8.0	7.6
Social and behavioral sciences	17.5	12.6	15.4	1.6	2.1	2.5

Notes: 1. Data on foreign students include temporary residents only.
1. NS&E = natural sciences and engineering.
2. *Percentage of all bachelor's degrees.
Source: Collected and compiled by the author from:
1. National Science Board (NSB), *Science and Engineering Indicators 2002* (Volume 1), p. 2-20 and p. 2-22.
2. National Science Board (NSB), *Science and Engineering Indicators 2002* (Volume 2), pp. A2-22–A2-24.

the two decades between 1977 and 1998, the percentage of bachelor's degrees earned by foreign students increased in all S&E fields. Though trends in degrees earned by foreign students show a decrease in some fields between 1985 and 1998, their percentage increased in mathematics, computer sciences, and social sciences while the proportion in engineering leveled off.

Comparative Trends in Master's Degrees Earned by U.S. Citizens/Permanent Residents and Foreign Students in S&E Fields

Trends of declining S&E degrees earned by U.S. citizens and permanent residents at the master's degree level resemble trends at the bachelor's degree level as seen in figure 2.4. The number of degrees earned in engineering increased rapidly for more than a decade since the early 1980s, peaked in 1994, declined for the next 3–4 consecutive years, and then leveled off. The number of degrees earned in social and behavioral sciences increased strongly in the 1990s and leveled off in the past few years. The statistical trends for mathematics and computer sciences have remained stable during the past few decades. The number of degrees earned in natural sciences heavily decreased during the period between

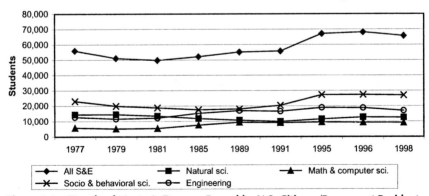

Figure 2.4. Trends of Master's Degrees Earned by U.S. Citizens/Permanent Residents in S&E Fields, 1977–1998

Source: Compiled by the author from: National Science Board (NSB), *Science and Engineering Indicators 2002* (Volume 2), pp. A2-35–A2-38.

the early 1980s and the mid-1990s. Then the numbers increased for a few years and slightly declined again from 12,803 in 1997 to 12,564 in 1998.

In contrast to the declining trends in master's degrees earned by U.S. citizens and permanent residents in S&E fields, the number of degrees earned by foreign students increased in all S&E fields during the same period (see figure 2.5). These strong increasing trends particularly took place between the late 1970s and the mid-1990s. After the mid-1990s the numbers slightly declined and then continued to increase in the subsequent years. This short-term decline was largely due to fewer Chinese students coming to the United States during the turbulent few years after the Tiananmen Square incident and the Chinese Students Protection Act. In the 1998–1999 academic year, the proportion of foreign students in some fields was considerably higher: foreign students earned about 42 percent of master's degrees awarded in engineering, about 35 percent awarded in mathematics and computer sciences, and close to 20 percent awarded in natural sciences. Even in social and behavioral sciences, foreign students earned about 11 percent of all master's degrees.

Comparative Trends in Doctoral Degrees Earned by U.S. Citizens and Non-U.S. Citizens in S&E Fields

As seen in figure 2.6, after a steady upward trend during the past two decades, the overall number of doctoral degrees earned by U.S. citizens

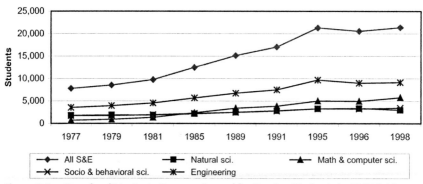

Figure 2.5.   Trends of Master's Degrees Earned by Foreign Students in S&E Fields, 1977–1998

Source: Compiled by the author from: National Science Board (NSB), *Science and Engineering Indicators 2002, volume 2, A2-35–A2-38.*

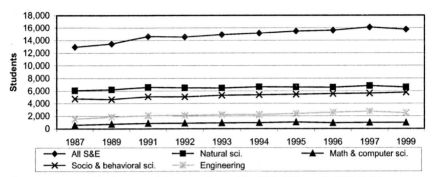

Figure 2.6. Trends of Doctoral Degrees Earned by U.S. Citizens in S&E Fields, 1987–1999

Source: Compiled by the author from: National Science Board (NSB), *Science and Engineering Indicators 2002, volume 2, A2-43.*

in S&E fields declined in 1999. Trends differ by fields. Degrees in natural sciences and in mathematics and computer sciences followed the overall pattern and declined in 1999. The number of degrees earned in engineering peaked in 1997 and declined for the next two years. However, the number of degrees earned in social and behavioral sciences kept increasing during this period.

When we turn to figure 2.7 we can see that, during the period between 1987 and 1996, the number of non-U.S. citizens earning all S&E doctoral

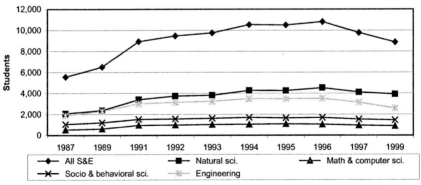

Figure 2.7. Trends of Doctoral Degrees Earned by Non-U.S. Citizens in S&E Fields, 1987–1999

Source: Compiled by the author from: National Science Board (NSB), *Science and Engineering Indicators 2002, volume 2, A2-43.*

degrees at universities in the United States steadily increased, with an increase of 7.8 percent annually, much greater than the increase in those earned by U.S. citizens (2 percent annually). After the peak year of 1996, the number of earned S&E degrees dropped off. The decline mirrors the declining enrollment of foreign students in doctoral programs from 1993 through 1996. As we mentioned previously, this short-term decline was partly due to fewer Chinese students coming to the United States during the few years after the Tiananmen Square incident and the Chinese Students Protection Act. Chinese student enrollment in U.S. S&E graduate programs declined from 28,823 in 1993 to 24,871 in 1995. Aside from the factors relating to China, there are other factors that explain the decline. The number of graduate S&E students from India, South Korea, Taiwan, Indonesia, and Malaysia also declined in various years in the 1990s because of expanded opportunities for graduate education within their own nations or regional economies. After the four-year drop-off in enrollment from 1993 through 1996, the number of foreign graduate students stabilized in 1997 and increased in 1998 and 1999. The number of non-U.S. citizens earning S&E doctoral degrees may increase within the next few years if their graduate enrollment in U.S. institutions continues to grow.

Though the number of doctoral degrees earned by non-U.S. citizens at universities in the United States decreased after 1996, their proportion of all doctoral degrees awarded increased. According to the NSB statistics, non-U.S. citizens earn a larger proportion of degrees at the doctoral level than at any other degree levels, including more than one-third of all S&E doctoral degrees awarded in 1999 as shown in figure 2.8. Similar to the master's degree level, in the 1999 academic year, the proportion of doctoral degrees earned by non-U.S. citizens in some S&E fields is very high and the ratio between the doctoral degrees earned by U.S. citizens and non-U.S. citizens is: 46:49 in engineering, 49:47 in mathematics and computer sciences, 60:36 in natural sciences, and 75:19 in social and behavioral sciences.

International Comparison of First University Degrees Earned in S&E Fields

The following sections will provide information for comparing the number of United States S&E first university and doctoral degrees and partici-

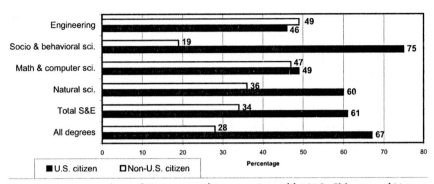

Figure 2.8.   Comparison of S&E Doctoral Degrees Earned by U.S. Citizens and Non-U.S. Citizens, 1999

Source: Compiled by the author from: National Science Board (NSB), *Science and Engineering Indicators 2002, volume 2, A2-43.*

pation rate in university degrees and S&E degrees with that in other selected nations and economies.

Figure 2.9 presents the statistics of first university degrees earned in S&E fields in selected regions in the world in 1999. In 1999, more than 2.6 million students worldwide earned a first university degree in S&E fields. Approximately 900,000 degrees were earned in fields within each

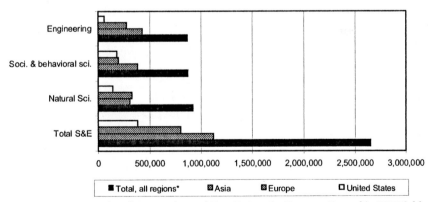

Figure 2.9.   International Comparison of First University Degrees Earned in S&E Fields in Selected Locations, 1999

Note: Total S&E include number of first university S&E degrees awarded in other parts of the world.
Source: Compiled by the author from: National Science Board (NSB), *Science and Engineering Indicators 2002, volume 2, A2-25–A-27.*

of the broad categories of natural sciences (917,721), social and behav-ioral sciences (872,629), and engineering (868,340).

From among reporting regions, 42.3 percent (1,119,405) of the 2.6 mil-lion S&E degrees were earned by Asian students at Asian universities. Students across Europe (including Eastern Europe and Russia) earned almost 800,000 first university degrees in S&E fields. Students in the United States earned only 384,674 S&E bachelor's degrees, less than half of the figure of Europe and close to one-third of the figure of Asia.

Students in Asia and Europe generally earn more first university degrees in engineering and natural sciences than in social sciences, whereas the converse is true for students in the United States. Asian nations and economies[6] produce close to half (49 percent) of all first uni-versity degrees awarded in engineering in the world. This number is approximately six times as many as the figure for the United States. In 1999, S&E first university degrees represented 73 percent of total bache-lor's degrees earned in China, 69 percent in Japan, 45 percent in Korea, and 40 percent in Taiwan,[7] whereas less than one-third (32 percent) in the United States.[8]

International Comparison of Participation Rates in First University Degrees and NS&E First University Degrees

Traditionally, the United States has been a world leader in providing broader access to higher education than most other nations in the world. The ratio of bachelor's degrees earned in the United States to the college-age cohort is relatively high—35.3 per 100 in 1998 as seen in figure 2.10. However, other nations and economies have expanded their higher educa-tion systems, and the United States is now one out of ten (1 of 10) coun-tries providing a college education to approximately one-third or more of their college-age population. Norway, the Netherlands, the United King-dom, and Australia now exceed the U.S. in the percentage of their college-age population to which they provide a college education.

In addition, in more than 17 countries and economies, the ratio of natural science and engineering (NS&E) first university degrees to the college-age population is higher than that in the United States (while in 1975, the United States ranked third) as seen in figure 2.10. The ratio of these

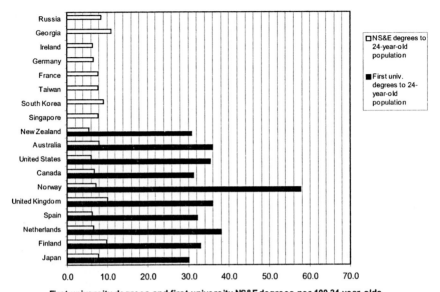

First university degrees and first university NS&E degrees per 100 24-year-olds

Figure 2.10. Ratio of Total First University Degrees and NS&E First University Degrees to 24-year-old population, by Nation or Economy, 1999 or most recent years

Source: Compiled by the author from: National Science Board (NSB), *Science and Engineering Indicators 2002, volume 2, A2-25–A-27.*

degrees to the population of 24-year-olds in the United States has been between 4 and 5 per 100 for two decades since 1975 and reached 6 per 100 in 1998. South Korea and Taiwan dramatically increased their ratios of NS&E first university degrees earned by 24-year-olds from 2 per 100 in 1975 to 9 per 100 in South Korea and almost 8 per 100 in Taiwan in 1999. At the same time, several European nations have doubled and even tripled the ratio of young people earning NS&E first university degrees to between 8 and 10 per 100.[9]

International Comparison of Doctoral Degrees Earned in S&E Fields

Figure 2.11 indicates the comparative trends in doctoral S&E degrees earned in selected Asian and European nations and economies and the United States during the last two decades from 1975 to 1998. Before the mid-1980s, the number of S&E doctoral degrees awarded annually in the

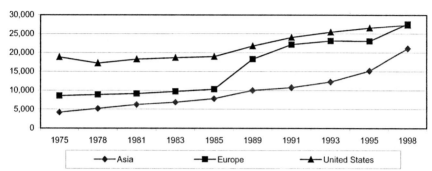

Figure 2.11.   Comparative Trends of Doctoral S&E Degrees in Selected Asian and European Nations and Economies and the United States: 1975–1998

Note:
  1. Asia includes China, India, Japan, South Korea, and Taiwan. Chinese S&E doctoral degrees were not available before 1985.
  2. Europe includes France, Germany, and the United Kingdom. French S&E doctoral degrees were not available before 1989.
  Source: Compiled by the author from: National Science Board (NSB), *Science and Engineering Indicators 2002, volume 2, A2-72–A-73.*

United States never exceeded 20,000. After the mid-1980s the number of S&E doctoral degrees earned in the United States steadily increased. This is largely attributable to the growing inflow of foreign students from Asia, particularly from China. For example, the number of foreign students earning doctoral degrees in S&E increased from 5,000 in 1986 to almost 11,000 in the peak year of 1996. During the 1986–1999 period, foreign students earned 120,000 doctoral degrees in S&E fields. China was the top country of origin of these foreign students: almost 24,000 Chinese students earned S&E doctoral degrees at universities in the United States during this period.

Europe (France, Germany, and the United Kingdom) has more than tripled their S&E doctoral degree production in the past two decades. With the data of French S&E doctoral degrees available after 1989, the number of S&E doctoral degrees earned in Europe has strongly increased since the mid-1980s. In 1998, for the first time in history, the total number of S&E doctoral degrees earned in Europe (France, Germany, and the United Kingdom) surpassed the figure of the United States: 27,593 to 27,309.

Developing Asian nations and economies, starting from a very low base in the 1970s and 1980s, have increased their S&E doctoral education by several orders of magnitude. Before the mid-1980s, the number of S&E doctoral degrees awarded annually in Asia (China, India, Japan, Korea, and Taiwan) never exceeded 10,000. Only after the mid-1980s when China resumed its doctoral education did the number of S&E doctoral degrees earned in Asia increase strongly. In 1998, the total number of S&E doctoral degrees earned in these countries and economies was 21,088: more than two-thirds of the number earned in the United States and Europe, respectively.

In 1998, Europe (France, Germany, and the United Kingdom) produced more S&E doctoral degrees (27,593) than the United States (27,309) or Asia (China, India, Japan, Korea, and Taiwan) (21,088). Within broad S&E fields, Europe produced more doctoral degrees in natural science and in math and computer sciences than the United States and Asia. (Data on Indian and Japanese doctoral degrees in the field of math and computer sciences are not available for 1998.) More doctoral degrees in engineering and agricultural sciences were awarded at Asian universities than in Europe and the United States. The United States took first place only in the field of social and behavioral sciences: it awarded more doctoral degrees than Europe and Asia combined* (see figure 2.12).

QUALITY ISSUES

The previous section presented readers with the quantity issues facing the U.S. education system. While the American people have only been concerned with the quantity issues for a decade, starting from the early 1990s, they have been troubled by the quality issues for several decades, going back to the 1950s. This section highlights the quality issues at the levels of both K–12 education and undergraduate education, particularly in the subjects of mathematics and science in K–12 education.

Mathematics and Science Performance

According to the statistics of the NSB, although performance on assessment tests for mathematics and science achievement provided by the

---

*Here the data on Indian doctoral degrees in the field of social and behavioral sciences are not available in 1998.

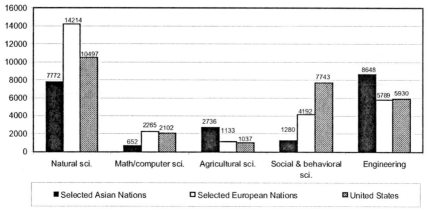

Figure 2.12.   Comparison of S&E Doctoral Degrees in Selected Asian and European Nations and Economies and the United States by Field, 1998

Note:
1. Asia includes China, India, Japan, South Korea, and Taiwan. Data on Indian and Japanese doctoral degrees in math and computer sciences are not available in 1998. Data on Indian doctoral degrees in social and behavioral sciences are not available in 1998.
2. Europe includes France, Germany, and the United Kingdom.
Source: Compiled by the author from: National Science Board (NSB), *Science and Engineering Indicators 2002, volume 2, A2-72–A-73.*

National Assessment of Educational Progress (NAEP) has improved since the 1970s, few students are attaining levels deemed Proficient or Advanced by a national panel of experts. Table 2.2 shows that only 17 percent of 12th-grade students scored at the Proficient level on the NAEP mathematics assessment in 2000. Only 2 percent of them scored at the Advanced level whereas more than one-third scored below the Basic level.

Although similar proportions of males and females scored at the Basic level or above on the 2000 NAEP mathematics assessment, boys were more likely to score at the Proficient or Advanced levels than girls. For example, 20 percent of 12th-grade males scored at the Proficient level compared with 14 percent of females, and the percentage of each group at the Advanced level was 3 and 1 percent, respectively.

Internationally, U.S. student relative performance becomes increasingly weaker at higher grade levels. On the Third International Mathematics and Science Study of 1995 (TIMSS) and 1999 (TIMSS-R), 9-year-olds tended to score above the international average, 13-year-olds near the average, and 17-year-olds below it. Even the most advanced students performed poorly compared with students in other nations taking advanced mathe-

Table 2.2.   Percentage of 12th-Grade Students at Each NAEP Mathematics Achievement Level: 1990 and 2000

Year and characteristic	Advanced	Proficient	Basic	Below basic
Total				
2000	2	17*	65*	35*
1990	1	12	58	42
Male				
2000	3	20	66*	34*
1990	2	15	60	40
Female				
2000	1	14*	64*	36*
1990	1	9	56	44

Note: *Significantly different from 1990 at 0.5 level.
Source: Cited by the author from: National Science Board (NSB), *Science and Engineering Indicators 2002* (Volume 1), p. 1–12.

matics and science courses. In some advanced subjects, such as advanced calculus, performance by the top 5 percent of U.S. students is matched by the top 10 to 20 percent of students in several other nations.

Mathematics and Science Coursework

Research suggests that, although most states have strengthened graduation requirements for high school students in the past two decades, the implication of state-level mandates for stronger course-taking requirements varies greatly across the country. As of 2000, 25 states required at least 2.5 years of math and 20 states required 2.5 years of science; in 1987, only 12 states required that many courses in math and 6 states required that many courses in science. A survey of states conducted by the Council of Chief State School Officers (CCSSO) in 2000 showed the following state totals for required credits in mathematics and science:

- Twenty-one states required between 2.5 and 3.5 credits of mathematics and four states required four credits.
- Sixteen states required between 2.5 and 3.5 credits of science and four states required four credits.
- Five states left graduation requirements to local districts.

The National Center for Education Statistics' (NCES) research undertaken in 2000 found that, although students in all racial and ethnic groups took more advanced mathematics and science courses in 1998 than before, black, Hispanic, and American Indian/Alaskan Native graduates still lag behind their Asian/Pacific Islander and white counterparts in advanced mathematics and science course-taking (see table 2.3). For example, the percentage of graduates in the class of 1998 who had taken algebra II ranged from 47 percent of American Indian/Alaskan Natives to 70 percent of Asian/Pacific Islanders. Percentages for white, black, and Hispanic graduates were 64.6, 55.6, and 48.3 percent respectively. Furthermore, Asian/Pacific Islanders were a third more likely than whites to take calculus (18.4 versus 12.1 percent) and approximately three times more likely than blacks, Hispanics, and American Indian/Alaskan Natives (about 6 percent each). This difference was more visible in AP/IB calculus: Asian/Pacific Islanders were almost twice as likely as whites to take this course (13.4 versus 7.5 percent) and approximately four times as likely as blacks and Hispanics (about 3.5 percent each). The situation is similar in science course-taking: more Asian/Pacific Islander and white

Table 2.3. High School Graduates Who Completed Selected Mathematics and Science Courses in High School, by Race/Ethnicity, 1998 (Percentage)

Courses (Carnegie units)	White	Black	Hispanic	Asian/ Pacific Islander	American Indian/Alaskan Native
Mathematics					
Algebra II (0.5)*	64.6	55.6	48.3	70.1	46.6
Calculus (1.0)	12.1	6.6	6.2	18.4	6.2
AP/IB calculus (1.0)	7.5	3.4	3.7	13.4	0.6
Science					
Biology (1.0)	93.7	92.8	86.5	92.9	91.3
AP/IB honors biology (1.0)	16.7	15.4	12.6	22.2	6.0
Chemistry (1.0)	63.2	54.3	46.1	72.4	46.9
AP/IB honors chemistry (1.0)	4.8	3.5	4.0	10.9	0.9
Physics (1.0)	30.7	21.4	18.9	46.4	16.2
AP/IB honors physics (1.0)	3.0	2.1	2.1	7.6	0.9

Notes:
1. AP = Advanced placement; IB = International Baccalaureate.
2. A Carnegie unit is a standard of measurement that represents one unit of credit for the completion of a one-year course.
3. *Includes algebra II/trigonometry and algebra II/geometry.
Source: National Center for Education Statistics, *Digest of Education Statistics 2000*, table 140, NCES 2001-034, (Washington, D.C.: U.S. Department of Education, Office of Educational Research and Improvement, 2001).

students took science courses than did their black, Hispanic, and American Indian/Alaskan Native peers, especially in physics. 46.4 percent of Asian/Pacific Islander graduates took physics in high school whereas blacks, Hispanics, and American Indian/Alaskan Natives were less than half as likely to do so.

Content Standards and Assessments

The CCSSO's 2000 research shows that most states approved policies aimed at improving the quality of K–12 education, implementing statewide curriculum guidelines and frameworks as well as assessments in the 1980s. At present, half of the states require students to pass some form of exit examination to graduate from high school, and others report they are developing such tests. In addition, by 2000, 49 states had established standards in mathematics and 46 states had established standards in science. Nearly all states conduct statewide assessments in mathematics, although the assessed grades and the types of tests vary widely. Underlying this reform agenda is the assumption that these standards and assessments will lead to higher student achievement. However, assessments and standards are not always tightly linked, and the implied performance incentives for students, teachers, and administrators vary across states.

The weak linkage between assessments and standards can been seen in the findings coming from a recent "Reality Check" Survey by Public Agenda, a nonprofit, nonpartisan research group (see figure 2.13). Employers and professors are far more disapproving than parents or teachers of how well young people are prepared for college and work, and large majorities continue to voice significant dissatisfaction about students' basic skills. This survey tracks whether efforts to set high education standards have made a difference by interviewing the students and teachers in public schools, the parents of those students, and the employers and college professors who deal with recent graduates. Employers and college professors were asked how they would rate recent job applicants/freshmen and sophomores across different topics, including clear writing, work habits, motivation and conscientiousness, and basic math skills. About two-thirds of professors found the basic math skills of recent freshmen and sophomores to be "fair" or "poor." About 80 percent stated that the ability of students to write clearly was "fair" or "poor." These results

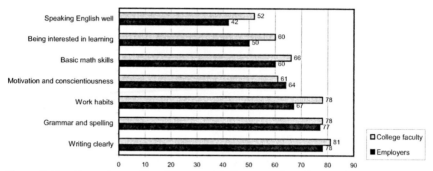

Figure 2.13.   Percentage of Employers and College Faculty Who Rated Job Applicants/ Freshman and Sophomore Students as "Fair" or "Poor" on Various Activities: 2000

Source: Compiled by the author from Public Agenda, *Reality Check 2001*, http://www.publicagenda.org/ specials/rc2001/reality6.htm (accessed July 12, 2003).

point to the continuing gap between student skill level and preparation for college and college professors' views of the adequacy of that preparation. Results were similar for employers regarding recent job applicants.

International Comparison of Curriculum and Textbook Content

International studies have shown that U.S. math and science textbooks cover comparatively more topics with less depth of coverage and development. Curriculum guides in the United States include more topics than is the international norm. Most other nations, particularly Japan and Germany, focus on a limited number of topics, and each topic is generally completed before a new one is introduced. In contrast, U.S. curricula follow a "spiral" approach: topics are introduced in an elemental form in the early grades, then elaborated and extended in subsequent grades. One result of this is that U.S. curricula are quite repetitive, because the same topic appears and reappears at several different grades as seen in figure 2.14. Another result is that topics are not presented in any great depth in the U.S. curriculum, but instead in a more shallow and unfocused manner.

Schmidt and his colleagues in their 1997 study found that U.S. curricula, especially in math, make fewer intellectual demands on students, delaying until later grades topics that are covered much earlier in other countries. U.S. mathematics curricula also were judged to be less

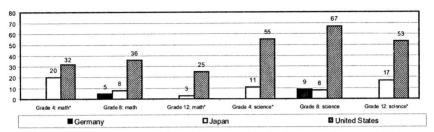

Figure 2.14. Textbook Topics of Grades 4, 8, and 12 in Germany, Japan, and the United States in Mathematics and Science Instruction: 1994–1995 (Number of topics)

Note: *Data for Germany are not available.

Source: Compiled by the author from National Science Board (NSB), *Science and Engineering Indicators 2002,* volume 1, 1–33.

advanced, less challenging, and out of step with the curriculum in other countries such as Japan and Germany (see figure 2.15). The middle school curriculum in most TIMSS countries, for example, covers topics in algebra, geometry, physics, and chemistry. Meanwhile, the grade 8 curriculum in U.S. schools is closer to what is taught in grade 7 in other nations and includes a fair amount of arithmetic. Textbooks reflect the same inadequacies documented by curriculum analyses: insufficient coverage of many topics and insufficient development of topics. Compared to textbooks used in other countries, science and mathematics textbooks in the

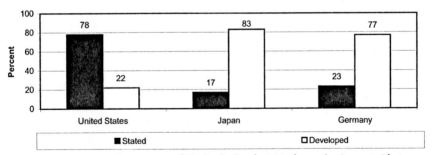

Figure 2.15. Average Percentage of Topics in Grade 8 Mathematics Lessons That Contained Topics That Were Stated or Developed* in the United States, Japan, and Germany: 1994–1995

Note: *A concept is coded as "stated" if it was simply provided by the teacher or students but was not explained or derived. A concept is coded as "developed" if it was derived and/or explained by the teacher or the teachers and students collaboratively in order to increase students' understanding of the concept.

Source: National Science Board (NSB), *Science and Engineering Indicators,* volume 1, 1–33.

United States convey less challenging expectations, are repetitive, and provide little new information in most grades.

International Comparison of Instructional Practices

Figure 2.16 presents the TIMSS video study of 8th-grade mathematics instructional practices in the United States, Japan, and Germany. Lessons in U.S., German, and Japanese classrooms were fully documented, including descriptions of the teachers' actions, students' actions, amount of time spent on each activity, content presented, and intellectual level of the tasks that students were given in the lesson.[10] These findings identified five key points:

- The content of U.S. mathematics classes requires less high-level thought than that of classes in Germany and Japan.
- The typical goal of U.S. mathematics teachers is to teach students how to do something, whereas the typical goal of Japanese teachers is to help them understand mathematical concepts.
- The U.S. teacher merely states the concept, demonstrates how to work the problems, and asks the students to practice the procedure on similar problems. Little time is spent developing connections and relationships between ideas; the focus is on practicing procedures.
- Japanese classes share many features called for by U.S. mathematics reforms, but U.S. classes are less likely to exhibit these features.

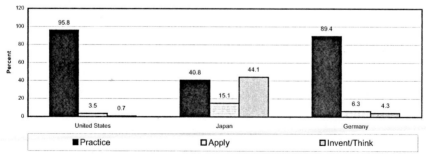

Figure 2.16. Percentage of Classwork Time Spent in Three Kinds of Tasks in the United States, Japan, and Germany

Source: Stigler, J., and Heibert, *The Teaching Gap,* New York: The Free Press, 1999, p. 71.

• Although most U.S. mathematics teachers report familiarity with reform recommendations, relatively few apply the key points in their classrooms.

Ratings by mathematicians of the quality of instruction in 8th-grade German, Japanese, and U.S. mathematics classrooms in 1994–1995 suggest a lower level of quality in U.S. instruction. 39 percent of lessons in Japanese classrooms were rated as "high quality," 51 percent were rated as "medium quality," and only 11 percent were rated as "low quality." In German classrooms, 28 percent of lessons received high ratings, 38 percent received medium ratings, and 34 percent received low ratings. In comparison, 89 percent of U.S. lessons were considered "low quality," 11 percent were considered "medium quality," and none were considered "high quality" (see figure 2.17).

Remedial Work for University Freshmen in Science and Mathematics

In 2000, the Higher Education Research Institute of UCLA conducted a survey and found that more than 20 percent of first-year college students intending to undertake an S&E major reported that they needed remedial work in mathematics; almost 10 percent reported they needed remedial work in the sciences. This percentage has been relatively stable during the past 25 years. There are some differences, however, by field of intended major as seen in figure 2.18. Students intending to major in mathematics,

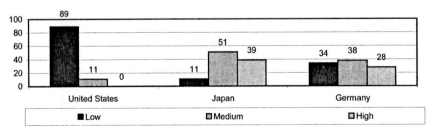

Figure 2.17.   Quality of Mathematics Content of Grade 8 Lessons in the United States, Japan, and Germany: 1994–1995 (Percentage of lessons having low, medium, and high quality)

Source: National Science Board (NSB), *Science and Engineering Indicators 2002*, volume 1, 1–33.

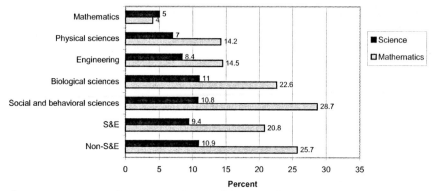

Figure 2.18.   U.S. Freshmen Reporting Need for Remedial Work in Science or Mathematics, by Intended Major: 2000

Note: Physical sciences include physics, chemistry, astronomy, and earth, atmospheric, and ocean sciences.
Source: Compiled by the author from: National Science Board (NSB), *Science and Engineering Indicators 2002*, volume 2, A2-15.

physical sciences, and engineering report a lesser need for remedial work than students in other fields. In contrast, students intending to major in social and biological sciences, as well as in non-S&E fields, report a greater need for remedial work.

Retention Rates of Students in the Fields of SMET

As a large number of freshmen in the United States are not ready for college-level coursework, particularly in mathematics and science, a considerable portion of them drop out of S&E programs. In 2000, the Center for Institutional Data Analysis and Exchange (C-IDEA) released a report of its longitudinal study, conducted from 1992 to 1998, of a cohort of college students. The study aimed to gather benchmark statistics on retention rates in science, mathematics, engineering, and technology disciplines (SMET). The study surveyed 119 colleges and universities ranging from small to large, liberal admission to highly selective admission, and bachelor's degree-only to doctorate-granting institutions. In 119 colleges and universities, about 25 percent of all entering first-time freshmen in 1992 declared their intention to major in an S&E field. By their second year, 33 percent of these students had dropped out of an S&E program. After six years, 38 percent of those that began in S&T had completed an

S&E degree. Women and underrepresented minorities dropped out of S&E programs at a higher rate than men and nonminority students. Consequently, degree completion rates in S&E fields were lower for women (35 percent) and underrepresented minorities (24 percent).[11]

Another longitudinal study made by the TX Higher Education Coordinator Board in TX LSAMP Partner Institutions in 2001 shows a similar trend (see table 2.4). From 1991 to 2000, more than 40 percent of all entering first-time freshmen or first-time transfers in the fields of SMET had dropped out of a SMET program by their second year. After six years, only between one-fourth and one-third of the cohort still remained in the fields of SMET.

CONCLUSION

The American readers may feel saddened by the dismal picture of the U.S. education system presented above. I fully understand that it is very difficult for the American people to acknowledge the fact that the average quality of U.S. students at the levels of K–12 education and undergraduate education is lagging behind that of other nations, while there is great

Table 2.4. Comparative Universal Retention by Cohort in the Fields of SMET: 1991–2000 (Percent)

	1991	1992	1993	1994	1995	1996	1997	1998	1999	2000
Fall 92	62.6%	0.0%	0.0%	0.0%	0.0%	0.0%	0.0%	0.0%	0.0%	0.0%
Fall 93	48.6%	59.2%	0.0%	0.0%	0.0%	0.0%	0.0%	0.0%	0.0%	0.0%
Fall 94	40.0%	42.5%	58.8%	0.0%	0.0%	0.0%	0.0%	0.0%	0.0%	0.0%
Fall 95	35.8%	34.2%	41.4%	56.7%	0.0%	0.0%	0.0%	0.0%	0.0%	0.0%
Fall 96	31.8%	29.9%	34.9%	41.8%	59.5%	0.0%	0.0%	0.0%	0.0%	0.0%
Fall 97	31.8%	27.8%	30.3%	34.2%	40.2%	56.7%	0.0%	0.0%	0.0%	0.0%
Fall 98	30.3%	26.7%	28.6%	28.7%	34.0%	48.2%	58.7%	0.0%	0.0%	0.0%
Fall 99	30.4%	26.2%	27.1%	26.4%	26.8%	42.6%	47.0%	59.2%	0.0%	0.0%
Fall 00	30.3%	27.5%	27.7%	27.6%	28.0%	27.5%	34.3%	43.7%	61.4%	0.0%
Fall 01	29.2%	25.7%	25.3%	24.9%	24.6%	22.8%	22.4%	26.2%	31.4%	52.7%

Notes:
1. "SMET" refers to science, mathematics, engineering, and technology disciplines.
2. Universal Retention is defined as students who remain enrolled in ANY community college or university.
3. SMET retention indicates the percentage of individuals of the original cohort that have remained in SMET majors.
Data Source: TX Higher Education Coordination Board. Sample of Minority SMET student population of 1st time freshmen or 1st time transfers in TX LSAMP Partner Institutions. 2001. Available at (22 June, 2003).

strength only at the highest educational levels, particularly at the level of doctoral education. The U.S. educators, researchers, parents, policy makers, and students themselves are under domestic pressure and challenges from abroad as well.

Fortunately, the United States has risen to meet comparable challenges before. As Jackson pointed out in 2002, whenever the American people have faced such challenges, economic and national security interests invariably have converged to marshal resources and build strength.[12] The American people are aware of the crisis and are going to meet bravely the challenges. On January 8, 2002, President Bush signed *No Child Left Behind* into law, opening a new era in the United States. As Secretary of Education Rod Paige has stated, "Never in the history of human civilization has a society attempted to educate all of its children. Under this new law, we will strive to provide every boy and girl in America with a high-quality education—regardless of his or her income, ability or background."[13]

Another wise decision has been made by President Bush, showing a very encouraging progress toward the integration of the U.S. education system into the international community of education. On September 12, 2002, President Bush announced that the United States will rejoin the United Nations Educational, Scientific, and Cultural Organization (UNESCO) after the United States withdrew from it in 1984. The President pledged to "participate fully in UNESCO's mission to advance human rights, tolerance, and learning."

Rejoining UNESCO represents a new opportunity for all parties in the U.S. education sector to share U.S. knowledge and strengths with other countries. It also provides an opportunity for the U.S. education community to participate more fully in a wide variety of informational education activities and to have broader access to information about international developments and innovations in the field of education. Under such good circumstances, the author will guide the readers across the Pacific Ocean to take a close-up look at the homelands of the U.S. "model minority"—Japan, Korea, Taiwan, China, and India. From this academic trip readers may, through comparison, draw inferences about the educational ideas and practices that have relevance for education reform in the United States.

NOTES

1. Colette Chabbott and Emerson J. Elliott, ed. *Understanding Others, Educating Ourselves*, (Washington, DC: the National Academies Press, 2003), 7.

2. Andrew C. Porter and Adam Gamoran, "Introduction," in *Methodological Advances in Cross-National Surveys of Educational Achievement*, ed. Porter, Andrew C. and Gamoran, Adam (Washington, DC: the National Academies Press, 2002), 3.

3. Shirley Ann Jackson, "The Quiet Crisis: Falling Short in Producing American Scientific and Technical Talent," *Building Engineering and Science Talent* 2002, <http://www.bestworkforce.org/publications.htm> (10 Sept. 2002), 1.

4. Greenspan, A. *Remarks of the Chairman*, Board of Governors of the Federal Reserve System to the National Governors' Association 92nd Annual Meeting (Washington, DC: July 11, 2000).

5. Jackson, "The Quiet Crisis," 2.

6. Asian nations and economies here include China, Hong Kong, India, Indonesia, Japan, Malaysia, Singapore, South Korea, Taiwan, and Thailand.

7. The ratio of S&E first university degrees to all first university degrees awarded in India is relatively low. In 1999, S&E first university degrees represented 24 percent of total bachelor's degrees earned in India (NSB, *Science and Engineering Indicators 2002*, Vol. 2, pp. A2-25–A2-27).

8. National Science Board (NSB), *Science and Engineering Indicators— 2002*, Vol. 1 (Arlington, VA: National Science Foundation, 2002), 2–38.

9. National Science Board (NSB), *Science and Engineering Indicators— 2002*, Vol. 1, 2–39.

10. James W. Stigler and James Hiebert, *The Teaching Gap* (New York, NY: The Free Press, 1999), 71.

11. National Science Board (NSB), *Science and Engineering Indicators— 2002*, Vol. 1, 2–19.

12. Jackson, "The Quiet Crisis," 4.

13. Rod Paige, the Secretary of Education, "Statement," *What to Know & Where to Go, Parents' Guide to No Child Left Behind*, Washington, DC: US Department of Education, Office of the Secretary, 2002.

Chapter Three

Profile of Japanese Education

Summary of findings: The story of Japan's educational success has been told many times in the past years. Its achievements in education are so striking and visible that many people attribute Japan's economic success to its education system. With a long tradition of respect for education that borders on reverence, Japan possesses a large pool of literate, educated, and increasingly skilled human resources. Its primary and secondary education was universalized a couple of decades ago and its gross enrollment in tertiary education reached more than 40 percent in 1999. The noteworthy features of the Japanese education system include a centrally controlled administration which is criticized as too rigid and hierarchical, the non-formal educational institutions which are closely connected with the formal system to cater to special educational needs, and the highly-developed private education sector, particularly at the level of tertiary education where the majority of students are enrolled. The efficient elementary and secondary education in Japan has long been attracting international praise though its entrance examination is so fierce that many foreigners call it "examination hell." Japan has been a leading sending country for international students to the United States for a long time, but, starting in the 1990s, it took steps to become a receiving nation by providing financial support to attract international students to study in Japan.

OVERVIEW

Growth of Japanese Education

Japan's current educational system had its foundations laid during the Meiji period when Japan embarked on a rapid modernization drive to compete with Western powers. Japan's defeat in World War II led to the introduction of important reforms during the U.S. occupation and the abolishment of ultra-nationalistic elements in the education system. Based on its own model, the Americans turned the Japanese education system into a democratic and egalitarian system. The old prewar multi-track system was replaced by the single-track 6-3-3-4 ladder which consists of six years of elementary school, three years each of junior and senior high school, and the old higher education. Higher education is characterized by a hierarchy of status integrated into two basic institutions: four years of university or two years of junior college, each of which offers general and specialized education. As a result of this reconstruction, by the time the American-guided education reform was over in 1952 more than 20 million students were enrolled in all levels of schools, from kindergartens to universities, including nearly half a million in higher education.

Table 3.1 indicates that postwar Japan has made enormous strides in providing expanded educational opportunities for its young people. In the forty years between the end of World War II and the mid-1980s, the number of students attending school in Japan increased by 1.5 times, from 16.78 million to over 24.48 million. In the mid-1980s virtually all the young people (99.99 percent) completed nine years of compulsory education, and an impressive 94.1 percent of these graduates went on to the noncompulsory senior secondary school; in turn, 30.5 percent of senior high school graduates advanced to colleges and universities. The percentage of upper secondary schools and higher education enrollment increased between 1948 and 1985: from 7.17 percent and 0.07 percent in 1948 to 21.15 percent and 9.07 in 1985, respectively. This rapid educational expansion was correlated with the Japanese economic development from the late 1950s to the 1980s, during which Japan achieved a tremendous economic growth based on technological innovation and productivity improvement. The stronger the economy became, the higher the quality it needed from the workforce. In turn, Japan was in a good position to invest more in education. In table 3.2 we can see that the expenditure

Table 3.1. Student Enrollment in Japan, 1948–1985

Year	Total	Elementary school No.	%	Lower secondary school No.	%	Upper secondary school No.	%	College & university No.	%
1948	16783097	10774652	64.20	4792504	28.56	1203963	7.17	11978	0.07
1949	17929608	10991927	61.31	5186188	28.93	1624625	9.06	126868	0.71
1950	18699055	11191401	59.85	5332515	28.52	1935118	10.35	240021	1.28
1951	19095325	11422992	59.82	5129482	26.86	2193362	11.49	349489	1.83
1952	19020432	11148325	58.61	5076495	26.69	2342869	12.32	452743	2.38
1953	19451971	11225469	57.71	5187378	26.67	2528000	13.00	511124	2.63
1954	20525698	11750925	57.25	5664066	27.59	2545254	12.40	565453	2.75
1955	21343885	12266952	57.47	5883692	27.57	2592001	12.14	601240	2.82
1956	21905731	12616311	57.59	5962449	27.22	2702604	12.34	624367	2.85
1957	22209704	12956285	58.34	5718182	25.75	2897646	13.05	637591	2.87
1958	22408542	13492087	60.21	5209951	23.25	3057190	13.64	649314	2.90
1959	22444565	13374700	59.59	5180319	23.08	3216152	14.33	673394	3.00
1960	22439947	12590680	56.11	5899973	26.29	3239416	14.44	709878	3.16
1961	22618016	11810874	52.22	6924693	30.62	3118896	13.79	763553	3.38
1962	22501599	11056915	49.14	7328344	32.57	3281522	14.58	834818	3.71
1963	22248432	10471383	47.07	6963975	31.30	3896682	17.51	916392	4.12
1964	22121566	10030990	45.34	6475693	29.27	4634407	20.95	980476	4.43
1965	21891163	9775532	44.66	5956630	27.21	5073882	23.18	1085119	4.96
1966	21376501	9584061	44.83	5555762	25.99	4997385	23.38	1239293	5.80
1967	20898726	9452071	45.23	5270854	25.22	4780628	22.88	1395173	6.68
1968	20473658	9383182	45.83	5043069	24.63	4521956	22.09	1525451	7.45
1969	20224350	9403193	46.49	4865196	24.06	4337772	21.45	1618189	8.00
1970	20111600	9493485	47.20	4716833	23.45	4231542	21.04	1669740	8.30
1971	20211392	9595021	47.47	4694250	23.23	4178327	20.67	1743794	8.63
1972	20356361	9696133	47.63	4688444	23.03	4154647	20.41	1817137	8.93
1973	20704458	9816536	47.41	4779593	23.08	4201223	20.29	1907106	9.21
1974	21085122	10088776	47.85	4735705	22.46	4270943	20.26	1989698	9.44
1975	21548231	10364846	48.10	4762442	22.10	4333079	20.11	2087864	9.69
1976	21986771	10609985	48.26	4833902	21.99	4386218	19.95	2156666	9.81
1977	22391514	10819651	48.32	4977119	22.23	4381137	19.57	2213607	9.89
1978	22852627	11146874	48.78	5048296	22.09	4414896	19.32	2242561	9.81
1979	23301316	11629110	49.91	4966972	21.32	4484870	19.25	2220364	9.53
1980	23749341	11826573	49.80	5094402	21.45	4621930	19.46	2206436	9.29
1981	24101285	11924653	49.48	5299282	21.99	4682827	19.43	2194523	9.11
1982	24317969	11901520	48.94	5623975	23.13	4600551	18.92	2191923	9.01
1983	24376285	11739452	48.16	5706810	23.41	4716105	19.35	2213918	9.08
1984	24410031	11464221	46.97	5828867	23.88	4891917	20.04	2225026	9.12
1985	24483029	11095372	45.32	5990183	24.47	5177681	21.15	2219793	9.07

Note: Data for college and university includes students enrolled in both two-year junior colleges and four-year universities.

Source: Computed and compiled by the author from: Ministry of Education, Culture, Sports, Science and Technology (MEXT), Japan, *Statistics*, 2001 <http://www.mext.go.jp/english/statist/xls/24-27.xls> (10 Oct. 2002).

Table 3.2.   Total Expenditure on Education in Japan, 1955–1998 (million yen)

Year	Expenditure on education, science, sports, and culture	Expenditure on education	
		No.	%
1955	437,350	407,482	93.17
1960	752,209	702,721	93.42
1970	3,547,031	3,237,318	91.27
1980	16,666,258	14,933,543	89.60
1985	20,424,657	18,258,314	89.39
1990	25,822,599	22,536,633	87.27
1995	30,102,175	25,734,808	85.49
1996	30,321,581	25,906,644	85.44
1997	30,380,268	25,990,317	85.55
1998	30,442,790	26,060,848	85.61

Source: Computed and compiled by the author from: Ministry of Education, Culture, Sports, Science and Technology (MEXT), Japan, *Statistics*, 2001 <http://www.mext.go.jp/english/statist/xls/168-169-1.xls> (10 Oct. 2002).

on education in 1985 was 45 times that of 1955. During the period of 1955 to 1985, the average percentage of expenditure on education was kept at over 90 percent of the total expenditure on education, science, sports, and culture.

Centrally Controlled Education Administration

It is important to point out that, although Japanese education became democratic and egalitarian, until the passage of a new National University Corporation Law on July 16, 2003, it was still very much controlled by a centralized authority.* Japanese education has benefited greatly from the jurisdictional authority of the Ministry of Education, to which prefecture governors and the prefecture boards of education report. The Ministry of Education makes educational policies and determines standards for text-

---

*Japan's parliament passed the National University Corporation Law on July 16, 2003, which will allow the biggest shake-up of the Japanese higher education system since the end of World War II. The legislation will turn state-run universities into independent administrative institutions and will eliminate the civil-service status of nearly 125,000 faculty members. This legislation paves the way for the MEXT to loosen restrictions on individual national universities and technical colleges and to allow the heads of the universities to make more independent decisions, including setting tuition within a determined range. The new laws take effect on October 1, 2003. If you would like to check the Japanese text of the National University Corporation Law, please see the following web page: <http://www.mext.go.jp/a_menu/koutou/houjin/index.htm> (29 Nov. 2003).

books, courses of study and the curriculum, teachers' qualifications, salaries, internships and in-service education, school financing, building specifications, class sizes, university entrance examinations, etc. The centralized system has been criticized by many as too rigid and hierarchical. But there are at least two merits worth noting. First, the centralized educational system makes it possible for the national government to set nationwide academic standards for all students to meet. That is why mass education in Japan does not have to be purchased with diluted quality. Time and time again, international achievements have placed the Japanese students at, or close to, the top in a variety of subjects. The National Research Council reported in 1989 that the performance of the top 5 percent of U.S. students in mathematics is matched by the top 50 percent of students in Japan.[1]

The other advantage of the centralized system is the egalitarian resource allocation. The postwar public concern with education has placed pressure on the central government to reduce inequalities in educational resource distribution including finance, teacher placement, class space, and equipment among public schools, regardless of whether each school is located in a metropolitan or a rural area. As early as 1980 William K. Cummings observed that there was virtually no variation at the compulsory level between prefectures in annual operating expenditures per student. Remarkable equality in distribution has been established with respect to the essentials. The government's equalizing measures are usually directed at disadvantaged social groups and remote areas. The measures include subsidizing children from low-income families to pay for school lunches and other regular activities, providing more equipment to raise the conditions of schools in remote areas, and authorizing hardship salary supplements so as to induce skilled teachers to take positions in these areas. For most categories of educational expenditures, such as salaries, textbooks, and lunches, the central government is required by law to pay up to half of the expenses required to realize the national standards. It is obviously the central system of finance for Japanese education that greatly facilitates the realization of equal expenditures nationwide.[2]

The Role of Non-formal Educational Institutions

The Japanese education system as a whole consists of the formal schools, which constitute the legally authorized backbone of the system, and the non-formal institutions, which cater to special educational needs. The parallel systems are so closely interconnected and mutually supporting of each other that without both systems the Japanese education system could barely function. Each stage of formal schooling is closely connected to a tremendous array of non-formal institutions and programs such as private college preparatory and cram schools and proprietary technical and vocational schools. Moreover, various lifelong learning and training programs are usually provided by corporate organizations as part of on-the-job training. Table 3.3 illustrates the dual structure of Japanese education.

The coexistence of these kinds of supporting institutions and formal schools contributes substantially to the functioning of the Japanese education system as a whole. Japan's school system has often been evaluated as the most effective system in the world in terms of low dropout rates, high academic achievements, and cost-effectiveness. However, it should be noted that such supremacy could not be maintained without extensive utilization of the huge non-formal support system that compensates for the inflexibility and uniformity of the formal education system.[3] Table 3.4 shows that, in 2000, close to one-third of elementary school students and upper secondary school students attended various kinds of cram schools. At the level of lower secondary schools, the figure was over 57.3 percent. Many parents bear heavy expenses in their children's tutoring and cram schools each year (see table 3.5). Tutoring and cram schools are a major industry in Japan.

The Role of the Private Sector

An important characteristic of Japan's education system is its dual structure, comprising a limited public sector controlled by central and local governments and an enormous market-driven private sector. Based on the founding principles of the school, private schools are developing their own unique and individualistic education and research activities, and are playing a significant role in Japanese education. In the year of 2000, 79.1 percent of kindergarten students and 29.4 percent of upper secondary students were enrolled in the private sector. The dominance of the private sector is more evident in higher education at least in terms of quantity: in 2000, 497 private junior colleges which comprised 86.9 percent of total junior colleges enrolled 91.2 percent of all junior college students; 478

Table 3.3. Parallel Structures of Japanese Education, 1987

Educational Stage	Formal Education (Types of Institutions)	Non-formal Education (Types of Institutions and Programs)
Infant Education	Kindergartens (6,263 schools and 470,000 students)	Nursery Schools (23,000 schools and 1.9 million students)
Compulsory Education	Primary Schools (25,000 schools and 11.1 million students)	Primary (16.5%, 1.8 million students)
		Secondary (44.5%, 1.8 million students)
		Remedial Juku (Hoshu-juku) Vocational & Technical Juku (Naraigoto-juku)
		Primary level (70.7%, 7.8 million students)
		Secondary level (27.4%, 1.6 million students)
	Junior High Schools (11,131 schools and 5.9 million students)	Cram Schools for entrance exam (Gakushu-juku) (50,000–100,000 institutions estimated)
Upper secondary Education	Senior High Schools (5,508 schools and 5.37 million students)	Technical and Vocational Schools (851 schools and 103,255 students)
		Miscellaneous Schools (3,918 schools and 466,049 students)
Short-cycle Higher Education	Junior Colleges (561 colleges and 437,000 students)	Specialized Technical Schools (2,581 schools and 483,000 students)
	Technical Colleges (62 colleges and 50,000 students)	Junior College Level Correspondence Education (13 colleges and 117,000 students)
		College Preparatory Schools (300 schools estimated and 200,000 students estimated)
Long-cycle Higher Education	Universities (474 universities and 1.9 million students)	Government's "Grand Schools" (15,000 students)
		Universities of the Air (17,000 students)
		University Level Correspondence Education (13 universities and 100,000 students)

(continues)

Table 3.3. (Continued)

Educational Stage	Formal Education (Types of Institutions)	Non-formal Education (Types of Institutions and Programs)
Post-Graduate Education	Graduate Schools (28 schools and 78,914 students)	Government & Private Research Institutes On-the-job Training programs
		Lifelong learning programs
		Adult Education

Source: Kitamura, Kazuyuki, "Japan" in Altbach, Philip G., ed. *International Higher Education: An Encyclopedia,* Vol. 1, Garland Publishing, Inc. 1991, pp. 492–93.

Table 3.4. Percentage of Japanese Children Attending Cram Schools, 1984–2000 (Unit: percent)

	Elementary School	Lower Secondary School	Upper Secondary School
1984	28.1	58	8.5
1985	36.5	58.6	14.6
1986	37	65.5	19.9
1987	33.5	69.7	16.6
1988	35.2	64.1	17.1
1989	36.2	63	20.4
1990	37.7	65.9	25.2
1991	38.5	66.4	21
1992	37.2	65.7	19.8
1993	49.5	64.2	35.8
1994	40.6	64.1	30
1995	31.5	62.7	29.7
1996	35.5	63.6	32.2
1997	38.6	65.3	34
1998	35.3	60	35.7
1999	31.1	57.8	29.5
2000	29.2	57.3	31.2

Source: Japan Information Network, Japan, *Statistics,* 2003, <http://www.jinjapan.org/stat/stats/16EDU-A1.html> (30 Nov. 2003).

private universities which comprised 73.7 percent of total universities enrolled 73.3 percent of all university students. The latest data on the number and percentage of Japanese private schools at different levels can been seen in table 3.6.

Although public higher education is fully financed by the Japanese government, the public institutions enroll only one-fourth of the student pop-

Table 3.5.   Expenditures for Tutors and Cram Schools in Japan, 2000 (Unit: yen)

		Expenditures for Tutors	Expenditures for Cram Schools
Kindergarten	Public	1,684	8,267
	Private	3,043	13,365
Elementary School	Public	10,174	43,593
Lower Secondary School	Public	37,688	162,357
	Private	52,444	109,959
Upper Secondary School	Public	26,112	66,181
(full-time)	Private	29,870	106,553

Note: Annual amount of expenditures per capita.
Source: Collected and compiled by the author from: Japan Information Network, Japan, *Statistics*, 2003, <http://www.jinjapan.org/stat/stats/16EDUA3.html> and <http://www.jinjapan.org/stat/stats/16EDUA4.html> (30 Nov. 2003).

Table 3.6.   Number and Percentage of Japanese Private Schools at Different Levels (2002)

Total	Private	%	Total	Private	%	Total	Private	%
Kindergarten			*Elementary School*			*Lower Secondary School*		
14,277	8,410	58.91	23,808	175	0.74	11,159	691	6.19
Upper Secondary School			*Technical College*			*Vocational School*		
5,472	1,321	24.14	62	3	4.84	3,467	3,152	90.91
Miscellaneous School			*Junior College*			*University*		
2,069	2,038	98.50	541	475	87.80	686	512	74.64
Master's Degree Program			*Doctoral Degree Program*					
1,337	822	61.48	993	582	58.61			

Source: Computed and compiled by the author from: Japan Information Network, Japan, *Statistics*, 2003, <http://www.jinjapan.org/stat/category_16.html> (30 Nov. 2003).

ulation, forcing the majority of young people to attend the more costly, but generally educationally disadvantaged and crowded private universities. Most of the public expenditures for higher education have been channeled into national institutions. Things are getting better in recent years. With the aim to maintain and improve the conditions of education and research and to alleviate the economic burdens for attending school, the central government is encouraging the efforts of private institutions by implementing various measures such as subsidy programs for supporting their running costs or the maintenance and expansion of their facilities and equipment, and long-term low-interest financings for the maintenance and expansion of their facilities and equipment. As early as 1975, the Japanese government issued the Private School Promotion Subsidy Law, which stipulated that the state could subsidize private universities up to a limit of 50 percent of their maintenance expenditure.[4]

In FY2002 MEXT started the "Special Assistance for Promoting the Advancement of the Education and Research of the Private University" program focusing on the excellent university with abundant potential and strong motivation and intending to transform it to a world-class private university, and the "Project for Promoting Industry-University Joint Research" to offer support to the research project conducted jointly by a university and a company. The statistics in figure 3.1 and figure 3.2 indicate that the financing provided to private institutions of upper secondary education increased by 5.2 times during the period of 1975 and 2002, from 979 billion yen to 6,112 billion yen. During the same period, the financial assistance to support the running costs of private institutions of higher education increased by 2.2 times, from 1,007 billion yen in 1975 to 3,198 billion yen in 2002. These measures improved the financial and other conditions of educational and research activities of private institu-

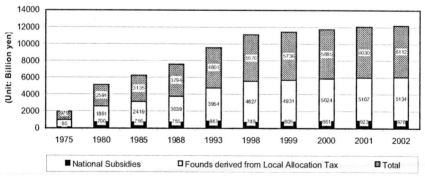

Figure 3.1.   Financing Provided to Private Institutions of Upper Secondary Education (1975–2002)

Source: MEXT, Japan, *the Role of the Ministry of Education, Culture, Sports, Science and Technology,* 2002, p. 25.

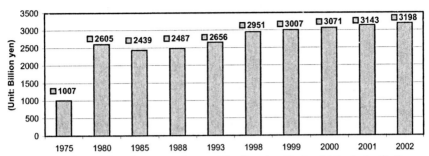

Figure 3.2.   Financial Assistance to Support the Running Costs of Private Institutions of Higher Education (1975–2002)

Source: MEXT, Japan, *the Role of the Ministry of Education, Culture, Sports, Science and Technology,* 2002, p. 25.

tions and alleviated the economic burdens of students enrolled in these institutions.

Present Educational Size and Trends

One of the important challenges during the period from the 1980s to 2002 in Japan was demographic change, which greatly affected the student enrollment at all levels except higher education. Since the 1980s, the young population in Japan has been decreasing. At the beginning of the 1980s, the age cohort for elementary school started to decrease and toward the beginning of the twenty-first century it fell to its lowest level since the post-World War II baby boom (see figure 3.3). Table 3.7 shows

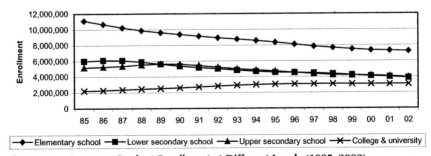

Figure 3.3.   Japanese Student Enrollment at Different Levels (1985–2002)

Source: Cited from table 3.7.

Table 3.7. Japanese Student Enrollment (1985–2002)

Year	Total	Elementary school No.	%	Lower secondary school No.	%	Upper secondary school No.	%	College & university No.	%
1985	24483029	11095372	45.32	5990183	24.47	5177681	21.15	2219793.00	9.07
1986	24306447	10665404	43.88	6105749	25.12	5259307	21.64	2275987.00	9.36
1987	24054884	10226323	42.51	6081330	25.28	5375107	22.35	2372124.00	9.86
1988	23747045	9872520	41.57	5896080	24.83	5533393	23.30	2445052.00	10.30
1989	23399111	9606627	41.06	5619297	24.02	5644376	24.12	2528811.00	10.81
1990	22978544	9373295	40.79	5369162	23.37	5623336	24.47	2612751.00	11.37
1991	22510275	9157429	40.68	5188314	23.05	5454929	24.23	2709603.00	12.04
1992	22020370	8947226	40.63	5036840	22.87	5218497	23.70	2817807.00	12.80
1993	21549432	8768881	40.69	4850137	22.51	5010472	23.25	2919942.00	13.55
1994	21129205	8582871	40.62	4681166	22.15	4862725	23.01	3002443.00	14.21
1995	20710746	8370246	40.41	4570390	22.07	4724945	22.81	3045165.00	14.70
1996	20250472	8105629	40.03	4527400	22.36	4547497	22.46	3069946.00	15.16
1997	19788767	7855387	39.70	4481480	22.65	4371360	22.09	3080540.00	15.57
1998	19387433	7663533	39.53	4380604	22.60	4258385	21.96	3084911.00	15.91
1999	19034861	7500317	39.40	4243762	22.29	4211826	22.13	3078956.00	16.18
2000	18702934	7366079	39.38	4103717	21.94	4165434	22.27	3067704.00	16.40
2001	18405495	7296920	39.65	3991911	21.69	4061761	22.07	3054903.00	16.60
2002	18084735	7239333	40.03	3862851	21.36	3929359	21.73	3053192.00	16.88

Note: Data for college and university includes students enrolled in both two-year junior colleges and four-year universities.

Source: Computed and compiled by the author from: Japan Information Network, Japan, Statistics, 2003, <http://www.jinjapan.org/stat/category_16.html> (30 Nov. 2003).

that the elementary school enrollment was over 11 million in 1985 and fell to about 7 million in 2002, a decrease of 53 percent. Starting from the late 1980s, junior and senior high school student enrollment followed a similar decreasing trend. Junior high school enrollment was close to 6 million in 1985 while senior high school enrollment was more than 5 million. Both fell to a little below 4 million in 2002, decreases of 55 percent and 32 percent, respectively. Japanese higher education was the only exception during this period due to two factors. First, the demographic change had not affected higher education as much as pre-tertiary education. Secondly, Japanese higher education kept up its expansion momentum and increased the enrollment rate of the college cohort population. These efforts accelerated the transition from "elite" to "mass" higher education in Japan. Between 1985 and 2002, the figure of post-secondary enrollment increased by 38 percent, from 2.2 million to a little over 3 million (with 267,114 junior college students and 2,786,078 four-year university students).

Statistically speaking, Japan has become one of the most education-oriented nations in the world. Compared with other industrial nations, Japan enrolls exceptionally high percentages of the appropriate age groups at each level of education. As the World Bank statistics show (see table 3.8), in 1999, both gross and net enrollment rates of male and female primary education students reached 102 percent; in secondary education females' enrollment rate, both gross and net, already exceeded males' as early as 1980, and in 1999 their gross enrollment reached 101 percent and 103 percent, respectively; in higher education, the male and female gross enrollment reached 47 percent and 40 percent respectively in 1999. In terms of these quantitative aspects, Japan has successfully developed an enormous mass education system in the relatively short period since the Westernization of the educational system was promoted by the Meiji government in the 1870s.

Table 3.8.   Japanese Educational Attainments (1980–1999)

	1980	1985	1990	1999
Gross enrollment rate (% of age group)				
Primary				
Male	101	102	100	102
Female	101	102	100	102
Secondary				
Male	92	94	96	101
Female	94	96	98	103
Tertiary				
Male	40	35	36	47
Female	20	20	23	40
Net enrollment rate (% of age group)				
Primary				
Male	101	102	100	102
Female	101	102	100	102
Secondary				
Male	92	..	..	..
Female	94	..	..	..
Expected years of schooling				
Male	13	..	..	14
Female	13	..	..	14

Source: the World Bank Statistics, 2002.

FEATURES AND CHANGES

In the previous section, a general sketch of the Japanese education system and its development in the past decades was provided. Now, I will summarize some of its features and changes, which might be of interest to the American people.

Entrance Examinations

Japanese schools evaluate students' performance on the basis of academic grades. For the transitions between the junior and senior high school levels, between the senior high school and university levels, or between the undergraduate and graduate levels, entrance examinations are utilized. This is one of the striking features that differentiates the Japanese system from the U.S. system, in which public high schools do not screen applicants, nor do universities administer their own entrance examinations. The competition resulting from Japanese entrance examinations is harsh. The sharp rise in the advancement rate of students wishing to attend universities has led to a situation in which both children and parents engage in excessive competition over entrance examinations, as schools demand higher grades. Whoever passes and does well in their tests can go to better senior schools, or to universities, including the most established and prestigious ones, or to graduate programs. Entrance examinations are the central focus of Japanese education, because there is a close connection between the quality of the schools or universities that students enter and the quality of their future employment. Graduates of the best universities are on the fast track to becoming top-level bureaucrats and executives of major corporations. As the results of entrance examinations greatly influence students' careers, both students and parents put great pressure on the schools to concentrate more on exam preparation and de-emphasize whole-person education. Apart from going to school, preparation also takes the form of attending extra-schools or hiring tutors. It is quite common for a youth to spend a year or two after high school focusing full-time on exam preparation. As the Japanese entrance examination is so fierce, many foreign scholars have called it "examination hell" or "examination war." It is said that a young person who spends more than four hours sleeping each night is sure to fail.[5]

This situation highlights the need to review and improve entrance examinations and ease the competition such exams produce. The reform measures that have been recently taken by the MEXT include allowing early university entrance for upper secondary students who have displayed academic excellence suited to the educational objective of that university and facilitating coordination between upper secondary schools and universities through, for example, university classes opened to upper secondary students. University entrance examinations, which used to be inclined to emphasize academic ability evaluation too much, have also been improved with the introduction of more diverse selection methods and criteria, the clarification of admission policy in each school, and the enhancement of multidimensional evaluation of the examinee's ability and qualification through Admission Office (AO) entrance examinations. In entrance selection of FY2001, 207 public and private universities carried out an Admission Office (AO) examination, which has been introduced by more and more universities.[6] The AO examination does not place a disproportionate emphasis on academic ability evaluation, and has the following features:

- an Admission Office does not require recommendations, and anyone who meets certain requirements can take this open examination;
- a university clarifies the qualifications desired of applicants; and
- an applicant is asked to submit various documents such as one describing the reasons for applying and an essay, and a university combines a detailed screening of the application documents and a thorough interview to judge in a comprehensive manner an applicant's willingness to study, learning ability, and sense of purpose, and to try to create a good match between the admitted applicants and the university.

Amid growing diversity in the roles of secondary schools and universities, appropriate and mutual selection between a student and university has become a guiding principle in university entrance.

Japanese Schools Are More Demanding

The centralization of the Japanese education system enables the state to exert considerable leverage over many aspects of the educational process, which includes drafting a detailed course of study, prescribing the contents of the curriculum, setting school days and hours, and inspecting commercial textbooks to ensure that they conform to the official standards. This system maintains higher standards than those of U.S. schools at the pre-college level, because the contents of national courses of study for each subject and each grade are systematically composed by the MEXT and its appointed Curriculum Council consisting of expert teachers, administrators, and scholars.

Japanese Elementary School Curriculum: Table 3.9 reflects the curriculum for Japanese elementary schools instituted in 1992, and table 3.10 shows the weekly timetable for a typical fifth grade class. There are several contrasts from U.S. elementary school curricula and timetables. First, the Japanese curriculum covers a wider range of subjects and pursues these in greater depth than is the case for the curriculum of a typical U.S. school. The differences are evident from the first grade of a primary school. Young Japanese pupils spend a larger proportion of their time than do American students in subjects such as arts, music, and physical education. While many U.S. schools do not offer a science curriculum at the primary school level, Japan does, starting from the third grade. In arith-

Table 3.9. Japanese Elementary School Curriculum:
Prescribed Subjects and Number of School Hours, 1992

Grade	1	2	3	4	5	6
Japanese Language	306*	315	280	280	210	210
Social Studies			105	105	105	105
Arithmetic	136	175	175	175	175	175
Science			105	105	105	105
Life Environment Studies**	102	105				
Music	68	70	70	70	70	70
Art and Handicraft	68	70	70	70	70	70
Homemaking					70	70
Physical Education	102	105	105	105	105	105
Moral Education	34	35	35	35	35	35
Special Activities***	34	34	34	34	34	34
Total	850	910	980	1,015	1,015	1,015

Note: *A one unit school hour is a class period of forty-five minutes.
**A new course replacing and combining social studies and science for first and second grades.
***Special activities include classroom activities, student council, club activities, and school events.
Source: Wray, Harry, *Japanese and American Education: Attitudes and Practice*, Bergin & Garvey, 1999, p. 258.

Table 3.10. Weekly Timetable for a Fifth Grade Class at Japanese Komiro Elementary School

	Monday	Tuesday	Wednesday	Thursday	Friday	Saturday
8:30–8:45	School assembly		Sports assembly		Student assembly	
8:45–8:50	Short meeting	Short meeting	Short meeting	Short meeting	Short meeting	Short meeting
8:50–9:35	Lang. Arts	Math	Lang. Arts	Math	Lang. Arts	Arts & craft
9:35–9:40	Break	Break	Break	Break	Break	Break
9:40–10:45	Math	Lang. Arts	Math	Lang. Arts	Lang. arts	Arts & craft
10:45–11:30	Science	Social studies	Home econ.	Social studies	Math	Social studies
11:30–11:35	Break	Break	Break	Break	Break	Break
11:35–12:20	Science	Math	Home econ.	Science	Homeroom	Gym
12:20–13:10	Lunch	Lunch	Lunch	Lunch	Lunch	Reflection
13:10–13:30	Cleaning	Cleaning	Cleaning	Cleaning	Cleaning	
13:30–13:50	Recess	Recess	Club Activity	Recess	Recess	
13:50–14:35	Moral ed.	Gym	Music	Gym		
14:35–14:50	Reflection	Reflection	Break	Reflection		

Source: Wray, Harry, *Japanese and American Education: Attitudes and Practice*, Bergin & Garvey, 1999, p. 259.

metic, a subject central·to both Japanese and U.S. curricula, the Japanese texts move faster than the typical U.S. text.[7]

Second, Japanese schools' weekly schedule runs 2,161 minutes, compared to the 1,850 minutes of the American school Shimahara and Sakai researched, New Jersey's Westville Upper Elementary School. This longer schedule gives Japanese schools greater flexibility to teach a more diversified curriculum. In order to cover the demanding curriculum, until recently the government required schools to operate an educational program for at least 240 days each year in contrast to 180 days for American schools. Before 1993, Japanese students spent 5.5 days in school each week. Japan eliminated one half-day on Saturday in 1993 and two half-days in 1995; in 2003 it will eliminate all Saturdays so that children attend school for only 5 days each week.[8]

Japanese Junior High School Curriculum: Japanese junior high schools continue to deal with many aspects of children. They allocate more curricular time than U.S. schools for field trips, clubs, ceremonies, homeroom, art, music, and moral education. Table 3.11 lists the new cur-

Table 3.11. Japanese Junior High School Curriculum: Prescribed Number of School Hours, 1993

Grade:	7	8	9
Japanese Language	175*	140	140
Social Studies	140	140	70–105
Mathematics	105	140	140
Science	105	105	105–140
Music	70	35–70	35
Fine Arts	70	35–70	35
Health and Physical Education	105	105	105–140
Industrial Arts & Homemaking	70	70	70–105
Moral Education	35	35	35
Special Activities	35–70	35–70	35–70
Elective Subjects (English is listed as an "elective")**	105–140	105–210	140–280
Total	1,050	1,050	1,050

Note: *One unit school hour is a class period of fifty minutes. Note that these are only minimum requirements. In practice, ambitious schools will exceed the minimum requirement for academic subjects. That flexibility is explained in number 2 below, regarding electives.

**Electives include a foreign language (English), but in fact English is not a true elective because it is required for at least 105 minutes. In academic and upward-bound schools English will be taught more during class hours. Thus, the amount of time for true electives is severely limited at the seventh and eighth grades. Schools are free to apply the extra time allotted for electives to required subjects.

Source: Wray, Harry, *Japanese and American Education: Attitudes and Practice*, Bergin & Garvey, 1999, p. 261.

riculum for junior high school students. Nine subjects are taught in Japan versus six in the U.S. curriculum. Two and one-third class periods a week are in vocational education. In theory, time for elective subjects increases slightly for seventh and eighth graders, and ninth graders can spend five and one-half hours each week taking them. In fact, since the standard school time spent on a foreign language (English) is 105 to 140 minutes at each of the three grade levels, a regrettable lack of time for taking electives at junior high schools exists. As a transition between the curriculum in the elementary and in the senior high school, the junior high school curriculum focuses on teaching both group life and knowledge. It is characterized by no skipping of grades, mainstreaming, or tracking, except for ninth grade mathematics. By this curriculum students experience both the severe academic pressure of passing entrance examinations for entering ranked high schools and the greater expectations to learn hierarchy and behavior appropriate to group life.[9]

Japanese Senior High School Curriculum: At the senior high school level there are three curricular courses: academic, specialized (vocational), and comprehensive. Table 3.12 lists the required curriculum for senior high school students. Four points can be highlighted about the academic high school curriculum. First, no life adjustment courses are offered; available elective courses are severely limited to traditional courses related to entrance examinations. Second, with the exception of classes in home economics for girls and boys, no courses are truly vocational in nature. Third, a literary or a science preference can be elected by students in their junior years. For example, literary students will take four credits of World History A, four credits of Japanese Language 1, and three credits each of Math, Physics, Biology, and English 1. Fourth, science and literary majors will be able to exercise slightly more choice than before the diversification.

All schools must teach in sequence the basic contents of Math 1, 2, and 3, and they may also select and teach topics from Math A, B, and C. Academic-track students who choose the literary option are still required to study four units (three years) each of science and math; students who choose the science and math curriculum option take a minimum of four units in integral and differential calculus, probability and statistics, and physics and chemistry. All Japanese tenth grade students must take Science 1, an integrated, general science course, for four credit hours. A

Table 3.12. Japanese Senior High School Curriculum for the Academic School Course: Standard Number of Credits for Each Subject, 1994

Subject areas	Subjects	Credits
Japanese Language Required: a	Japanese Language 1 (a) Japanese Language 2 Japanese Lang. Expression Comtemporary J'se Language Contemp. J'se Use and Usage Classics 1 Classics 2 Appreciation of Classics	4 4 2 4 2 3 3 2
Geography and History Required: a or b; and c, or d, or e, or f	World History A (a) World History B (b) Japanese History A (c) Japanese History B (d) Geography A (e) Geography B (f)	2 4 2 4 2 4
Civics Required: a; or b and c	Contemporary Society (a) Ethics (b) Politics and Economics (c)	4 2 2
Mathematics Required: a	Mathematics 1 (a) Mathematics 2 Mathematics 3 Mathematics A Mathematics B Mathematics C	4 3 3 2 2 2
Science Required: one subject each from two subject groups a, b, c, d, or e	Integrated Science (a) Physics 1 A (b) Physics 1 B (b) Physics 2 Chemistry 1 A (c) Chemistry 1 B (c) Chemistry 2 Biology 1 A (d) Biology 1 B (d) Biology 2 Earth Science 1 A (e) Earth Science 1 B (e) Earth Science 2	4 2 4 2 2 4 2 2 4 2 2 4 2
Health and Physical Education	Physical Education (required) Health (required)	7–9 2

Art	Music 1 (a)	2
Required: a, or b, or c, or d. Students	Music 2	2
who take further classes usually	Music 3	2
continue with the same subject	Fine Arts 1 (b)	2
	Fine Arts 2	2
	Fine Arts 3	2
	Crafts Production 1 (c)	2
	Crafts Production 2	2
	Crafts Production 3	2
	Calligraphy 1 (d)	2
	Calligraphy 2	2
	Calligraphy 3	2
Foreign Languages	English 1 (a)	4
Not "required" but all usually take a,	English 2 (b)	4
b, c, and either d or e	Oral Communication A (c)	2
	Oral Communication B	
	Oral Communication C	2
	Reading (d)	4
	Writing (e)	4
Home Economics	General Home Economics (a)	4
Required: a, or b, or c	Home Life Techniques (b)	4
	General Home Life (c)	4

Source: Wray, Harry, *Japanese and American Education: Attitudes and Practice*, Bergin & Garvey, 1999, pp. 264–265.

larger percentage of Japanese students than American students take physics (25 percent versus 16 percent), chemistry (42 percent versus 35 percent), biology, and earth science in the eleventh and twelfth grades.[10]

A study by Stigler and Stevenson shows that American students spend fewer hours in school than Japanese students and that U.S. schools allocate less time to core instruction than do other industrialized nations. For example, core academic time in U.S. schools was estimated at 1,460 hours during the four years of high school compared with 3,170 hours in Japan.[11]

The New Courses of Study: The standardization of education due to excessive egalitarianism and cramming of too much knowledge into children in Japan has been for a long time criticized. Education and instruction at school have been provided more or less uniformly to go in tandem with the level of understanding of average children, making classroom lessons boring to children with a quick understanding and difficult for children who need longer to understand. As a consequence, there has emerged a noticeable trend that levels of understanding and satisfaction decline as grades go up. It has also been pointed out that the present Japanese education system has not been constructed in a manner that encourages the maximum growth of individuality and capability in each and every child. In response to such criticism, the MEXT has recently tended to promote education geared more to fit the individuality and capabilities of children by reforming curriculum.

In order to keep up with advancements in science, industry, and culture, the MEXT has continuously revised the Courses of Study since the 1970s through carefully selecting the contents of curriculum and reducing the number of class hours. The new Courses of Study especially considers:

- transferring relatively advanced content to higher grades or educational stages to make the school curriculum more systematic, understandable, and consistent; and
- removing content that overlaps between schools, grades, or subjects.

Since April, 2002, the elementary schools and the lower secondary schools have been nationally using the new Courses of Study, which aim at the education of students to firmly acquire basic knowledge and to cultivate a "zest for living," which means the ability to learn and think independently by and for themselves. In implementing the new Courses of Study the MEXT is promoting "academic ability" and "moral education" as the two major pillars. For improvement of "academic ability" schools are required to make active efforts to provide learning to deepen understanding beyond the scope of the Courses of Study for those children who adequately understand the contents designated by the Courses of Study, and to repeat instruction in the basics for those children who do not adequately understand the contents designated by the Courses of Study.

High Quality of Japanese Students in Mathematics and Science

The efficient elementary and secondary education in Japan has long been winning international praise and several studies over the past decades have demonstrated the success of Japan's systematized and sequential curriculum, which has enabled Japanese students to place at, or close to, the top in international mathematics and science tests. Table 3.13 shows the 1995 TIMSS and 1999 TIMSS-R of 4th and 8th grade students in 17 countries as well as the change in their performance relative to the international average scores. Here we cite only figures from Japan and the United States. In mathematics, Japanese 4th graders were ranked 3rd in 1995, scoring 567, above the international average score by 50, while the American 4th grade score was 517, similar to the international average. Four years later when they became 8th graders in 1999, these students again took the TIMSS-R mathematics test. Japanese 8th graders were ranked fourth, scoring 579, above the international average score by 55, while the American 8th grade score was 502, below the international average. In science, the Japanese 4th and 8th graders performed excellent and were ranked third; their scores were much above the international average in both 1995 and 1999. The American 4th graders did a good job in science in 1995; however, when they grew up to be 8th graders, their scores decreased and their rank declined, to 34 points below the score of Japanese students.

Table 3.14 provides further evidence of the high quality of Japanese students in the fields of mathematics and science. According to international research that has been conducted by the International Association

Table 3.13. TIMSS-R Mathematics and Science Achievement of Japanese and American Students

Mathematics						
Country	Fourth grade, 1995	Score	Ranking	Eighth grade, 1999	Score	Ranking
Japan		567	3		579	4
United States		517	9		502	12
Average		517			524	

Science						
Country	Fourth grade, 1995	Score	Ranking	Eighth grade, 1999	Score	Ranking
Japan		553	3		549	3
United States		542	4		515	12
Average		514			524	

Source: Compiled by the author from: National Science Board (NSB), *Science and Engineering Indicators 2002*, Vol. 1, p. 1–17

Table 3.14. Mathematical and Scientific Achievements of Japanese Students in International Research

Year	Elementary School	Lower Secondary School	Year	Elementary School	Lower Secondary School
1964 (1st)	N/A	2nd/12 countries	1970 (1st)	1st/16 countries	1st/18 countries
1981 (2nd)	N/A	1st/20 countries	1983 (2nd)	1st/19 countries	2nd/26 countries
1985 (3rd)	3rd/26 countries	3rd/39 countries	1995 (3rd)	2nd/26 countries	3rd/41 countries
1999 (3rd, supplement research)	N/A	5th/38 countries	1999 (3rd, supplement research)	N/A	4th/38 countries

Source: Compiled by the author from: Ministry of Education, Culture, Sports, Science and Technology (MEXT), Japan, *Japanese Government Policies in Education, Culture, Sports, Science and Technology 2001: Educational Reform for the 21st Century,* 2002, p. 33.

for the Evaluation of Educational Achievement (IEA) in the past 35 years, Japanese students have high levels of skill and knowledge in mathematics and science among the international community. These findings indicate that the academic achievement of Japanese students has generally been good throughout the postwar era.

Many other international mathematics and science tests demonstrate the high achievement of Japanese students. According to the U.S. Department of Education, "In comparison to Japan, the scores of America's best students, who are at the 95th percentile for the whole nation, are significantly below the scores of the top quarter of Japanese students, who perform at their nation's 75th percentile."[12]

JAPANESE HIGHER EDUCATION

Unlike elementary and secondary education, Japanese higher education has long been the target of intense criticism both at home and abroad. I am not intent to examine the reasons for the shortcomings in Japanese higher education. I would rather reveal some of its characteristics and recent trends.

Tertiary Enrollment and Gender Distribution: In 2002, boys and girls were represented in almost equal proportion in Japanese senior high school enrollment. However, gender-specific differences became striking at the tertiary education level. Female enrollment at four-year universities in Japan is lower than that in any Western industrialized nation. As table 3.15 shows, the main tertiary track for women is two-year junior colleges (88.7 percent in 2002) rather than four-year universities (38.0 percent in 2002). And female graduate students made up only one-fourth of both master's and doctoral enrollment in 2000. However, this could be considered considerable progress in view of the very small base of female enrollment 47 years ago. Between 1955 and 2002, the female share in junior college and four-year university enrollment increased by 34.7 percentage points and 25.6 percentage points, respectively, from 54.0 percent to 88.7 percent in junior college enrollment and from 12.4 percent to 38.0 percent in four-year university enrollment. The enormous growth is also shown in the absolute number of both men and women in the total junior college and four-year university enrollment, which increased by over 5 times from 1955 to 2002. Japan used to invest little in graduate education, with only 153,423 students enrolled in 1995 when there were fewer graduate school students per capita in Japan than in other advanced nations: 1.1 graduate students per 1,000 people in 1994 in comparison to 7.7 in the United States (1992), 2.4 in the United Kindom (1992), and 3.6 in France (1993).[13] However, driven by the globalization of the knowledge economy in the late 1990s, Japan greatly expanded its graduate education. In 2002, Japanese graduate enrollment reached 223,512, increasing by 31.4 percent relative to 1995. Women are usually less represented in Japan's graduate education and they constituted a little over one-fourth of both master's students and doctoral students (see table 3.15). Women's major subject choices are heavily biased toward "general education" areas such as humanities and fine arts and typically female areas such as home economics and education.

Fields of Study of Tertiary Education: Based on the data available in table 3.16, I will examine the fields of study in four levels of education: junior colleges, four-year universities, master's programs, and doctoral programs.

Junior College Level: In 2000, 18.7 percent of junior college students

Table 3.15. Japanese Tertiary Education Enrollment: Female Percentage, 1955–2002

Year	Junior College Total	Female	Female (%)	Four-year University Total	Female	Female (%)	Master's Student Total	Female	Female (%)	Doctoral Student Total	Female	Female (%)
1955	77,885	42,061	54.0	523,355	65,081	12.4						
1960	83,457	56,357	67.5	626,421	85,966	13.7	8,305			7,429		
1965	147,563	110,388	74.8	937,556	152,119	16.2	16,771			11,683		
1970	263,219	217,668	82.7	1,406,521	252,745	18.0	27,714			13,243		
1975	353,782	305,124	86.2	1,734,082	368,258	21.2	33,560			14,904		
1980	371,124	330,468	89.0	1,835,312	405,529	22.1	35,781			18,211		
1985	371,095	333,175	89.8	1,848,698	434,401	23.5	48,147			21,541		
1990	479,389	438,443	91.5	2,133,362	584,155	27.4	61,884			28,354		
1995	498,516	455,439	91.4	2,546,649	821,893	32.3	109,649			43,774		
1996	473,279	429,290	90.7	2,596,667	864,147	33.3						
1997	446,750	402,929	90.2	2,633,790	899,434	34.1						
1998	416,825	375,372	90.1	2,740,023	992,312	36.2	123,255			55,646		
1999	377,852	339,741	89.9	2,701,104	959,490	35.5	132,118			59,007		
2000	327,680	293,690	89.6	2,740,023	992,312	36.2	142,830	37,885	26.5	62,481	16,331	26.1
2001	289,198	258,107	89.2	2,765,705	1,026,398	37.1	150,797			65,525		
2002	267,114	237,043	88.7	2,786,078	1,059,931	38.0	155,267	43,694	28.1	68,245	19,051	27.9

Source: Computed and compiled by the author from:
1. Ministry of Education, Science, Culture and Technology (MEXT), Japan, *Statistics*, 2001, <http://www.jinjapan.org/stat/category_16.html> (13 Dec. 2002).
2. Japan Information Network, Japan, Statistics, 2003, <http://www.jinjapan.org/stat/category_16.html> (2 Dec. 2003).
3. Ministry of Education, Culture, Sports, Science and Technology (MEXT), *Statistical Abstract, 2003 Edition*, pp. 86–90.

Table 3.16. Japanese Tertiary Education Students by Field of Study, 2000 and 2002

Junior College Students by Field of Study (2000)

	Total	All S&E	Eng.	Agri.	Social sci.	Health	Gen. culture	Humanities	Home economics	Education & teacher	Arts	Others
Male												
	32,563	20,431	10,098	1,468	8,865	3,241	190	3,135	1,296	1,945	1,958	367
	(10.2)	(34.4)	(76.4)	(49.7)	(20.5)	(9.6)	(2.3)	(4.9)	(1.7)	(3.2)	(12.5)	(8.2)
Female												
	285,695	38,940	3,115	1,483	34,342	26,468	7,970	60,259	75,922	58,282	13,756	4,098
	(89.8)	(65.6)	(23.6)	(50.3)	(79.5)	(93.4)	(97.7)	(95.1)	(98.3)	(96.8)	(87.5)	(91.8)
Sub Total												
	318,258	59,371	13,213	2,951	43,207	29,709	8,160	63,394	77,218	60,227	15,714	4,465
	(100.0)	(18.7)	(4.2)	(0.9)	(13.6)	(9.3)	(25.6)	(19.9)	(24.3)	(18.9)	(4.9)	(1.4)

Four-year University Students by Field of Study (2000)

	Total	All S&E	Sci.	Eng.	Agri.	Social sci.	Humanities	Med./ Health	Mercantile mar.	Home eco.	Education	Arts	Others
Male													
	1,558,533	1,246,101	65,619	420,673	41,981	717,828	135,246	65,947	803	2,160	56,455	20,114	31,707
	(63.1)	(77.4)	(74.2)	(90.0)	(59.7)	(72.8)	(32.9)	(45.9)	(88.7)	(4.9)	(41.0)	(30.8)	(54.5)
Female													
	913,222	364,887	22,282	46,489	28,327	267,789	275,733	77,690	102	42,138	81,160	45,094	26,418
	(36.9)	(22.6)	(25.8)	(10.0)	(41.3)	(27.2)	(67.1)	(54.1)	(11.3)	(95.1)	(59.0)	(69.2)	(45.5)

(continues)

Table 3.16. (Continued)

	Total	All S&E	Sci.	Eng.	Agri.	Social sci.	Humanities	Med./ Health	Mercantile mar.	Home eco.	Education	Arts	Others	Adult students
Sub Total	2,471,755 (100.0)	1,610,988 (65.2)	87,901 (3.6)	467,162 (18.9)	70,308 (2.8)	985,617 (39.9)	410,979 (16.6)	143,637 (5.8)	905 (0.0)	44,298 (1.8)	137,615 (5.6)	65,208 (2.6)	58,125 (2.4)	

Master's Students by Field of Study (2002)

	Total	All S&E	Sci.	Eng.	Agri.	Social sci.	Humanities	Med./ Health	Mercantile mar.	Home eco.	Education	Arts	Others	Adult students
Male														
	111,573 (71.9)	87,303 (82.2)	10,409 (78.4)	55,815 (90.8)	5,276 (65.9)	15,803 (67.4)	5,877 (45.5)	4,141 (47.3)	37 (75.5)	134 (13.7)	5,933 (50.4)	1,286 (38.5)	6,842 (60.9)	11,458 (58.5)
Female														
	43,694 (28.1)	18,918 (17.8)	2,872 (21.6)	5,660 (9.2)	2,732 (34.1)	7,654 (32.6)	7,039 (54.5)	4,610 (52.7)	12 (24.5)	847 (86.3)	5,847 (49.6)	2,055 (61.5)	4,366 (38.9)	8,121 (18.6)
Sub Total														
	155,267 (100.0)	106,221 (68.4)	13,281 (8.6)	61,475 (39.6)	8,008 (5.2)	23,457 (15.1)	12,916 (8.3)	8,751 (5.6)	49 (0.0)	981 (0.6)	11,780 (7.6)	3,341 (2.2)	11,228 (7.2)	19,579

Doctoral Students by Field of Study (2002)

	Total	All S&E	Sci.	Eng.	Agri.	Social sci.	Humanities	Med./ Health	Mercantile mar.	Home eco.	Education	Arts	Others	Adult students
Male														
	49,194 (72.1)	24,403 (81.0)	5,142 (83.1)	11,173 (89.4)	3,236 (73.7)	4,852 (68.8)	3,581 (49.1)	15,925 (72.8)		51 (16.8)	834 (49.1)	253 (48.7)	4,147 (64.5)	9,973 (73.4)

Female

19,051	5,728	1,047	1,326	1,154	2,201	3,713	5,946	252	864	266	2,282	3,619
(27.9)	(19.0)	(16.9)	(10.6)	(26.3)	(31.2)	(50.9)	(27.2)	(83.2)	(50.9)	(51.3)	(35.5)	(26.6)

Sub Total

68,245	30,131	6,189	12,499	4,390	7,053	7,294	21,871	303	1,698	519	6,429	13,592
(100.0)	(44.2)	(9.1)	(18.3)	(6.4)	(10.3)	(10.7)	(32.0)	(0.4)	(2.5)	(0.8)	(9.4)	(19.9)

Note:
1. The figures in parentheses refer to percentage.
2. The Data on junior college and four-year university students are for 2000 while the data on master's and doctoral students are for 2002.
Source: Computed and compiled by the author from:
1. Ministry of Education, Culture, Sports, and Technology, Statistics, Japan (MEXT), 2001.
2. Ministry of Education, Culture, Sports, Science and Technology (MEXT), Statistical Abstract, 2003 Edition, pp. 86–90.

were enrolled in S&E fields, with 65.6 percent of the S&E students being women and 34.4 percent men. The highest proportions of total enrollment are concentrated in general culture (25.6 percent), home economics (24.3 percent), humanities (19.9 percent), and education (18.9 percent), successively. The men's largest share is in engineering (76.4 percent) and agriculture (49.7 percent) while women dominate all other fields: 98.3 percent in home economics, 97.7 percent in general culture, 96.8 percent in education, and 93.4 percent in health.

Four-year University Level: In 2000, 65.2 percent of four-year university students were enrolled in S&E fields, with 22.6 percent being women and 77.4 percent men. The highest proportions of total enrollment are concentrated in social science (39.9 percent), engineering (18.9 percent), and humanities (16.6 percent), successively, while the lowest proportions are in mercantile marines (0.04 percent), home economics (1.8 percent), arts (2.6 percent), and agriculture (2.8 percent), successively. However, dramatic differences by gender exist. Engineering consists of 90 percent male students, mercantile marine 88.7 percent, science 74.2 percent, and social science 72.8 percent while female students are strong in home economics (95.1 percent), arts (69.2 percent), humanities (67.1), and education (59 percent).

Master's Program Level: In 2002, 68.4 percent of master's students were enrolled in S&E fields, with 82.2 percent being men and only 17.8 percent women. The highest proportions of total enrollment are concentrated in engineering (39.6 percent), social science (15.1 percent), science (8.6 percent), and humanities (8.3 percent). Male student enrollment dominates in most fields, particularly in engineering (90.8 percent), science (78.4 percent), mercantile marine (75.5 percent), social science (67.4 percent), and agriculture (65.9 percent) while female students have higher proportions only in home economics (86.3 percent), arts (61.5 percent), humanities (54.5 percent), and medicine (52.7 percent).

Doctoral Program Level: In 2002, 44.2 percent of doctoral students were enrolled in S&E fields, with 81.0 percent being men and only 19.0 percent women. The highest proportions of total enrollment are concentrated in medicine (32.0 percent), engineering (18.3 percent), humanities (10.7 percent), social science (10.3 percent), and science (9.1 percent), and, successively. Similar to the master's programs, male student enrollment dominated in most fields, particularly in engineering (89.4 percent), science (81.1 percent), agriculture (73.7 percent), medicine (72.8 percent), and social science (68.8 percent) while female students have higher proportions in home economics (83.2 percent), arts (51.3 percent), education (50.9 percent), and humanities (50.9 percent).

A few features in the distribution of fields of study need to be noted. First, women are heavily represented in junior colleges, but usually less represented in four-year universities and graduate education. Second, women's major subject choices are heavily biased toward "general education" areas such as humanities and fine arts and typically female areas such as home economics and education, while men's choices are heavily biased toward engineering, science, and mercantile marine. Third, Japanese four-year universities and graduate programs strongly stress S&E fields, especially engineering.

JAPANESE INTERNATIONAL EDUCATION AT HOME AND ABROAD

The success of the Japanese economy has been largely attributed to the absorption of foreign knowledge and technology. There can be no doubt that in the past decades there has been an increasing demand for people with international minds and the knowledge necessary to perform in an internationally competitive economic climate. Japan has now become both home and host country of international students.

Japan is a Leading Home Country of International Students in the United States: In the past two decades, Japan has been one of the major sending countries for international students to the United States. Throughout both the 1980s and 1990s, Japan and China were the leading home countries of international students in the United States. Table 3.17 and figure 3.4 clearly show the dramatically increasing enrollment and ratio of Japanese students among total foreign students in U.S. universities from 1980 to 2003: in the first half of the 1980s, Japanese students were the largest population in foreign student enrollment in U.S. universities. During the period from the mid-1980s to the early 1990s, Japan ceded the lead to China. However, Japan re-took the lead (in total foreign student enrollment in America) in 1994–1995, and remained the first leading

Table 3.17. Japanese and Chinese Students Enrolled in U.S. Universities, 1980–1981 to 2002–2003

	1980–1981 No.	%	1985–1986 No.	%	1989–1990 No.	%	1991–1992 No.	%	1993–1994 No.	%	1994–1995 No.	%
Total	311,880	100	343,780	100	386,850	100	419,590	100	449,704	100	452,635	100
China	2,770	0.9	13,980	4.1	33,390	8.6	42,940	10	44,381	9.9	39,403	8.7
Japan	13,500	4.3	13,360	3.9	29,840	7.7	40,700	9.7	43,770	9.7	45,276	10

	1995–1996 No.	%	1998–1999 No.	%	1999–2000 No.	%	2000–2001 No.	%	2001–2002 No.	%	2002–2003 No.	%
Total	453,787	100	490,933	100	514,723	100	547,886	100	582,996	100	585,323	100
China	39,613	8.7	51,001	10	54,466	10.6	59,939	10.9	63,211	10.8	64,757	11.1
Japan	45,531	10	46,406	9.9	46,872	9.1	46,497	8.49	46,810	8.03	45,960	7.85

Source: Computed and compiled by the author from:
1. U.S. Department of Education, *Digest of Education Statistics 1996 and 1997*, p 450 and p. 456.
2. Institute of International Education (IIE), *Open Doors*, 1999, 2000, and 2003.

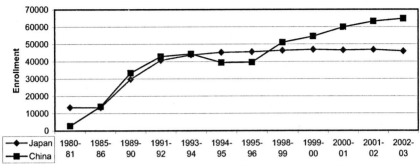

Figure 3.4. Japanese and Chinese Students Enrolled in U.S. Universities: 1980/81 to 2002/03

Source: Cited from table 3.17.

sender for five years until 1998–1999. Since then, Japan has fallen to fourth due to surges in enrollment from India, China, and Korea while numbers from Japan remained virtually flat for the past five years, due in part to economic conditions. The 2 percent decline in the 2002–2003 academic year marked the first drop in number of Japanese students coming to the United States since 1998.

From 1980 to 2003, the number of Japanese students in the United States increased 3.4 times from 13,500 to 45,960 while the proportion rose from less than 4.3 percent to 7.9 percent. The majority of Japanese students study at the undergraduate level. In 2002–2003, 20.7 percent of them were enrolled as graduate students, 68.5 percent as undergraduate students while 10.8 percent were enrolled in other types of schools.

Main Host Countries of Japanese International Students: The Japanese MEXT provides scholarships to Japanese students going abroad for study, cooperates with foreign governments in recruiting and screening Japanese students who study under their respective scholarship programs, and provides information related to study abroad. As a result, the number of Japanese students who go abroad to study has been increasing year by year. According to the Japanese government's statistical report, the number of Japanese studying abroad was 193,779 students in 2000. In addition to the students sent to the United States which constituted 46 percent of all Japanese students abroad in 2000, Japan sent over one-quarter to

Europe and the remaining one-quarter went to Asia, Africa, and Oceania (see figure 3.5 and figure 3.6).

Host Country of Foreign Students: In order to strengthen the Japanese competitive power of economics and S&T in the world, Japan started to attract foreign students to study in Japan. As early as 1983 Japan initiated the "Foreign Students Plan" which aimed at increasing Japan's intake of foreign students to 100,000 by the year 2000. Although this target was not met—largely as a result of the economic problems in Asia in the late 1990s—there has been a significant increase each year, especially in 1998 when Japan offered government scholarships to 8,323 foreign students.[14] As a result, during the period from 1991 to 2003, the number of foreign students in Japan more than doubled (see figure 3.7). According to the latest report from Japan's MEXT, by November 2003, the number of foreign students in Japan had reached close to 110,000, and the goal of 100,000 foreign students in Japan was realized in 2003.[15]

The Japanese government provides funds to both public and private universities to help them accommodate more foreign students. In 1999, 56,308 foreign students were enrolled in Japanese universities, making up 2.1 percent of the total enrollment in Japanese higher education. In undergraduate programs, foreign student enrollment constituted 1.4 percent (33,877), while in graduate programs foreign students' proportion was 11.74 percent (22,431). More than half of foreign students were enrolled in S&E fields. Almost 90 percent of foreign students in Japan are from

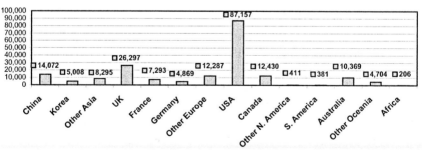

Figure 3.5. Distribution of Japanese Students Studying in Main Countries and Regions in 2000

Source: Computed and compiled by the author from: Japan Information Network, Japan, *Statistics,* 2003, <http://www.jinjapan.org/stat/category_16.html> (2 Dec. 2003).

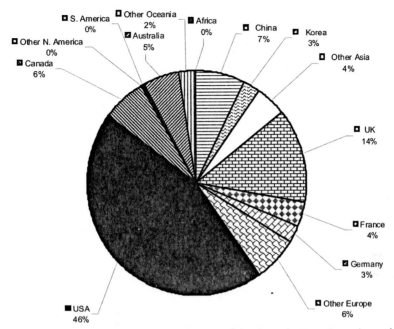

Figure 3.6. Percentage of Japanese Students Studying in Main Host Countries and Regions in 2000

Source: Computed and compiled by the author from: Japan Information Network, Japan, *Statistics,* 2003, <http://www.jinjapan.org/stat/category_16.html> (2 Dec. 2003).

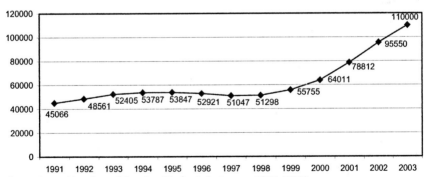

Figure 3.7. Number of Foreign Students in Japan: 1991–2003

Note: The number for 2003 is estimated.
Source: Collected and compiled by the author from: Japan Information Network, Japan, Statistics, 2003, http://www.jinjapan.org/stat/category_16.html> (accessed 2 Dec. 2003); and "Two-thirds of Foreign Students Studying in Japan Are from China," *china.org.cn,* November 12, 2003, http://www.china.org.cn/chinese/kuaixun/440795.htm (accessed Dec. 2, 2003).

Asia, with China and South Korea the leading home countries of the international students (see table 3.18). The proportions of Chinese and Korean students combined accounted for 77.5 percent of foreign students in 2002.

The Japan's MEXT has been carrying out a wide range of measures on a comprehensive basis in order to promote international student exchange. These measures include the Japanese Government scholarship (Monbukagakusho scholarship) for the youth of Asia and other countries, financial aid to privately finance foreign students, the promotion of student exchange in cutting-edge areas, assistance with living accommodations, the improvement of teaching and guidance for foreign students at universities, the full-scale implementation of testing for foreign students wishing to study in Japan, the dissemination of information related to study in Japan, and improved follow-up service after the students return to their homes.

For the time being, we have finished our travel in Japan and will continue our journey to other designated Asian nations and economies. Before we go, I would point out the interesting phenomenon that all the East Asian nations and economies (India differs) have, in large degree, inherited the ancient Chinese culture and tradition, which is deeply rooted in these societies. This culture and tradition plays such a great role that, though Japan, Korea, China, and Taiwan implement different political and socioeconomic systems, their educational systems still remain similar in many aspects such as centralized administration, rigid screening mechanisms, high respect for knowledge, the emphasis on S&T, and the high demand for education as we have seen in Japan's profile. I will guide you

Table 3.18. Number and Percentage of Foreign Students in Japan by Country of Origin, 2002

China		Taiwan		Korea		Malaysia		U.S.A.		Thailand	
No.	%	No.	%	No.	%	No.	%	No.	%	No.	%
58,533	60.98	4,266	4.44	15,846	16.51	1,885	1.96	1,217	1.27	1,504	1.57

Indonesia		Philippines		Brazil		Bangladesh		Others		Total	
No.	%	No.	%	No.	%	No.	%	No.	%	No.	%
1,441	1.50	483	0.50	347	0.36	823	0.86	9,205	9.59	95,990	100.00

Source: Computed and compiled by the author from: Japan Information Network, Japan, Statistics, 2003, <http://www.jinjapan.org/stat/stats/16EDU61.html> (2 Dec. 2003).

more quickly through the aspects that Korea, China, and Taiwan share with Japan to avoid repetition.

NOTES

1. National Research Council, *Everybody Counts: A Report to the Nation on the Future of Mathematics Education* (Washington, DC: National Academy Press, 1989), 77.

2. William K. Cummings, *Education and Equality in Japan* (Princeton, New Jersey: Princeton University Press, 1980), 9.

3. Kazuyuki Kitamura, "Japan," in *International Higher Education: An Encyclopedia,* Vol. 1, ed. Philip G. Kitamura, (New York & London: Garland Publishing, Inc. 1991), 490.

4. Kitamura, "Japan," 494 and 497.

5. William K. Cummings, *Education and Equality in Japan*, 167.

6. Ministry of Education, Culture, Sports, Science and Technology (MEXT), Japan, *Japanese Government Policies in Education, Culture, Sports, Science and Technology 2001: Educational Reform for the 21st Century* (Tokyo, Japan: MEXT, 2002), 43.

7. Cummings, *Education and Equality in Japan*, 10.

8. Harry Wray, *Japanese and American Education: Attitudes and Practices* (Westport, CT: Bergin & Garvey, 1999), 4.

9. Wray, *Japanese and American Education: Attitudes and Practices*, 261–62.

10. Wray, *Japanese and American Education: Attitudes and Practices*, 262.

11. National Science Board (NSB), *Science and Engineering Indicators—2002*, Vol. 1 (Arlington, VA: National Science Foundation, 2002), 1–30.

12. U.S. Department of Education, National Center for Education Statistics, *Pursuing Excellence*, by Lois Peak, (Washington, DC: U.S. Government Printing Office, 1996), 25.

13. Kaori Okano and Motonori Tsuchiya, *Education in Contemporary Japan: Inequality and Diversity* (Cambridge, United Kingdom: Cambridge University Press, 1999), 215.

14. Christopher P. Hood, *Japanese Education Reform: Nakasone's Legacy* (New York, NY: Routledge, 2001), 67.

15. "Two-thirds of Foreign Students Studying in Japan Are from China," *china.org.cn,* 11/12/03, <http://www.china.org.cn/chinese/kuaixun/440795.htm> (2 Dec. 2003).

Chapter Four

Profile of Korean Education

Summary of findings: In contrast to Korea's thin endowment of natural resources this nation has a large pool of human resources. The Korean people have made major investments in education, well beyond those of most other Asian NIEs and other developing countries. One of the most striking attributes of Korean parents is their strong commitment to education. This commitment is the principal reason why Korea has been able to upgrade its economy within a relatively short period and compete in more advanced industries. High motivation and expectations originated from the Confucian culture which places a high value on education. Since 2000, Korean higher education has expanded to such an extent that its total enrollment has surpassed both those in the middle and high schools. In the past decade, though Korea has been one of the leading countries of origin of international students to the United States, it also has succeeded in enticing many of its students to return home. Korea has become one of the few countries in the world to successfully turn its brain drain into a brain gain.

OVERVIEW

For several millennia prior to the twentieth century Korea was politically and culturally linked with China whose social philosophy and culture have exerted great influence on the former nation. In education, the continuing impact of Chinese influence is still visible in the context of studies as well as in the structure of educational advancement. In the twenty-first century Korea has begun breaking away from China's influence. Its culture and education system are now developing through Korea's interactions with diverse foreign nations such as Japan, the United States, and certain European nations. After Korea was liberated from Japanese rule in 1945, a new era arrived, enacting a dramatic shift from a colonial political system to a democratic system. During the past half century, Koreans have not only transformed their nation from an unprosperous Japanese-ruled agricultural nation into a self-governing industrial power, but they also have changed their society from a closed system to an open one. Korea's rapid economic growth during the 1950s and the 1970s enabled it to join the group of "Newly Industrialized Economies" (NIE) by the 1970s.

The new era brought Koreans the opportunity for education, which the Japanese had denied them. A single-track 6-3-3-4 school system was adopted. According to the Education Law, which was legislated and promulgated in 1949, every citizen was entitled to free elementary education and equal opportunity for further education. A unique feature of Korea is that its education system's growth and evolution paralleled and often led national economic and social development and changes. By the 1990s, the quantitative dimensions of the Korean educational effort, reflected in enrollment rates at the various educational levels, resembled more closely the enrollment rates in Western European nations than those in most of the third world.

Growth of Korean Education

As table 4.1 shows, in the past half century Korean education has experienced rapid growth at all levels. This growth started in the 1950s and accelerated in the 1960s, during which time the Korean economy grew at an average annual rate of approximately 10 percent (see table 4.2). This economic growth rate is attributed both to increased industrial output and to the drop in the population growth rate (from 2.9 percent in 1961 to 1.7 percent in 1971). No nation-state was more committed to economic development during the undeclared "development decade," i.e., the 1960s, than Korea.[1]

Table 4.1. Korean Student Enrollment and Ratio at All Levels (1945–2002)

Year	Total	Elementary school No.	%	Middle school No.	%	High school No.	%	Higher education No.	%
1945	1495603	1366685	91.38	80828	5.40	40271	2.69	7819	0.52
1950	3040000	2658000	87.43	249000	8.19	133000	4.38		0.00
1955	3765000	2947000	78.27	475000	12.62	265000	7.04	78000	2.07
1960	4525753	3622685	80.05	528593	11.68	273434	6.04	101041	2.23
1965	6224000	4941000	79.39	751000	12.07	426000	6.84	106000	1.70
1970	7904927	5794301	73.30	1318808	16.68	590382	7.47	201436	2.55
1975	8958000	5599000	62.50	2027000	22.63	1123000	12.54	209000	2.33
1980	10442243	5658002	54.18	2471997	23.67	1696792	16.25	615452	5.89
1990	10918886	4868520	44.59	2275751	20.84	2283806	20.92	1490809	13.65
2000	11315547	4019991	35.53	1860539	16.44	2071468	18.31	3363549	29.73
2001	11332314	4089429	36.09	1831152	16.16	1911173	16.86	3500560	30.89
2002	11352352	4138366	36.45	1841030	16.22	1795509	15.82	3577447	31.51

Sources: Computed and compiled by the author from:
1. Ministry of Education and Human Resources Development (MOEHRD), Korea, *Education in Korea: 2001–2002*, 2002, p. 17 and p. 19 and *Education in Korea: 2002–2003*, 2003, p. 15.
2. McGinn, Noel F., Snodgrass, Donald R., Kim, Yung Bong, Kim, Shin-bok and Kim, Quee-young, *Education and Development in Korea*, Council on East Asian Studies, Harvard University, 1980, p. 132.

In keeping with the emphasis on state-managed economic development, education was viewed essentially as an institution for developing human capital and as a process for preparing members of the corporate state. The educational slogan for the 1950s had been "one skill for one person"; the slogan for the 1960s was "education for economic development" or "nation-building through education." Figure 4.1 reflects education's rapid growth: in 1945 the Korean primary enrollment was 1,366,685 and in 1960 the enrollment was 3,622,685, an increase of 2.7 times. In 1945 the Korean primary education enrollment ratio was 45 percent of the 6-to-12-year-old cohort; by 1960 more than 90 percent of this age group was enrolled in school. In 1970 the elementary school gross enrollment rate reached 100.7 percent and obtained its peak number of 5,794,301, 1.6 times the number in 1960. After the early 1980s the number of elementary students decreased due to the declining birthrate.

A similar growth has been reflected in middle school education since 1945. Following the abolition of the entrance examination to middle school in 1968, all candidates from elementary schools were assigned to a school in their residential district through the lottery. Rates of advancement to the middle school rose immediately in 1969 to 62 percent and to

Table 4.2. GNP Growth and Ratio to GNP in Korea, 1954–2000

Year	GNP (Billion) (won)	Ratio of Central Government Expenditures on Education (%)	
		to Government Budget	to GNP
1954	890.2	4.0	0.9
1957	1,014.4	9.2	1.6
1960	1,129.7	14.9	2.5
1963	1,328.3	13.8	2.2
1966	1,719.2	17.2	2.4
1969	2,400.5	15.5	2.8
1972	3,023.6	16.4	3.0
1974	3,810.4	15.5*	2.2*
1980			4.0
1985			4.0
1990	178,628.3		3.0
1992	245,387.7		
1993	277,107.5		
1996	417,108.4		
1997	450,853.3		
1998	444,3665		
1999	4,827,442		4.0
2000	5,170,968		

*This indicates that the data is from 1975.
Source: Computed and compiled by the author from:
1. McGinn, Noel F., Snodgrass, Donald R., Kim, Yung Bong, Kim, Shin-bok and Kim, Quee-young, *Education and Development in Korea*, Council on East Asian Studies, Harvard University, 1980, p 16 and p 134.
2. Ministry of Education and Human Resources Development (MOEHRD), Korea, *Education in Korea: 2001–2002*, 2002, p 9.
3. World Bank Statistics, 2002.

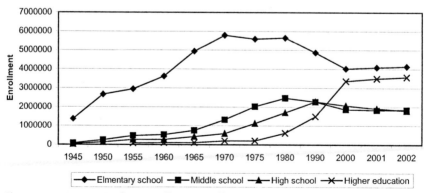

Figure 4.1. Korean Student Enrollment at All Levels (1945–2002)
Source: Cited from table 4.1.

70 percent in 1970. By 1990, the national advancement rate was 99.7 percent. In effect, nine-year universal education was achieved by the mid-1980s.[2] Middle school students' enrollment has steadily increased, with a peak of 2.7 million in 1985. Since then the absolute number of students has decreased, again due to the falling birthrate.

High schools are of two kinds: academic and vocational. In 2002, 99.6 percent of all middle school graduates entered high school. Between 1970 and 1990, high school enrollment quadrupled. The peak year was 1989 when 2,326,062 students were enrolled. After that, the number of students fell slightly in both academic and vocational high schools.

Examining the expansion rate of Korean education enrollment at all levels reveals the important phenomenon that the growth rate of higher education enrollment increased much more than any other level of enrollment between 1945 and 2002: 457.5 times as opposed to 3.0 times, 22.8 times, and 44.6 times for elementary, middle, and high school, respectively. When the elementary, middle, and high school students' enrollment fell during the 1980s and 1990s, higher education enrollment in Korea still kept going upward. In 2002, 87.0 percent of all graduates of academic high schools entered higher education institutions while 49.8 percent of all graduates of vocational high schools entered higher education institutions.[3] The Korean higher education system has expanded so rapidly that by 1990 its enrollment already exceeded one-third of the 18-to-21-year-old cohort, a higher ratio of enrollment than among any of the other NIEs, e.g., Taiwan, Singapore, and Malaysia. Most important in Korean higher education development is that since the late 1990s the absolute number of higher education students' enrollment has gradually surpassed both that of middle and high school students' enrollment (see table 4.1). In 2002, Korean higher education enrollment reached 3,577,447 while enrollment for middle school and high school were only 1,841,030 and 1,795,509, respectively. The ratio of higher education enrollment was 31.51 percent as opposed to 16.22 percent and 15.82 percent for middle and high school enrollment, respectively.

The remarkable achievements in educational development in the past several decades provided a large quality workforce for Korea's economic sector. Table 4.2 illustrates the rapid growth of GNP from 1954 to 2000. In turn, the economic sector invested aggressively in education. The Korean central government has annually allocated a large share of its expenditure and GNP to education since the 1950s. And in recent years it has continued to increase the education budget for the improvement of the quality of education in an attempt to match the outstanding quantitative growth thus far accomplished. Table 4.3 shows that in 2002 the central government allocated 17.4 percent of its total budget to education, whose share is the second largest next to that for economic development.

Educational Administration and Finance

Educational Administration: From 1945 to 1991, similarly to the situation in Japan, all education in Korea, from the preschool through tertiary levels, in both public and private sectors, was under the control of the Ministry of Education and Human Resources Development (MOEHRD), which issued ministerial decrees and had authority over the education budget, administration, policies, personnel, curriculum and instruction methods, higher education admission quota, approval of textbook adoption, and the licensing and establishment of institutions. As a central authority, the Korean MOEHRD held such broad power that it had the right to recommend the presidents of all public universities and approve the presidents of all private universities. Following the local autonomy law of 1991, administration became decentralized and the MOEHRD del-

Table 4.3.   Composition of the Korean Education Budget with Other Government Budgets, 2002

(General Account)	(Unit: million won)	
Classification	Budget for the year 2001	Ratio (%)
Education Expenditure	18,460,852	17.4
Defense Expenditure	17,106,006	16.2
Social Development Expenditure	13,900,887	13.1
Economic Development Expenditure	27,454,506	25.9
Legislative & Election Expenditure	518,672	0.5
Judicial/Police Expenditure	5,856,169	5.5
General Administration	3,665,678	3.5
Local Finance	11,821,170	11.2
Repayment of Government Debt & Others	4,553,631	4.3
Special Support in Finance	2,539,100	2.4
Total	105,876,671	100

Sources: Ministry of Education and Human Resources Development (MOEHRD), Korea, *Education in Korea: 2002–2003*, 2003, p. 28.

egated much of its budget, planning, and major administrative decisions to local authorities.

It is worth noting that in Korea's modern history, most new presidents' first goal has been education reform. The Minister of Education and Human Resources Development is a member of the National Council of the President of Korea and participates in top-level decisions within the central government. The Presidential Commission on Education and Human Resource Policy was established on the basis of Presidential Order No. 16977 of September 30, 2000. The Presidential Commission is to provide the President of Korea with advice concerning strategies and policies for education and human resource development geared toward producing the human talent suitable for the knowledge-information society of the twenty-first century. The Presidential Commission is comprised of eight ministers of the ministries related to education and human resources development and a number of education experts who form three subcommittees in different areas. The founding of this Presidential Commission will strengthen the Korean educational reform and better meet the needs of the knowledge-economy in the twenty-first century.[4]

Educational Finance: Among Korea's educational institutions, elementary, middle, and high schools are under the control of regional entities, i.e., the metropolitan and provincial offices of education. Funding for Korea's education comes from the central government, the local governments, and the independent resources of private schools. The central government's education budget provides funding for the offices of education which control elementary and secondary school education, the operating finances of the national universities, some support for private universities, and some support for educational administrative and research organizations. The central government's education budget is supported by the nation's tax.

The local government education funds are given to elementary and secondary school education; 83 percent of the financial resources of local governments are from the central government. Private schools exist at every level of education from elementary to college. Up to 80 percent of junior colleges and universities are private schools. The funding sources for private schools include tuition from parents, support from national or regional entities, and resources from school foundations. Reliance upon parents' tuition still remains high.

Of the 20 trillion won annual educational expenditure of the central government in 2001, 83.1 percent, or 16.6 trillion won, was transferred to the local educational authorities for funding elementary and secondary education; the remaining 16.9 percent, 3.37 trillion won, was directly managed and distributed as national funds by the MOEHRD to state-run institutions.[5]

FEATURES AND CHANGES

Korea shares many features with Japan in its education system and educational practices. Given that fact, it is reasonable to skip some details such as entrance examinations at the levels of Korean middle to high schools and high schools to colleges.[6] The other trait to be skipped is Korea's non-formal education system, which, like that in Japan, includes numerous supplementary classes and programs, cram schools, preparation schools, and private tutors.

Contribution of Korean Private Schools

The expansion of the Korean education system since 1945 was made possible only through the active involvement of the private schools. The pragmatic quality of national policies encouraging freer markets and private school activities has been interpreted as a contributing factor to industrialization. Private education is frequently described as making a crucial contribution to the extension of educational opportunities—a claim particularly true in secondary and higher education. With its limited resources and its commitment to primary education, the Korean government has to rely on private institutions to accommodate much of the demand at the secondary and higher education levels. In 1945 private secondary schools made up only 17 percent of the total, yet by 1957 the figure had increased to 40 percent. As table 4.4 and table 4.5 indicate, in 2001 private high schools made up 46.6 percent, with an enrollment of 1,040,391 (53.8 percent of total high school enrollment). The private sector has also played an important role throughout the growth of higher education. Since the mid-1960s private colleges and universities have accounted for the majority of higher education schools and enrollment.

Table 4.4.   Korean Schools by Type, 2001

	Number of Schools (unit: school)					
		National		Public		Private	
Classification	Total	Number	%	Number	%	Number	%
Grand Total	19058	102	0.5	12650	66.4	6306	33.1
Kindergarten	8407	3	0.03	4207	50.0	4197	49.9
Elementary School	5323	17	0.3	5229	98.2	77	1.5
Middle School	2785	10	0.4	2091	75.1	684	24.5
High School	2035	17	0.8	1070	52.6	948	46.6
Special School	134	5	3.7	42	31.3	87	65.0
Junior College	159	6	3.8	9	5.7	144	90.5
Undergraduate University	197	44	22.3	2	1.0	151	76.7
Graduate School	18(887)	(139)		(12)		18(736)	

Note: The figures in parentheses are not included in the grand total.
Source: Computed and compiled by the author from: Ministry of Education and Human Resources Development (MOEHRD), Korea, *2001 Brief Statistics of Korean Education*, 2002 <http://www.moe.go.kr/English/> (12 Dec. 2002).

Table 4.5.   Korean Student Enrollment by School Type, 2001

	Number of Schools (unit: person)					
		National		Public		Private	
Classification	Total	Number	%	Number	%	Number	%
Grand Total	11929584	960968	8.1	6508799	54.5	4459817	37.4
Kindergarten	545142	263	0.1	122152	22.4	422727	77.5
Elementary School	4089569	11367	0.3	4026320	98.4	51882	1.3
Middle School	1835897	7174	0.4	1428062	77.8	400661	21.8
High School	1934647	17768	0.9	876488	45.3	1040391	53.8
Special School	23769	1217	5.1	8881	37.4	13671	57.5
Junior College	953294	13775	1.4	23765	2.5	915754	96.0
Undergraduate University	2303996	837724	36.4	20115	0.9	1446157	62.7
Graduate School	243270	71680	29.5	3016	1.2	168574	69.3

Source: Computed and compiled by the author from: Ministry of Education and Human Resources Development (MOEHRD), Korea, *2001 Brief Statistics of Korean Education*, 2002 <http://www.moe.go.kr/English/> (12 Dec. 2002).

In 2001 private higher education institutions made up 84.0 percent of all institutions of higher education and private student enrollment accounted for 72.3 percent of all enrollment.

The rapid expansion of Korean private education has been largely due to such factors as an explosion in demand for higher education fueled by

Koreans' traditional enthusiasm for education, the salary differences between graduates from different educational levels, and the government policy of developing highly qualified people for national economic development. However, in spite of the fact that the Korean private institutions enroll more than fifty percent of the high school students and close to three-quarters of higher education students, the Korean government provides little financial support for the private sector. Before 1989, there were no direct government grants at all to private universities. Starting only in 1990, the Korean government promised financial aid to private universities and colleges, including a five-year commitment to increase grants to up to 10 percent of private institutions' total operating expenses. Although the 10 percent goal was not reached, the Korean government's contribution to private schools' operating expenses had reached 2.4 percent by 1994. The major source of financing for private institutions is the entrance fees and tuition fees. Compared with private universities and colleges in the United States, Korean private institutions receive very few donations. Among the total income of Korean private universities and colleges, less than 5 percent is provided by private donations.[7]

However, the situation is now improving for Korean private institutions. In 2001, the Korean government enacted a law exempting private schools from taxation on the acquisition and sale of properties, and the government is providing subsidies to cover the shortage of remuneration and operating costs. Loans are provided to help private schools with the expansion and renovation of facilities.[8] Although the government's coverage of research grants, students' activities, scholarship, and annuities is increasing, reliance on parents' tuition still remains quite high (see table 4.6).

Uniqueness of Education Growth in Korea

In the past two decades, many observers have pointed out a unique feature of education growth in Korea since 1945: a high level of human resources was developed early and despite low per capita income. Adams (1993)[9] noted that between the 1950s and the 1960s Korean education expanded more rapidly than the economy, although in this respect Korea was little different from several other developing nations. However, unlike many nations, Korea was able to achieve a well-developed system of primary

Table 4.6. Revenue and Expenditures of Private Schools in Korea, 2001
(Unit: million won)

Schools	Tuition No.	%	Grants No.	%	Transfer from Foundation No.	%	Others No.	%	Total No.
Elementary School	926	74.92	12	0.97	218	17.64	80	6.47	1236
Middle School	2800	27.68	6837	67.59	253	2.50	225	2.22	10115
High School	15013	51.86	12450	43.01	604	2.09	882	3.05	28949
University	55308	64.76	2575	3.02	14224	16.65	13299	15.57	85406
Total	74047	58.90	21874	17.40	15299	12.17	14486	11.52	125706

Source: Computed and compiled by the author from: Ministry of Education and Human Resources Development (MOEHRD), Korea, *Education in Korea: 2001–2002,* 2002, p 36.

education prior to large-scale efforts at economic modernization. Indeed, growth at all levels of education in Korea preceded the period of rapid economic growth. During most periods since World War II, Korea's education level was similar to that of nations with a much higher economic level.

For example, McGinn (1980)[10] found that Korea's 1960 level of primary school enrollment (59 percent of the age group) stood fairly close to the normal pattern of human resource development for a nation with a mean per capita GNP of nearly $200, despite the fact that Korea's per capita income was $90. (Then, the average nation with a per capita income of $90 could be expected to enroll only 22 percent of the age group.) In 1965, with a per capita income of $107, Korea's primary school enrollment (82 percent) was equivalent to that of nations with a GNP per capita of $380. (Then, the average nation with a per capita income of $107 could be expected to enroll only 62 percent of the age group.)

Differences at the secondary and tertiary levels were even more impressive. From 1960 to 1965, enrollment in secondary schools comprised about 27 percent of the 15- to 19-year-old group, which was as high as the average proportion enrolled in nations with per capita incomes of $380. Korea's enrollment in higher education was also very high, equivalent to countries with per capita incomes three or four times as large, such as Chile, Hungary, Venezuela, and Italy.

A comparison of Korea's educational growth during its period of industrial development with the educational growth patterns of other newly industrialized nations/economies is provided in table 4.7. It can be seen

Table 4.7. Total Enrollment Ratios by Levels and Stages of Development in Selected NIEs

Development Stage	Pre Takeoff	Takeoff	Post Takeoff	Pre Takeoff	Takeoff	Post Takeoff	Pre Takeoff	Takeoff	Post Takeoff
Country	Brazil			Greece			Hong Kong		
3rd Level	2.23	5.26	10.90	9.81	12.02	26.9	4.38	7.33	13.20
2nd Level	17	27	34	52	69	95	24	41	72
1st Level	72	83	99	111	109	102	91	120	104
Year	1965	1970	1980	1965	1970	1986	1960	1970	1984
Country	Indonesia			Israel			Malaysia		
3rd Level	6.5			10.91	20.04	34.2	1.99	4.30	6.7
2nd Level	42			48	48	83	34	48	57
1st Level	118			98	95	95	91	93	102
Year	1988			1960	1965	1987	1970	1980	1988
Country	Singapore			Korea			Taiwan		
3rd Level	10.01	9	11.8	4.58	10.3	37.7	4	15	35.8
2nd Level	45	52	71	27	56	86	33	48	78
1st Level	105	110	115	94	107	100	96	98	99
Year	1965	1975	1985	1960	1975	1989	1960	1965	1988
Country	Thailand			Tunisia			Turkey		
3rd Level	1.54	2.02	13.1	1.89	2.87	7	4.38	6.09	10.4
2nd Level	12	17	49	16	23	44	16	28	46
1st Level	78	81	99	91	91	113	101	109	117
Year	1965	1970	1980	1965	1970	1988	1965	1970	1987
Country	Yugoslavia			Mean					
3rd Level	8.61	20	18.3	5.45	9.52	18.83			
2nd Level	34	76	80	30.76	44.2	66.25			
1st Level	96	103	94	95.53	99.91	103			
Year	1960	1975	1988						

Source: Adams, Don and Gottlieb, Esther E., *Education and Social Change in Korea*, Garland Publishing, Inc., 1993, pp. 161–62.

that all NIEs have highly developed primary levels of education prior to the time of industrial takeoff. However, enrollment ratios at the second and third levels of education vary widely during early periods of industrialization, with Korea and its neighbor Taiwan exhibiting comparatively high enrollment ratios at these levels.[11]

It is difficult for some popular theories such as human capital theory and modernization theory to offer a fully satisfactory explanation of the early stages of Korea's educational development. Several factors might be critical. First, per-student public expenditures on education in Korea were lower than those in most developing nations, even those with similar levels of GNP. Secondly, high parental demand for education for children, coupled with a governmental inability to provide educational facilities and the encouragement of the U.S. military government to decentralize educational decision-making in the 1950s, resulted in private contributions to a large percentage of the total educational expenditure, sometimes amounting to almost 50 percent of the total educational expenditure (the contribution of Korean parents to the education system will be discussed in the next section). Thirdly, the acceptance by the Korean government of external pressure to create a strong capitalist state with constitutional rights for all citizens led to the correlative assumption of the necessity for extensive literacy and basic education, since these are considered basic human rights. The universalization of primary education was high on the agenda of each successive Korean government from 1948 to the present. Fourthly, the emphasis on developing the education system conforms to the respect for education inherited originally from Confucianism and deeply rooted in Korean society. The Confucian legacy left a zeal for learning, an ideal of the cultured, accomplished person, and a drive for education at all costs. Finally, the possibility of global influences on Korean educational expansion should not be ignored. There are competing explanations of the manners in which factors exogenous to an educational system influence educational growth. From the unique Korean educational development we can conclude that it was the pool of available talent that made possible the economic takeoff in Korea.

Contribution of Korean Families

The other impressive feature of Korean educational development is the strong financial support from students and their families. In the past fifty years, the pattern of paying for education in Korea has not been like the typical pattern of third world nations where little cost is incurred by students or their families for education. Instead, the Korean government has transferred the cost of education to the private sector. In Korea parents have been traditionally expected to make a financial contribution to education above their contribution through taxes. Thus, parents not only pay fees in support of public schools, but also financially back up a large system of private schooling. As early as the 1950s, the central government was financing only about 10 percent of the total cost of education while at the local level parents contributed over 50 percent of the cost of local schools.[12] Private as well as national and other public higher education institutions rely heavily on student tuition and fees for their funding, about 80 percent and 40 percent, respectively. Corresponding figures for government aid are 20 percent and 55 percent, respectively.[13]

Table 4.8 shows the costs paid by parents at different education levels. The average tuition/fees and Parent Teacher Association (PTA) fees account for close to half of total educational expenditures. These costs are rising as students move upward. The percentage borne by parents has increased to 72.62 percent and 82.57 percent at the high school and junior college levels, respectively. As shown in table 4.9, during the period between 1968 and 1985 the private costs of education persisted at a high rate and by 1985 private individuals shouldered about 50 percent of total educational costs.

Table 4.8. Composition of Revenue Sources of Korean School Expenditures by Levels, 1989 (unit: percent)

Source	Average	Primary School	Middle School	High School	Junior College	College/Univ.
Total	100.00	100.00	100.00	100.00	100.00	100.00
Public Source	56.04	97.84	59.32	26.87	17.43	27.6
Central Government	46.99	97.59	45.55	18.57	7.54	9.54
Local Government or Others	9.05	0.25	13.77	8.3	9.89	18.07
Private Source	43.85	2.16	40.68	72.62	82.57	72.4
Tuition/Fees	30.73	0.98	30.51	58.81	55.85	43.08
PTA Fees	13.12	1.18	10.17	13.81	26.72	29.32

Source: Adams, Don and Gottlieb, Esther E., Education and Social Change in Korea, Garland Publishing, Inc., 1993, p. 168.

Table 4.9. Share of Private Costs in School Education by Levels, 1968–1985 (unit: percent)

Levels	1968	1970	1977	1982	1985
Average	37.48	36.87	33.51	37.09	50.19
Primary School	51.15	37.3	36.51	37.29	50.5
Middle School	55.76	44.57	33.03	44.06	53.29
High School	47.4	45.93	30.72	40.34	58.6
College/University	38.54	27.65	26.6	34.1	41.71

Source: Adams, Don and Gottlieb, Esther E., Education and Social Change in Korea, Garland Publishing, Inc., 1993, p. 169.

In addition, there are some hidden costs borne by parents and students, which add to the financial burden of educational attainment. Severe competition for admission to college and universities, for example, has brought additional financial burdens to families, who support extra-school preparation for entrance examination such as private tutoring and the purchase of expensive instructional materials and equipment. According to some surveys, the amount spent by Korean parents on private tutoring exceeds the national budget for education.[14]

There are a few factors that could account for this strong private financial support in Korean society. The most significant one, it seems to me, is the important role of cultural support, which includes the traditional honor and respect shown for the accomplishment of educated persons, the enormous continuing prestige of formal education as a process, and the high achievement motivation of students and parents. These values have translated into educational outlays. Unlike in the leading developed nations today, in Korea no financial or other incentives were needed to encourage parents to send their children to school. It is common that Korean parents sacrifice their own standard of living to educate their children and stories are widely told of parents who sold their only ox to pay for school fees. Such efforts may well have been an indispensable key to the continued growth of Korea's education system and to the maintenance of minimum standards of quality during both the pre- and post-economic takeoff stages.

School Curricular Changes at the Levels of Primary and Secondary Education

The Korean Ministry of Education and Human Resources Development (MOEHRD) promulgates the national school curriculum, as described by Article 23 of the Elementary and Secondary School Education Law, in order to ensure the quality of all education. The MOEHRD determines the curriculum for all school levels and provides the guidelines for developing textbooks. The national curriculum is revised on a periodic basis to reflect the emerging needs of a changing society and the new frontiers of academic disciplines. The Korean government has made six large-scale curriculum revisions since 1953, mostly through the changing of textbooks. The latest curriculum revision was made in 1997 and recently came into effect, beginning with the 1st and 2nd grades of elementary schools in 2000, followed by the 3rd and 4th grades in 2001 and by the 5th and 6th grades in 2002. In middle and high schools, this curriculum revision applied to first year students and freshmen beginning in 2001 and 2002, respectively, and gradually takes effect up to the third year of high school (12th grade) by 2004. I will first examine the old curriculum and then briefly introduce the new one so as to show the differences between them.

Korean Primary School Curriculum: Table 4.10 shows the Korean elementary school curriculum. As in most countries, the national language takes more time in the schedule than any other subject. Also typical is the significant level of attention given to arithmetic, science, and social studies. The teaching hours given to these three subjects account for 34.2 percent of the grand total of teaching hours during the six school years. Korean schools differ from schools in many other countries in their emphasis on health and physical education, music, crafts, and moral education. As seen in table 4.10, these four subjects account for approximately one-third of the class hours per week in elementary schools.

Korean Middle School Curriculum: The objectives of the middle school, as indicated in table 4.11, are much wider. In addition to the continuation of subjects offered at the elementary school level, the middle

Table 4.10.   Korean Primary School Curriculum (unit: teaching hours)

Subject/Classification	1st Year	2nd Year	3rd Year	4th Year	5th Year	6th Year
Moral Education			68(2)	68(2)	68(2)	68(2)
Korean Language	330(11)	374(11)	238(7)	204(6)	204(6)	204(6)
Social Studies			102(3)	102(3)	136(4)	136(4)
Arithmetic	180(6)	204(6)	136(4)	136(4)	170(5)	170(5)
Science			102(3)	136(4)	136(4)	136(4)
Physical Education			102(3)	102(3)	102(3)	102(3)
Music	180(6)	238(7)	68(2)	68(2)	68(2)	68(2)
Fine Arts			68(2)	68(2)	68(2)	68(2)
Crafts			. . .	68(2)	68(2)	68(2)
Extracurricular Activities	*30(1)	*34(1)	68(2)	68(2)	68(2)	68(2)
Grand Total	790(24)	850(25)	952(28)	1020(30)	1088(32)	1088(32)

*The hours shown in this table represent the minimum school hours for 34 weeks per year.
*Extracurricular Activities in 1st and 2nd year are the principal's optional subjects.
*Figures in parentheses are hours taught per week.
Source: Adams, Don and Gottlieb, Esther E., *Education and Social Change in Korea*, Garland Publishing, Inc., 1993, p. 48.

Table 4.11.   Korean Middle School Curriculum (unit: teaching hours)

Subject/Classification	7th Grade	8th Grade	9th Grade
Moral Education	68(2)	68(2)	68(2)
Korean Language	136(4)	170(5)	170(5)
Korean History	. . .	68(2)	68(2)
Social Studies	102(3)	68–102(2–3)	68–102(2–3)
Mathematics	136(4)	102–136(3–4)	136–170(4–5)
Science	136(4)	102–136(3–4)	136–170(4–5)
Physical Education	102(3)	102(3)	102(3)
Music	68(2)	68(2)	34–68(1–2)
Fine Arts	68(2)	68(2)	34–68(1–2)
Classical Chinese	34(1)	34–68(1–2)	34–68(1–2)
English	136(4)	102–170(3–5)	102–170(3–5)
Vocational Skills (Boys)			
Home Economics (Girls)	Se 1: 102(3)	Se 1: 136–204(4–6)	. . .
Agriculture, Technical,			
Commerce, Fisheries,			
Housekeeping	. . .	. . .	Se 1: 136–204(4–6)
Elective	0–68(0–2)	0–68(0–2)	0–68(0–2)
Extracurricular Activities	68(2)	68(2)	68(2)
Grand Total	1156–1224(34–36)	1156–1224(34–36)	1156–1224(34–36)

*The hours shown in this table represent the minimum school hours alloted for 34 weeks per year.
*One teaching hour in this table represents 45 minutes.
*Se: Select.
*Figures in parentheses are hours taught per week.
Source: Adams, Don and Gottlieb, Esther E., *Education and Social Change in Korea*, Garland Publishing, Inc., 1993, p. 51.

school curriculum introduces first foreign languages (English and classical Chinese) and vocational skills for boys and home economics for girls. Since 1987, aside from the new science education program and the use of computers, emphasis has been placed on writing skills and English as a foreign language. A total of thirteen subjects are taught rather than the nine and six taught in the American systems. Each year Korean middle schools require 100 teaching hours more than are required in American middle schools. Also, a much larger proportion of teaching hours are allocated to the subjects of mathematics and science than the proportion in American middle schools.

Korean High School Curriculum: High schools in Korea are of two kinds: academic and vocational. I will only examine academic schools whose main objective is to promote advanced general studies preparing the students for higher education. The academic high school curriculum is shown in table 4.12. As an academic curriculum, it includes no vocational

Table 4.12.   Korean General (Academic) High School Curriculum, 1990

Classification	Subjects	Required Subjects Units (10th Grade)	Students Select One of Three Majors		
Moral Education	Moral Education	6			
Korean Language	Korean Language	10			
	Literature	8	8		
	Composition	6	4		4
	Grammer	4			
Korean History	Korean History	6			
Social Studies	Political Economy	6			
	Geography	4			
	World History	4	4		
	Social Studies/Culture	4			4
	World Geography	4			
Mathematics	Mathematics	8	10	18	6
Science	Science (1–2)	10	8		
	Physics		8		
	Chemistry		8	4	
	Biology		6		
	Earth Science		6		
Physical Education	Physical Education	6	8	8	8
Military Training	Military Training	12			
Music	Music	4			
Fine Arts	Fine Arts	4			2
Classical Chinese	Classical Chinese		8	4	4
Foreign Language	English (1–2)	8	12	12	8
	German				
	French				
	Spanish				
	Chinese				
	Japanese				
Industrial Arts and	Industrial Arts (Boys)				
Home Economics	Home Economics (Girls)				
	Agriculture				
	Technology				
	Commerce				
	Fisheries				
	Housekeeping				
Elective			2	2	2
Extracurricular Activities		12			
Grand Total			204–216		

Source: Adams, Don and Gottlieb, Esther E., *Education and Social Change in Korea*, Garland Publishing, Inc., 1993, p. 57.

subjects. The continued heavy emphasis on mathematics and science at the high school level should be noted. Science is further divided into four courses: physics, chemistry, biology, and earth science. Military training through the Student Defense Corps is a requirement. In addition to English, students elect another foreign language that they study up to 10 hours a week in the second and third years of high school. At the end of the first year, students select between humanities and natural science majors as preparatory courses for entrance to college.

New Reform of Korean Elementary, Middle, and High School Curriculum: The seventh curriculum, the latest version made on December 30, 1997, took effect for the first and second grades of elementary school in 2000 and it will gradually take effect up to the third year of high school (12th grade) by 2004.

The new curriculum seeks a fundamental change in the conventional "spoon-fed" classroom instruction, which has remained one-dimensional and uniform, in order to develop the human resources capable of leading the globalized, knowledge-information society of the twenty-first century. To meet this goal, the quantity of learning for each curricular subject has been optimized, a level-appropriate curriculum that takes into account the differences among students in ability and individuality has been adopted, and autonomous activities aimed at elevating the self-directed learning ability suitable for a knowledge-based society has been adopted and expanded.

The new curriculum is divided into the basic common curriculum and the elective-centered curriculum. The basic common curriculum covers ten years of schooling, starting from the first year of elementary school through the first year of high school, and the elective-centered curriculum for the final two years of high school.

Korean New National Common Basic Curriculum: The new national common basic curriculum differs much from the previous one (see table 4.13). The new curriculum introduces ten basic common subjects, autonomous activities, and special activities which cover the ten years from the first year of elementary school through the first year of high school. During this period, every citizen is expected to be educated in the elementary and basic knowledge required in the life of the Korean citizen. The elective subjects for the final two years of high school are designed to provide

Table 4.13. Korean National Common Basic Curriculum

	Schools	Elementary School						Middle School			High School		
	Grades	1	2	3	4	5	6	7	8	9	10	11	12
Subjects													
Subject Areas	Korean Language / Korean	238	204	204	204	170	136	136	136				
	Moral Education — Korean Language 210 238	34	34	34	34	68	68	34	34				
	Social Studies — Mathematics 120 136	102	102	102	102	102	102	136	170 (Korean History 68)				
	— Disciplined Life 60 68												
	Mathematics	136	136	136	136	136	136	102	136				
	Science — Intelligent Life 90 102	102	102	102	102	102	136	136	102				
	Practical Arts	...	...	68	68	Technology and Home Economics 68	102	102	102				
	— Pleasant Life 180 204												
	Physical Education	102	102	102	102	102	102	68	68				
	Music	68	68	68	68	68	34	34	34				
	Fine Arts — We are the first graders 80	68	68	68	68	34	34	68	34				
	Foreign Languages (English)	34	34	68	68	102	102	136	136				
Optional Activities		60	68	68	68	68	68	136	136	136	204		
Extracurricular Activities		30	34	34	68	68	68	68	68	68	68	8 units	
Grand Total		830	850	986	986	1088	1088	1156	1156	1156	1224	144 units	

(Right-most vertical heading for grades 11–12: Elective Courses)

Note:
1. The above table shows the minimum numbers of total annual instruction hours by subject and grade level during the period of national common basic education, 34 school weeks a year.
2. For grade 1, the standard number of school weeks assigned to subject matter, optional and extracurricular activities is 30. The number of instructional hours allocated to "We Are First Graders" represents the number of instructional hours in March.
3. In principle, one instructional hour covers 40 minutes in elementary school, 45 minutes in middle school, and 50 minutes in high school. However, the school is entitled to adjust the duration of each instructional hour depending on the weather and seasonal changes, the individual school situation, the developmental level of the students, the nature of learning, and so forth.
4. The number of extracurricular activities and the annual grand total for Grad 11 and Grade 12 represents the number of units to be completed to those two years.
Source: Ministry of Education and Human Resources Development (MOEHRD), Korea, *Education in Korea: 2002–2003*, 2003, p. 37.

student choice in consideration of individual differences in aptitude and career desires.

More emphasis is placed on the subject of science in this new curriculum. The goals of science education defined by the new curriculum are to instill in students curiosity and interest in natural phenomena and to help them acquire investigative skills and a healthy attitude toward nature. From table 4.13 we can see that science in the national common basic curriculum is being taught to students in grades three through ten. Students from grades three through five take the elementary course and those from grades six through ten take the enrichment supplementary course building on the elementary course.

Curricular hours for science during the first and second elementary years, under the subject title "Intelligent Life," are a minimum of 90 hours for the first year and 102 hours for the second year. From the third year on, there is an independent science subject, and the yearly hours allocated for different levels are 102 hours for the third through seventh year, 136 hours for the eighth through ninth year, and 102 hours for the tenth year.

However, subject matters for grades 1 and 2 are integrated in Korean Language, Mathematics, Disciplined Life, Pleasant Life, and We Are the First Graders. Optional activities are divided into subject matter optional activities and creative optional activities. Extracurricular activities are comprised of student government activities, adaptive activities, self-development activities, social service activities, and event activities. In addition, to expand foreign language education, starting from 2001, English has been taught as a part of the regular curriculum, one to two hours per week, beginning with the third grade. For this purpose, the allocation of English teachers is taken into consideration, and competent language teachers are given priority. A total of 856 native speakers of English have been invited by the government from the United States, Canada, Australia, New Zealand, the United Kingdom, and Ireland and placed in elementary, middle, and high schools in order to prepare for the "Age of Internationalization."[15]

Korean New High School Elective-Centered Curriculum (General Subjects): The elective-centered curriculum covers the second and third years of high school, during which students are given opportunities to decide their curriculum, track, and courses and thereby become educated in a variety of areas that fit their individual aptitude and career development (see table 4.14). The elective-centered curriculum includes humanities, natural sciences, vocational training, and other necessary subjects.

Similar to the national common basic curriculum, science subjects are underlined in the elective-centered curriculum. The elective-centered curriculum for high school consists of nine subjects: common science, physics I and II, chemistry I and II, biology I and II, and earth science I and II. All students are required to take eight units of common science. Students in the humanities and social science track are required to choose four units among physics I, chemistry I, biology I, and earth science I; students in the science track are required to choose eight units among physics II, chemistry II, biology II, and earth science II. Choosing the subjects for the two tracks follows the direction set by the metropolitan and provincial office of education.

Unlike the prior curriculum, the new curriculum is characterized by its emphases upon the talent, individuality, and creativity of the students who are the consumers of education. This new curricular revision focuses on learner-centered education with specific goals of developing:

- a person who seeks individuality on the basis of growth of the whole personality;
- a person who exerts creativity with fundamental capability;
- a person who pioneers a career path within a wide spectrum of culture;
- a person who creates new value on the basis of understanding his/her own culture as well as the cultures of other nations; and
- a person who contributes to the development of the community on the basis of democratic civil consciousness.[16]

High Quality of Korean Students in Mathematics and Science

I have noted in the previous sections the great quantitative growth of the Korean education system and the details of the curriculum. What about the quality of Korean education? Performing similarly to Japanese students and sometimes even better, the Korean primary and secondary

Table 4.14. Korean High School Elective–Centered Curriculum (General Subjects)

Subject Areas	Classification	National Common Basic Subjects	Elective Courses	
			General Elective Courses	Intensive Elective Courses
	Korean Language	Korean Language (8)	Korean Language Life (4)	Speech (4), Reading (8), Composition (8), Grammar (4), Literature (8)
	Moral Education	Moral Education (2)	Civic Ethics (4)	Ethics and thought (4), Traditional Ethics (4)
	Social Studies	Social Studies (10), Korean History (4)	Human Society and Environment (4)	Korean Geography (8), World Geography (8), Economic Geography (6), Korean Modern and Contemporary History (8), World History (8), Law and Society (6), Politics (8), Economics (6), Society and Culture (8)
	Mathematics	Mathematics (8)	Practical Mathematics (4)	Mathematics I (8), Mathematics II (8), Differentiation and Integration (4), Probability and Statistics (4), Discrete Mathematics (4)
	Science	Science (6)	Life and Science (4)	Physics I (4), Chemistry I (4), Biology I (4), Earth Science I (4) Physics II (6), Chemistry II (6), Biology II (6), Earth Science II (6)
	Technology Home Economics	Technology Home Economics (6)	Information Society and Computers (4)	Agricultural Science (6), Industrial Technology (6), Enterprise Management (6), Ocean Science (6), Home Science (6)

(continues)

Table 4.14. (Continued)

Subject Areas	Classification	National Common Basic Subjects	Elective Courses	
			General Elective Courses	Intensive Elective Courses
	Physical Education	Physical Education (4)	Gymnastics and Health (4)	Gymnastic Theory (4), Practice in Physical Education (4 or more)*
	Music	Music (2)	Music and Life (4)	Music Theory (4), Practice in Music (4 or more)*
	Fine Arts	Fine Arts (2)	Art and Life (4)	Art Theory (4), Practice in Art (4 or more)*
	Foreign Languages	English (8)		English I (8), English II (8), English Conversation (8), English Reading Comprehension (8) English Composition (8)
			German I (6), French I (6), Spanish I (6), Chinese I (6), Japanese I (6), Russian I (6), Arabic I (6)	German II (6), French II (6), Spanish II (6), Chinese II (6), Japanese II (6), Russian II (6), Arabic II (6)
	Chinese Characters and Classics		Chinese Characters and Classics (6)	Chinese Classical Literature (6)
	Military Training		Military Training (6)	

Liberal Arts	Philosophy (4), Logic (4), Psychology (4), Education (4), Life Economics (4), Religion (4), Ecology and Environment (4), Future Career & Occupation (4), Others (4)		
Total Units	(56)	24 or more	112 or fewer
Optional Activities	(12)		
Extracurricular Activities	(4)	8	
Grand Total Units		216	

Note:
1. The figure in ( ) are the numbers of units to be completed, and one unit means the amount of school learning in a 50-minute period of instruction per week for one semester (equivalent to 17 weeks).
2. The number of units allocated to the national common basic and optional activities and 4 units for extracurricular activities are to be completed in Grade 10.
3. The in-depth programs of Physical Education, Music and Fine Arts courses followed by an asterisk (*) should be selected from such specialized subjects as Physical Education and Arts.
4. In an in-depth elective program as a free elective is deemed necessary, the school may either select from the specialized subjects or create a new course in accordance with the guidelines of each Metropolitan or Provincial Office Education.
5. This table shows only general subjects.
6. * Specialized subjects include such areas as Agriculture, Industry, Commerce, Fishery and Marine Industry, Home Economics and Vocational Education, Science, Physical Education, Arts, Foreign Languages, International Affairs, etc. High schools aiming at specialized education should offer subjects at least 82 units as required courses from the specialized courses.

Source: Ministry of Education and Human Resources Development (MOEHRD), *Korea, Education in Korea: 2002–2003,* 2003, pp. 41–42.

school students have always ranked at the top level in international mathematics and science tests.

Table 4.15 shows the results of the 1995 TIMSS and 1999 TIMSS-R of 4th and 8th grade students of 17 nations as well as the changes in their performance relative to the international average scores. Here I cite only Korea and the United States. In mathematics, Korean 4th graders were ranked second in 1995, scoring 580, above the international average score by 63, while the American 4th grade score was 517, similar to the international average. Four years later when they became 8th graders in 1999, these students once again took the TIMSS-R mathematics test. Korean 8th graders were again ranked second, scoring 587, above the international average score by 63, while American 8th graders' score was only 502, and below the international average. In science, the Korean 4th and 8th graders performed excellently and were ranked first and fourth respectively; Korean students' scores were much above the international average in both 1995 and 1999. The American 4th graders performed well in science in 1995. However, when they grew up to be 8th graders, their scores decreased and their ranking declined, to 33 points below the ranking of Korean students.

Case 1. Mathematics and Science Achievement for TIMSS 1995 and TIMSS-R 1999.

Table 4.15. Mathematics and Science Achievement of Korean and American Students

	Mathematics					
Country	*Fourth grade, 1995*	*Score*	*Ranking*	*Eighth grade, 1999*	*Score*	*Ranking*
Korea		580	2		587	2
United States		517	9		502	12
Average		517			524	

	Science					
Country	*Fourth grade, 1995*	*Score*	*Ranking*	*Eighth grade, 1999*	*Score*	*Ranking*
Korea		576	1		548	4
United States		542	4		515	12
Average		514			524	

Source: Compiled by the author from: NSB, *Science and Engineering Indicators 2002*, pp. 1–16—1–20.

Case 2. Many other international mathematics and science tests also demonstrate the successful achievements of Korean students. In 1991, the Educational Testing Service initiated the International Assessment of Educational Progress. An international study was undertaken of science and mathematics proficiency. Fourteen industrialized nations and economies assessed nationally representative samples of their 13-year-olds, while 10 others assessed nationally representative samples of 9-year-olds. Comparing the overall averages for mathematics, U.S. students ranked at or near the bottom, with scores significantly lower than those of students from Korea, Hungary, Taiwan, the former Soviet Union, and Israel. The American 13-year-olds correctly answered about 55 percent of the mathematics problems, compared with Koreans and Taiwanese who correctly answered 73 percent.

The above two cases may suffice to convince us of the high level of achievement of Korean students in mathematics and science.

Vocational Education in Vocational High Schools

Despite their quantitative growth until the mid-1990s and their strong contribution to the nation's economic development through the training and supply of a quality technical workforce to the industry, vocational high schools have faced an identity crisis due to such recent changes as the transformation of the occupational world triggered by the arrival of the knowledge-based society and the dependence upon high technology in industrial structure; increasing demand for higher education following the elevated income level of the nation and of the average nuclear family; and the decrease in size of the school-aged population. As of 2001, 33.1 percent of the total number of high school students were attending vocational high schools; the number has been decreasing since 1996. About 57.7 percent of the graduates of vocational high schools became employed and 37.4 percent of them entered college; the rate of the graduates becoming employed is decreasing while that of those entering college is increasing.[17]

Understanding that the development of human resources is one of the key factors for determining the competitiveness of the nation as a whole as well as that of individual corporations, the Korean government has shifted its emphasis in vocational high schools away from the training of the technical workforce of the past to a curriculum that pursues simultaneously "continuing education" aimed at advancing to higher education and "terminal education" aimed at employment. A systemic change is underway, as the new emphasis was applied to schools in 2002.

Depending on the founding body, vocational high schools are classified as national, public, or private schools (see table 4.16). They are categorized in such specialized fields as agriculture, technology, commerce, fishery and marine industry, and home economics; in addition, there are corporate and comprehensive high schools. The required period of study in vocational high schools is three years. Table 4.16 indicates that the majority students in vocational education were enrolled in technical, commercial, and vocational/comprehensive high schools.

Vocational schools are of diverse types: high schools designed to train the workforce for the nation's key industries; specialized high schools designed to help students work in such fields as shoe manufacturing, cooking, and the animated film industry; and the "2 + 1 technical high school system" designed to train the workforce needed in the industries through two-year schooling and one-year training in industrial fields. Such diversity is intended to strengthen vocational education at the high

Table 4.16. Current Status of Vocational High Schools in Korea (2002)

Classification	Schools National & Public	Private	Total	Students National & Public	Private	Total	Teachers National & Public	Private	Total
Agricultural High Schools	28 (6.5)	0	28 (3.8)	16408 (5.7)	0	16408 (2.9)	1394 (6.4)	0	1394 (3.5)
Technical High Schools	132 (30.7)	77 (24.8)	209 (28.2)	131863 (45.4)	74665 (26.0)	206528 (36.0)	9650 (43.9)	4828 (26.9)	14478 (36.3)
Commercial High Schools	92 (21.4)	129 (41.5)	221 (29.8)	63234 (21.8)	138615 (48.2)	201849 (35.2)	4541 (20.7)	8197 (45.7)	12738 (31.9)
Fishery & Marine High Schools	8 (1.9)	0	8 (1.1)	4619 (1.6)	0	4619 (0.8)	373 (1.7)	0	373 (0.9)
Vocational/Comprehensive High Schools	170 (39.5)	105 (33.8)	275 (37.1)	74504 (25.6)	74465 (25.9)	145969 (25.5)	6004 (27.3)	4919 (27.4)	10923 (27.4)
Total	430 (100.0)	311 (100.0)	741 (100.0)	290628 (100.0)	287745 (100.0)	573373 (100.0)	21962 (100.0)	17944 (100.0)	39906 (100.0)

Note: The figures in parenthesis refer to percentage.
Source: Computed and compiled by the author from: Ministry of Education and Human Resources Development (MOEHRD), Korea, Education in Korea: 2002–2003, 2003, p. 87.

school level. Also, the Korean government has implemented the "2 + 2 curricular connection" project which connects the second and third-year courses of vocational high school to the first and second-year courses of junior college, not only to promote the development of vocational education, but also to satisfy the students' and parents' desire for opportunity in higher education.

In addition to vocational training in agriculture, technology, commerce, fishery and oceanography, industry, and home economics, students in vocational high schools are also required to be trained in advanced general education. They are required to take eight units of common science. For other subjects, they either take courses following the direction of the metropolitan and provincial office of education or take courses autonomously as electives. The Korean government is striving to devise a means to develop and support vocational high schools and to extend their roles as industry becomes more scientific and highly developed. The Korean government has provided incentives for vocational education as the major source of skilled manpower for the rapidly industrializing nation.

New College Entrance System

As we mentioned before, the Korean entrance examinations at different education levels might be more fierce than Japan's. Aware of the shortcomings of its entrance examination system, the Korean government has continued conducting reform of this system. The college entrance system has been changed more than ten times since 1945. Until 2001, however, students who applied for college entrance were evaluated based on their test scores and grade point averages. These criteria have put immense pressure on students as well as the economic burden on parents of supporting private tutoring. For example, the old college entrance system resulted in secondary education being characterized by rote-learning and memorization as valid methods of preparing for university admission.

The MOEHRD thus proposed a new college entrance system in order to root out these problems and to cultivate the individual talents and characteristics of students. The new system is characterized by three words: diversification, specialization, and autonomy. The new college entrance system allows each university or college to develop its own criteria for admitting students. Therefore, universities and colleges may require varying application materials from students in order to determine their different talents, such as School Activities Records, essays, interviews, recommendations, etc.

Principles for the New College Entrance System: All universities are allowed to develop their screening system in regards to pursuing diversification, specialization, and autonomy. The reform of the college entrance system has made it possible for elementary and secondary schools to offer a more appropriate and desirable education to their students. Also, it is expected to lessen the overheated zeal for private tutoring.

Student Recruitment: All universities are allowed to recruit students on a year-round basis, as part of the full degree of autonomy allocated to them in academic affairs. Universities select eligible applicants based on optional materials such as their School Activities Records, College Scholastic Abilities Test, essay-writing, letter of recommendation, interview, and/or performance-based test. They can also select eligible applicants based upon extenuating circumstances such as being a resident of a rural area or a fishing village, an orphan, and/or a winner of certain contests.

Materials for Selecting Eligible Applicants:

- School Activities Records;
- College Scholastic Ability Test;
- Tests administered by individual universities/colleges (essay-writing, interview, aptitude test, etc.);
- Letters of Recommendation;
- Aptitude Tests;
- Awards and prizes.

School Activities Records: The Presidential Commission on Educational Reform announced on May 31, 1995, that individual students' School Activities Records should be constructed by teachers. The purpose of this new evaluation system is to get not only summative information but also diagnostic and formative information about students' academic achievements, as well as a record of the development of social behaviors.

College Scholastic Ability Test: The College Scholastic Ability Test (CSAT) is administered once a year on the national level. The purposes of the CSAT are:

- To screen candidates' eligibility for higher education;
- To contribute to the improvement of high school education, and
- To provide valid, reliable, and objective data for selecting new students for colleges and universities.

The CSAT is divided into three options. The first option is for students on the humanities and social science track, the second for students on the natural science track, and the third for students on the sports and arts track. There are differences in both test content and test scores for each track. For example, the maximum score in the social studies test for the humanities and social science track and the arts and sports track students is 72, but for natural science track students it is 48. The maximum test score in science for the humanities and social science track and arts and sports track students is 48, but for natural science track students it is 72.

Since 1998 a standardized scale score has been adopted to adjust the differences in scores from elective subject tests. The student report card for the SCAT gives raw scores for each subject, percentile scores of the raw scores, and standardized T-scores and weighted standardized T-scores for each track and area (see table 4.17).

Table 4.17.   Format of the College Scholastic Ability Test (CSAT) in Korea (2002)

Content Area	Number of Items	Raw Scores	Period of Time (minutes)	Item Types
Language Ability (Korean)	60	120	90	5-option multiple-choice items
Mathematics	30	80	100	5-option multiple-choice items (24) & short answer items (6)
Social Studies & Science	80	120	120	5-option multiple-choice items
English	50	80	70	5-option multiple-choice items
Total	220	400	380	
Second Foreign Language	30	40	40	Elective (Not included in the total score)

Source: Ministry of Education and Human Resources Development (MOEHRD), Korea, *Education in Korea: 2002–2003*, 2003, p. 126.

Enrollment Distribution of Higher Education Students by Gender and Field of Study

Enrollment Distribution by Gender: Unfortunately, the latest data available on the gender enrollment distribution in Korean higher education are from 1995. Since World War II, female student enrollment in higher education has dramatically increased, showing an expansion rate that is by far the highest among female student enrollment at all levels of the formal education system. However, the statistical data shows that the actual percentage of female students making up the student body of tertiary education changed much less over the years. Table 4.18 shows that the total enrollment of female students in the higher education system was 25.2 percent in 1965. This percentage has been slowly increasing over the years and reached 30.5 percent in 1990, with a total gain of only 5.3 percent.

The data also reveals that the percentage of female students in teacher's colleges has always been the highest among all types of higher education institutions (42.1 percent in 1965 and 64.5 percent in 1990). This suggests that a strong traditional notion that teaching is a woman's job persists over the years.[18] It is important to note that the percentage of women enrolled in graduate schools has also increased quite a bit over the years, from 7.8 percent in 1965 to 22.5 percent in 1990. However, the percentage of women in junior colleges and four-year universities has not increased as much compared to the percentage of women in other institutions (from 29.4 percent and 22.5 percent in 1965 to 38 percent and 32 percent in 1995, respectively).

Table 4.18. Percentage of Female Students in Korea by Type of Higher Education Institutions, 1965–1995

Year	Total	Junior College	Teachers College	Four-Year University	Graduate School
1965	25.2	29.4	42.1	22.5	7.8
1970	24.6	24.8	54.3	22.3	12.2
1975	27.6	28.3	58	26.5	16.4
1980	24.2	25.9	81.9	22.4	17
1985	28.8	36	72.9	26.8	18.3
1990	30.5	36.9	64.5	28.5	22.5
1995		38		32	

Source: Weidman, John C. and Park, Namgi, *Higher Education in Korea: Tradition and Adaptation,* Falmer Press, 2000, pp. 134–135.

The data in table 4.19 shows an imbalance of gender in Korean higher education. In 1975, female students constituted 61 percent of the junior college student body. This was due to the predominance of the tradition-ally female fields of study in the earliest junior colleges to be established. However, as the number of junior colleges increased and the available fields of study expanded, the percentage of women decreased dramatically and then stabilized at a ratio of about one-third. The gender ratio of students enrolled in four-year universities has improved since 1945. How-ever, the female-to-male student ratio remained at .46 in 1995, indicating that there were more than twice as many male as female students on cam-puses of four-year universities in Korea. Even though the percentage of female students had increased since 1975 in both junior colleges and four-year universities, the percentage of female students in junior colleges con-tinued to be higher than in four-year universities.

Enrollment Distribution by Field of Study: Unfortunately, the latest data available on the enrollment distribution by field of study in Korean higher education are again from 1995. In Korea, students are expected to choose their major or field of study before they apply for a certain college

Table 4.19. Enrollment Distribution of Higher Education Students in Korea by Gender, 1975–1995

	1975	1980	1985	1990	1995
Junior College Students					
Total	3,787	151,199	242,114	323,825	569,820
Female	2,352	39,883	87,123	119,345	214,310
(%)	(61)	(26)	(36)	(36)	(38)
Male	1,435	111,316	233,991	204,480	355,510
(%)	(39)	(74)	(64)	(64)	(62)
F/M Ratio	1.63	.36	.56	.58	.60
Four-Year University Students					
Total	208,986	402,979	931,884	1,040,166	1,187,735
Female	55,439	90,634	250,088	296,129	378,418
(%)	(27)	(22)	(27)	(28)	(32)
Male	153,547	312,345	681,796	744,037	809,317
(%)	(73)	(78)	(73)	(72)	(68)
F/M Ratio	.36	.29	.37	.40	.46

Note: The figures in parenthesis refer to percentage.
Source: Weidman, John C. and Park, Namgi, *Higher Education in Korea: Tradition and Adaptation,* Falmer Press, 2000, p. 135.

or university. One of the personal factors that has a great impact on such a decision is the student's gender. Since there is a clear segregation by gender among academic fields of major, it is very difficult for females to apply for traditionally male fields of study and to expect to succeed in those majors. Table 4.20 represents the distribution of junior college and four-year university students by gender and field of study. The data clearly show a strong segregation among college majors: traditionally, male-dominated fields of study are social sciences, natural sciences, and engineering and medical programs; teacher education, humanities, home economics, and fine arts are areas considered more suitable as women's majors.

Although there was a steady increase in women's enrollment in higher education in general, a noticeable difference in the representation of women in fields of study in 1995 was that junior colleges showed a higher percentage of female students in all fields of study compared with the same fields in four-year universities. These results imply that during the expansion of higher education in Korea in the early 1990s, men benefited

Table 4.20.   Enrollment Distribution of Higher Education Students in Korea by Field of Study, 1995

	All Fields	Humanities	Social Sciences	Natural Sciences	Medicine, Pharmacy	Arts, Physical Ed.	Teacher Ed.
Junior College Students							
Total	569,820	22,793	119,662	296,306	56,982	56,982	17,095
(%)	(100)	(04)	(21)	(52)	(10)	(10)	(3)
Female	214,310	12,859	55,721	57,864	364,333	6,433	17,145
(%)	(100)	(6)	(26)	(27)	(17)	(16)	(8)
Male	355,510	10,665	60,437	238,192	21,331	24,886	0
(%)	(100)	(3)	(17)	(67)	(6)	(7)	(0)
F/M Ratio	.38	.55	.48	.20	.64	.57	1.00
Four-Year University Students							
Total	1,187,735	166,283	308,811	522,603	47,509	83,141	59,387
(%)	(100)	(14)	(26)	(44)	(4)	(7)	(5)
Female	378,418	87,036	79,468	109,741	18,921	49,194	41,626
(%)	(100)	(23)	(21)	(29)	(5)	(13)	(11)
Male	809,317	80,932	226,609	412,752	24,280	40,466	24,280
(%)	(100)	(10)	(28)	(51)	(3)	(5)	(3)
F/M Ratio	.32	.52	.26	.21	.39	.56	.65

Source: Weidman, John C. and Park, Namgi, *Higher Education in Korea: Tradition and Adaptation,* Falmer Press, 2000, pp. 138–139.

with more opportunities to gain access to a four-year college education as opposed to two years of higher education. This occurred because the Korean government allowed the establishment or expansion of traditionally male dominated major fields in four-year universities while it encouraged junior colleges to build or expand traditionally female dominated majors and departments.[19]

Taken together, these data suggest very strongly that, despite some gains in past years before the mid-1990s, there continued to be significant gender segregation by field in Korean higher education. Therefore, female students were situated less favorably than men.

Distribution of Korean Undergraduate and Graduate Students by Field of Study in 2001: figure 4.2, figure 4.3, figure 4.4, figure 4.5, table 4.21, table 4.22, and table 4.23 reveal the latest data of distribution by major of the whole body of Korean undergraduate and graduate education in 2001.

From figure 4.2 and table 4.21 we can see that emphasis is placed on the majors such as engineering, natural sciences, and social sciences in almost all types of higher education institutions. Engineering, natural sciences, and social sciences combined together account for 69 percent of all higher education enrollment.

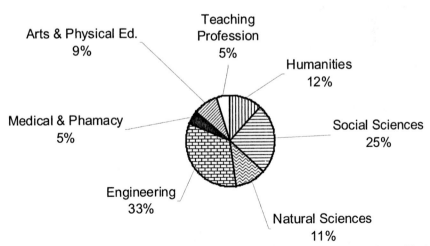

Figure 4.2. Enrollment Distribution of Higher Education Students in Korea by Field of Study, 2001.

Source: Cited from table 4.21.

Table 4.21.   Enrollment Distribution of Higher Education Students in Korea by Field of Study, 2001 (Unit: person)

Classification	Humanities	Social Sciences	Natural Sciences	Engineering	Medical & Pharmacy	Arts & Physical Ed.	Teaching Profession
Grand Total	381,979	815,778	367,886	1,083,335	157,153	287,347	163,812
University	232,363	465,999	222,674	527,372	62,992	149,878	68,460
University of Education	. . .	. . .	. . .	. . .	. . .	. . .	21,418
Industrial University	8,939	39,844	13,681	100,334	737	15,299	1,234
Technical College	. . .	99	. . .	99	. . .	. . .	. . .
Air & Corr. University	104,221	128,926	39,224	29,877	20,534	. . .	47,879
Junior College	35,228	180,486	92,306	425,653	72,890	121,295	24,791
Miscellaneous School (Junior College)	40	. . .	. . .	. . .	. . .	605	. . .
Miscellaneous School (College)	1,288	424	1	. . .	. . .	270	30

Source: Ministry of Education and Human Resources Development (MOEHRD), Korea, *2001 Brief Statistics of Korean Education*, 2002 <http://www.moe.go.kr/English/> (12 Dec. 2002).

At the graduate education level, things are a little different (see table 4.22, figure 4.3 and figure 4.4). First, in 2001 master's students and doctoral students made up 86.3 percent and 13.7 percent of higher education students, respectively; secondly, the largest proportion of degrees sought at the master's level are in social sciences (27 percent), the teaching pro-

Table 4.22.   Enrollment of Graduate Students in Korea by Field of Study, 2001 (Unit: person)

Classification	Grand Total	Master's Degree Course	Doctor's Degree Course
Grand Total	243,270	209,865	33,405
Humanities	24,867	21,273	3,594
Social Sciences	60,658	55,084	5,574
Natural Sciences	20,859	15,266	5,593
Engineering	49,251	39,469	9,782
Medical & Pharmacy	18,968	12,804	6,164
Arts & Physical Ed.	16,166	15,016	1,150
Teaching Profession	52,501	50,953	1,548

Source: Ministry of Education and Human Resources Development (MOEHRD), Korea, *2001 Brief Statistics of Korean Education*, 2002 <http://www.moe.go.kr/English/> (12 Dec. 2002).

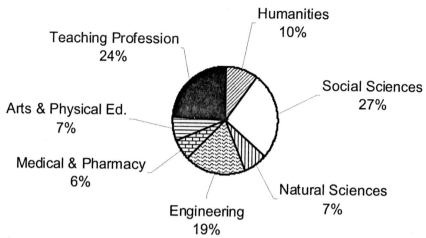

Figure 4.3. Enrollment of Master's Degree Student in Korea by Field of Study, 2001
Source: Ministry of Education (MOE), Korea, *Educational Statistics,* 2002.

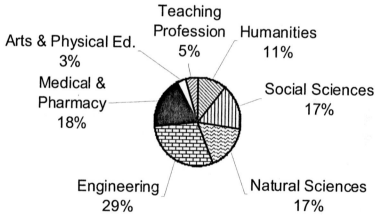

Figure 4.4. Enrollment of Doctoral Students in Korea by Field of Study, 2001
Source: Cited form table 4.22.

fession (24 percent), and engineering (19 percent), while at the doctoral level engineering accounts for close to one-third (29 percent), followed by medical and pharmacy (18 percent), natural sciences (17 percent), and social sciences (17 percent).

Since the mid-1980s, doctoral degrees awarded in Korea have been steadily increasing. As figure 4.5 shows, within the five years between 1996 and 2001 the number of doctoral degrees awarded in Korea increased by 72 percent, from 4,786 in 1996 to 6,646 in 2001. As the capacity of doctoral degree training has been growing, according to the statistics of the US National Science Board, in 1991 Korean students earned more S&E doctoral degrees at home than at universities in the United States.[20] Table 4.23 shows that the largest proportion of the earned doctoral degrees in 2001 were in engineering (28.1 percent), followed by degrees in medicine and pharmacy (24.4 percent) and in natural sciences (21.4 percent).

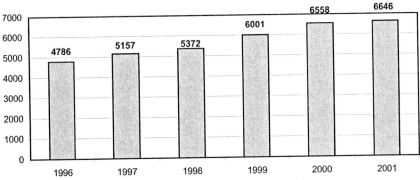

Figure 4.5.   Doctoral Degrees Awarded in Korea, 1996–2001

Source: Cited form table 4.23.

Table 4.23.   Doctoral Degrees Awarded in Korea by Field of Study, 1996–2001 (Unit: person)

Year	1996 Degree	(%)	1997 Degree	(%)	1998 Degree	(%)	1999 Degree	(%)	2000 Degree	(%)	2001 Degree	(%)
Humanities	683	14.3	700	13.6	717	13.3	708	11.8	746	11.4	716	10.8
Social Science	636	13.3	649	12.3	627	11.7	697	11.6	810	12.4	761	11.5
Education	129	2.7	144	2.8	154	2.9	182	3	209	3.2	224	3.4
Natural Science	918	19.2	1,018	19.7	1,116	20.8	1,214	20.2	1,340	20.4	1,420	21.4
Engineering	1,259	26.3	1,420	27.5	1,500	27.9	1,720	28.7	1,803	27.5	1,865	28.1
Medicine	1,125	23.5	1,187	23	1,233	22.9	1,433	23.9	1,605	24.5	1,622	24.4
Fishery	7	0.2	6	0.1	6	0.1	11	0.2	5	0.1	10	0.2
Home Economics	29	0.6	33	0.6	19	0.4	40	0.7	40	0.6	28	0.4
Total	4,786	100	5,157	100	5,372	100	6,001	100	6,558	100	6,646	100

Source: Computed and compiled from: Ministry of Education and Human Resources Development (MOEHRD), Korea, *2001 Brief Statistics of Korean Education*, 2002 <http://www.moe.go.kr/English/> (12 Dec. 2002).

KOREAN INTERNATIONAL EDUCATION AT
HOME AND ABROAD

As Adams pointed out in 1993, one major indicator of Western influence on the development of the Korean knowledge system is the number of Korean students studying abroad. To meet the demands of the age of internationalization, overseas studies have been liberalized in Korea. As early as 1956, the Korean government provided testing, guidance, and scholarship assistance for students who wanted to pursue overseas study. Opportunities for Koreans to study abroad during the period of the 1950s and 1960s were largely limited to those students who had received scholarships from the United States government, from private foundations, or directly from United States institutions. During the 1970s, a policy change on the part of the Korean government allowed students to study abroad at their own expense. Between 1953 and 1979, 15,206 Korean students studied abroad (85.1 percent of them in the United States, 3.9 percent in West Germany, 2.1 percent in France, and the rest in other countries).[21] As a result of the policy, the number of students seeking graduate study outside Korea expanded considerably.

In 1980 the Korean government not only eased the qualification test for study abroad but also opened the way for undergraduate study overseas. It was reported that out of 13,113 students studying abroad in 1983, most studied in graduate schools (72 percent in the United States). By 1988 Korean undergraduate students were also found in a significant number in the United States.

Aside from sending students abroad for study, the Korean government also supports sending professors and other experts to foreign universities and research institutes for the purpose of importing advanced foreign knowledge and comparing domestic academic development to the global standard.[22] Such support has contributed to training Korean experts in various specialized fields. The Korean Research Foundation selects and sends approximately 100 scholars overseas every year. The number was increased to 110 in 2001.

Korea is a Leading Home Country of International Students in the United States: From figure 4.6 we can see a few features of Korean international students in the United States. First, in the past sixteen years since

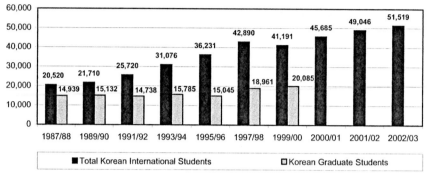

Figure 4.6.   Enrollment of Korean International Students in U.S. Universities, from 1987/88 to 2002/03

Source: Collected and compiled from: 1. NSB, *Science and Engineering Indicators 2002*, pp. A2-31–A2-32. Institute of International Education (IIE), *Open Doors*, 2001, 2002 and 2003.

the mid-1980s the number of Korean international students in the United States has increased rapidly: from 20,520 in the 1987–1988 academic year to 51,519 in the 2002–2003 academic year, an increase of 60.2 percent. Secondly, its graduate students make up a larger proportion of the total Korean international students: the graduate students accounted for about two-thirds before the 1990s and for about a half after 1990. In the 2002–2003 academic year its graduate students accounted for 47.8 percent, undergraduate students for 42.3 percent while others for 10.0 percent.[23] Thirdly, in the 2001–2002 academic year, Korea surpassed Japan as the third leading nation in sending international students to the United States: Korea's 51,519 students now represent 8.8 percent of the total number of international students in the United States, an increase of 5 percent from the 2001–2002 academic year, marking the third year of large increases after decreases in the late 1990s reflecting the Asian economic crises.[24]

Korea is a new attractive center for both foreign students and overseas Korean students: Since the mid-1980s, the Korean government has shifted its goal from sending students overseas to receiving students from overseas. Concrete means to this goal include participation in student-recruiting fairs in various countries; strengthening advertising for studying in Korea through a "Study in Korea Fair"; and supporting foreign students studying in Korea through simplification of the various regulations on foreign students' life in Korea. The number of foreign students in Korea has indeed been growing. According to Adams' report in 1993, between 1965 and 1986 a total of 1,222 foreign students studied in Korea. As table 4.24 shows, the total number of foreign students studying in Korea in 1998 was 2,143.

As a part of the effort to spread deep understanding of Korea and promote international exchange in learning and culture, MOEHRD scholarships are provided to foreign students who wish to study in Korea for advanced degrees. The Invitation to Study in Korea program started in 1967, and 780 students invited from 79 countries were studying in Korea as of the end of 2002 (see table 4.25).

Table 4.24. Foreign Students at Korean Universities, 1998

Nationality	Total	Undergraduate	Graduate	Others
Total	2,143	1,279	803	61
China	466	181	291	14
Taiwan	444	398	37	
Japan	395	242	149	4
United States	299	122	115	3
Malaysia	130	99	1	30
Canada	58	27	31	0
Argentina	49	44	4	1
Paraguay	28	27	1	0
Germany	14	9	5	0
Others	240	122	115	3

Source: Yamamoto, Shinichi, "*Graduate Education Reform and International Mobility of Scientists in Japan and Related Information for Korea,*" in *Graduate Education Reform in Europe, Asia and the Americas and International Mobility of Scientists and Engineers: Proceedings of an NSF Workshop,* US National Science Foundation, April 2000, p. 83.

Table 4.25. Number of Foreign Students Invited by the Korean Government from 1967 to 2002

Year	1967–1993	1994	1995	1996	1997	1998	1999	2000	2001	2002	Total
No. of invited students	293	26	41	54	70	45	78	73	46	54	780
No. of countries of origin	67	18	24	25	29	21	30	30	19	24	79

Source: Ministry of Education and Human Resources Development (MOEHRD), Korea, *Education in Korea: 2002–2003,* 2003, p. 103.

In addition to receiving foreign students, the Korean government has also been trying to attract and encourage Korean overseas students to return home. So far their efforts have been successful in comparison with the efforts of other Asian nations and economies. Table 4.26 indicates that of the Korean holders of doctoral degrees earned in the United States in the 1992–1993 academic year, only 9 percent were still working in the United States in 1997, compared with 92 percent of doctoral degree recipients from China, 83 percent from India, and 36 percent from Taiwan.

Table 4.26. Asian Foreign Students Earning Doctoral S&E Degrees in 1992–1993 Who were Working in the United States in 1997, by Nation

Nation of Origin	Foreign Doctoral Recipients	Percent (%) Working in US in 1997
S&E Fields, Total	16,391	53%
Taiwan	2,149	36%
Korea	2,056	9%
China (PRC)	4,010	92%
Japan	214	21%
India	1,549	83%

Source: Johnson, Jean, "Collaboration in S&T Information Exchange between the United States and China," paper presented at CIES 2000 Conference, San Antonio, Texas, March 7–11, 2000.

NOTES

1. Don Adams and Esther E. Gottlieb, *Education and Social Change in Korea* (New York, NY: Garland Publishing, Inc., 1993), 26.

2. Adams and Gottlieb, *Education and Social Change in Korea*, 49.

3. Ministry of Education and Human Resource Development (MOEHRD), Korea, *Education in Korea: 2002–2003* (Seoul, Korea: 2003), 42.

4. Ministry of Education and Human Resource Development (MOEHRD), Korea, *Education in Korea: 2001–2002,* (Seoul, Korea: 2002) <http://www.moe.go.kr/English/> (16 Nov. 2002), 31.

5. Ministry of Education and Human Resource Development (MOEHRD), Korea, *Education in Korea: 2001–2002,* (Seoul, Korea: 2002), 33.

6. Though the Korean entrance examinations at different educational levels might be more fierce than Japan's, which are described as "battlefield" rather as "struggle" or "competition." We will make an introduction of the Korean new college entrance system later.

7. Namgi Park, "Continuing Debates: Government Financial Aid to the Private Higher Education Sector and Faculty Tenure," in *Higher Education in Korea: Tradition and Adaptation, ed.* John C. Weidman and Namgi Park (New York, NY: Falmer Press, 2000), 117.

8. Ministry of Education and Human Resource Development (MOEHRD), Korea, *Education in Korea: 2001–2002,* (Seoul, Korea: 2002), 36.

9. Adams and Gottlieb, *Education and Social Change in Korea,* 160.

10. Noel F. McGinn, Donald R. Snodgrass, Yong Bong Kim, Shin-bok Kim and Quee-young Kim, *Education and Development in Korea,* (Cambridge, Mass.: Council on East Asian Studies, Harvard University: Distributed by Harvard University Press, 1980), 62.

11. Adams and Gottlieb, *Education and Social Change in Korea,* 160 and 163.

12. Adams and Gottlieb, *Education and Social Change in Korea,* 166.

13. Namgi Park, "The 31 May 1995 Higher Education Reform," in *Higher Education in Korea: Tradition and Adaptation, ed.* John C. Weidman and Namgi Park (New York, NY: Falmer Press, 2000), 170.

14. Namgi Park and John C. Weidman, "Battlefield for Higher Education," in *Higher Education in Korea: Tradition and Adaptation, ed.* John C. Weidman and Namgi Park (New York, NY: Falmer Press, 2000), 178.

15. Ministry of Education and Human Resource Development (MOEHRD), Korea, *Education in Korea: 2001–2002,* (Seoul, Korea: 2002), 43.

16. Ministry of Education and Human Resource Development (MOEHRD), Korea, *Education in Korea: 2002–2003,* (Seoul, Korea: 2003), 33–34.

17. Ministry of Education and Human Resource Development (MOEHRD), Korea, *Education in Korea: 2002–2003,* (Seoul, Korea: 2003), 87.

18. Jaelim Oh and Jeannie Myung-suk Pang, "Female Students and Faculty," in *Higher Education in Korea: Tradition and Adaptation, ed.* John C. Weidman and Namgi Park (New York, NY: Falmer Press, 2000), 134.

19. Oh and Pang, "Female Students and Faculty," 137 and 140.

20. National Science Board (NSB), *Science and Engineering Indicators—2002,* Vol. 2 (Arlington, VA: National Science Foundation, 2002), A2-74.

21. Adams and Gottlieb, *Education and Social Change in Korea,* 106.

22. Ministry of Education and Human Resource Development (MOEHRD), Korea, *Education in Korea: 2002–2003,* (Seoul, Korea: 2003), 100.

23. Institute of International Education (IIE), *Open Doors,* 2003.

24. Institute of International Education (IIE), *Open Doors,* 2002.

Chapter Five

Profile of Taiwanese Education

Summary of findings: Due largely to the same culture and tradition, the education system in Taiwan shares with Korea many common and similar traits, which include the high value attached by people and society to education, universalization of primary education prior to the economic takeoff, a high average level of education in the workforce, efficient vocational education, and the rapid expansion of higher education so that total enrollment actually surpasses enrollment in senior and junior high schools. The Taiwanese education system has also been distinguished for its highly-developed private education sector which accommodates about one-half of the student population at the tertiary education level and also offers supplementary education which provides people with an alternative way to achieve their educational goals. Achievements in education helped Taiwan to join the group of NIEs as early as the 1970s. Taiwan has been one of the leading economies of origin of international students in the United States and has relied heavily on the United States for advanced training for many years. However, the turning point came in 1998 when Taiwanese, for the first time, earned more S&E doctoral degrees at Taiwanese universities than at universities in the United States. As in the Korean situation, a very important feature is that the longstanding efforts of the Taiwanese government to attract Taiwanese students back home have been successful over the past decade and Taiwan has become one of

the few economies in the world that have successfully turned
brain drain into brain gain.

OVERVIEW

Taiwan, an island to the southeast of Mainland China, is one of the most
densely populated areas in the world: 35,873 square kilometers in size
with more than 22 million inhabitants. Taiwan was a part of China before
it was ceded to Japan in 1895. During the 50 years of Japanese occupation, a Western-style system of education was first introduced into Taiwan
via the Japanese. One university, one high school, and three junior colleges were established during that time. The enrollment was very small,
and the function of these institutions was to provide research capability
and high-level manpower in support of Japan's policies of colonization
and expansion.

At the end of World War II in 1945, Taiwan was restored to China. The
island's education system was soon replaced by the one adopted on the
mainland in 1922, which mainly follows the American prototype: 6-3-
3-4 single track. The Constitution of the Republic of China, which was
promulgated in 1947, unequivocally states that all citizens shall have
equal opportunities for receiving an education and that the poor shall be
given financial assistance.[1] After the Chinese National Party moved its
seat to Taiwan in 1949, Chinese education policy was imposed on the
island more thoroughly than before and Japanese influence diminished
further.

Growth of Taiwanese Education

Since 1949, Taiwan has witnessed a remarkable educational expansion
that led Taiwan to become one of the most highly educationally developed
economies in the world. To meet the needs of immediate economic development and the growing demand for skilled human resources, education
in Taiwan rapidly expanded over the past half century between the 1950–
1951 academic year and 2002–2003 academic year. By examining figure
5.1 and table 5.1, we see the characteristics of Taiwan's education system,
which resemble those of Korea's education system. First, student enroll-

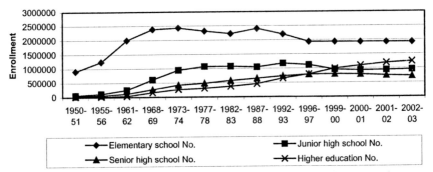

Figure 5.1.   Student Enrollment in Taiwan at All Levels (from 1950/51 to 2002/03)

Source: Cited from table 5.1.

Table 5.1.   Student Enrollment and Ratio at All Levels in Taiwan (from 1950–1951 to 2002–2003)

Academic Year	Total	Elementary school		Junior high school		Senior high school		Higher education	
		No.	%	No.	%	No.	%	No.	%
1950–51	1010440	906950	89.76	61082	6.05	35743	3.54	6665	0.66
1955–56	1436582	1244029	86.60	116192	8.09	58187	4.05	18174	1.27
1961–62	2402754	1997016	83.11	252107	10.49	115228	4.80	38403	1.60
1968–69	3431782	2383204	69.45	617225	17.99	270016	7.87	161337	4.70
1973–74	4076410	2431440	59.65	948872	23.28	425203	10.43	270895	6.65
1977–78	4191246	2319342	55.34	1075455	25.66	487866	11.64	308583	7.36
1982–83	4266038	2226699	52.20	1082358	25.37	581285	13.63	375696	8.81
1987–88	4572548	2400614	52.50	1053923	23.05	653347	14.29	464664	10.16
1992–93	4763755	2200968	46.20	1179028	24.75	730597	15.34	653162	13.71
1996–97	4639238	1934756	41.70	1120716	24.16	788219	16.99	795547	17.15
1999–00	4677496	1927179	41.20	957209	20.46	798825	17.08	994283	21.26
2000–01	4731572	1925981	40.70	929534	19.65	783955	16.57	1092102	23.08
2001–02	4797165	1925491	40.14	935738	19.51	748711	15.61	1187225	24.75
2002–03	4838285	1918034	39.64	956823	19.78	723136	14.95	1240292	25.63

Note: Data on senior high schools include the enrollments of both senior high schools and senior vocational high schools while data on higher education include the enrollments of two-year junior colleges, four-year universities, master's degree programs and doctoral degree programs.

Source: Computed and compiled by the author from: Ministry of Education. *Educational Statistics of the Republic of China (ROC), 2003 Edition*, pp. 20–23.

ment quickly expanded at all levels after World War II: student enrollment at all levels increased by 4.8 times from 1,010,440 in 1950–1951 to 4,838,285 in 2002–2003. Enrollment in elementary school, junior high school, senior high school, and higher education increased by 2.1 times, 15.7 times, 20.2 times, and 186.1 times, respectively. Second, the number of higher education institutions at the tertiary education level in Taiwan increased much more greatly than the number at any other level during this period. Most surprising is that the absolute number of higher education enrollment surpassed that of both senior high school in 1996 and junior high school in 1999, successively. In 2002–2003, higher education enrollment was 1,240,292 while that of junior high and senior high school were 956,823 and 723,136, respectively. The ratio of Taiwanese higher education enrollment was 25.63 percent as opposed to 19.78 percent and 14.95 percent for junior and senior high school enrollment, respectively.

It is worth noting that Taiwan and Korea are the only two of the five Asian economies we are examining whose higher education enrollment proportion is larger than that of secondary education and the reasons accounting for this uniqueness are also similar: First, policy makers in Taiwan have for a long time believed that Taiwan's economic growth has to be supported by large investment expenditures on human resources through education to supply a qualified workforce. The Taiwanese government has emphasized the impact of education on economic performance. This is reflected in the fact that the educational expenditures of Taiwan have gradually but consistently increased during the past fifty years. Figure 5.2 reveals this persistent growth of Taiwan's educational expenditures as a percentage of GNP from 1951 to 2001–2002. During this period, the figure increased from 1.73 percent to 6.09 percent. (In the peak year of 1993, the figure was 6.98 percent.) Such vast investment in education makes it possible for many students to advance to the next higher level of education. In 2002, 95.48 percent of junior high school graduates entered senior high schools while 69.01 percent of senior high school graduates entered higher education. Secondly, from the 1980s onward, enrollment in junior high schools and then senior high schools in the 1990s decreased due largely to the decline of birth rate.

Taiwan's striking development in higher education was also spurred by the political reform that occurred in the late 1980s. Since the 1970s, greater economic affluence and an expanded educational perspective

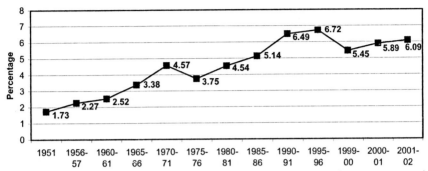

Figure 5.2. **Educational Expenditure and its Percentage of GNP in Taiwan, 1951–2001/ 2002**

Sources:
1. Ministry of Education (MOE) (ROC), *Education Statistical Indicators,* Republic of China (ROC), 2001, p. 48.
   2. Ministry of Education (MOE) (ROC), *Education Statistics of the Republic of China,* 2003 Edition, p. 47.

increased public demand for a more open society, prompting the government to liberalize the strictly controlled political environment. Starting in 1987, the Taiwanese government implemented a series of political reforms that included the lifting of martial law, permission for people to travel to mainland China, the lifting of restriction on the formation of political parties, the opening of newspapers, and permission for students to go abroad to study at their own expense. The smooth transformation from an authoritarian society into a democratic one resulted in a quite remarkable growth in higher education enrollment over the next fifteen years. This political reform led to a more open and democratic higher education system, which is now a better position to meet the growing demand of college-age cohorts for higher education.

EDUCATIONAL ADMINISTRATION, FINANCE, AND REFORMS

Educational Administration

As in Japan and Korea, a very significant feature of Taiwan's education system is its strong centralization, though in recent years several reforms have taken place to decentralize some aspects. The Ministry of Education in Taiwan has a great deal of power over educational institutions. This

power includes approving and controlling the establishment of departments, programs, schools, and universities at all levels, the sizes of enrollment, tuition rates, required courses, minimum graduation credits, and
other factors at all institutions, both public and private. Presidents of public institutions are chosen and appointed by the Ministry of Education.
Those of private ones are appointed by their board of trustees with the
approval of the Ministry of Education.

Educational Finance

Educational expenditure in Taiwan is borne by the central government,
local governments, and the private sector. Before 1961, the expenditure
on private education at all levels was less than ten percent of the total
educational expenditure. Subsequently, under the government's encouragement and subsidy, private schools have boomed. By 2002, the educational expenditure on private education had reached 30.25 percent of total
educational expenditure while that of public education was 69.74 percent.
In 2003, the educational expenditure of the government at all levels
accounted for 18.52 percent of the total budget and the central government bore 33.13 percent of all educational expenditures.[2] In 1999, the
Education Basic Law was promulgated, stipulating that all levels of government set more generous budgets for educational purposes and calling
for a more rational allocation of educational resources. Priority was given
to assistance for remote areas. The law also calls for more guarantees for
education-related budgets, with budget methods and guarantees to be for-
mally legislated later. The total educational expenditure at all levels in
2002 was distributed as follows: 3.04 percent for kindergarten education,
47.39 percent for compulsory education (starting from 1996, compulsory
education was extended from 9 years to 10 years), 15.01 percent for senior
secondary education, and 33.98 percent for higher education (see table
5.2).

Educational Reform

Following economic expansion and the development of democracy, the
Ministry of Education in Taiwan has moved gradually toward a more
flexible policy concerning the education system, especially at the higher

Table 5.2.   Total Educational Expenditure and Ratio at All Levels of Schools in Taiwan, 2002 (Unit: NT$1,000)

Total		Kindergarten		Compulsory Education		Sr. Secondary Education		Higher Education	
No.	%	No.	%	No.	%	No.	%	No.	%
563677854	100	17138458	3.04	267166738	47.39	30108261	15.01	191582647	33.98

Note: Compulsory Education includes elementary school and Junior high school, Sr. Secondary education includes Sr. high school and Sr. vocational high school, and higher education includes junior college, independent college and university.

Source: Computed and compiled by the author from: Ministry of Education. *Educational Statistics of the Republic of China* (ROC), 2003 Edition, p. 44.

education level. Starting from 1994, a series of education reforms have taken place with the goal of decentralizing the educational system. The four major reforms are as follows:

Reform in the Entrance System: As in Japan and Korea, higher education in Taiwan has recruited students through the University Joint Entrance Examination, which persisted for more than 40 years, from 1954 to 2001. Examination of the Japanese and Korean cases has already shown the role and significance of this system in the life of students and the society at large. This examination system has long been criticized for its shortcomings, including fierce competition that places too much pressure on students. In 2001, the University Joint Entrance Examination System in Taiwan was replaced with a multiple-channel admission. Universities can now recruit students from high schools, and students have the choices of either completing a recommendation/exam procedure or filing an application to select a university and department of their choice. This system will not only provide more of an even matching of students and universities, but it also will get rid of the old system that included "an exam that determined one's whole life." By the same token, this reform strengthens university rights for self-governance, along with acting out of respect for students' rights and choices.

University autonomy: Under the newly implemented education reform policy, the main function of the Ministry of Education is to "oversee" and "guide" universities instead of "governing" them, and all public universities have been granted the right of self-governance. Specifically, university presidents will no longer be appointed by the Ministry of Education, but will be selected either by a search committee or by votes from all faculty members in the university. However, the University Act revised in 1994 still specifies that the Ministry of Education holds final power over the appointment of presidents of national universities.[3] Deans, chairpersons, and new faculty members to be employed are also determined by the faculty. Original core courses are no longer mandatory as all requirements can be set by the decision of the curriculum committee of the faculty senate of the university.

Diversifying budgets: The Ministry of Education will no longer allocate the complete budget to each public university. Instead, support will be limited to an allocation of a ceiling of up to 80 percent of the total overall budget requested for a given fiscal year. Each institution must undertake efforts to raise funds and find resources from the society at large, rather than being solely dependent on the government.

Transfer of credits: A new policy on the transfer of credits has also been approved under the current reform campaign. Students do not have to restrict themselves to a single university. They are now allowed to take courses at other universities, if time permits. They are even allowed to transfer credits earned overseas during summer programs on the condition that the corresponding university is an accredited institution of higher learning.

University Academic Excellence Development Projects: As of the 2002–2003 academic year, Taiwan had a total of 154 colleges and universities. As the enrollment of higher education has been growing, a five-year US $400 million dollar Academic Excellence Development Project was launched in 1994 to improve the quality of university standards. According to the US NSF's statistics, between 1994 and 1999 Taiwan ranked about 20th in the world in the total number of research papers published in journals and listed in the Science Citation Index (SCI). This indicates that the research capability of Taiwanese university professors places them among the leaders for the world.[4]

Many other reforms are still under way, including the implementation of an integrated curriculum for a nine-year compulsory education program; the raising of the professional standards of elementary and junior high school teachers through the promotion of lifelong learning advanced study programs; the replacement of the conventional senior high school joint entrance examination with an academic proficiency examination; the promoting of vocational education and redirection of this education back into the mainstream of the education system, and so on. These reforms reflect the trends of decentralization, democratization, and internationalization of education in Taiwan in the past several years.

FEATURES AND CHANGES

Supplementary School System

Like the Japanese and Korean systems, the Taiwanese education system consists of formal schools and nonformal institutions, known as the supplementary school system. Supplementary education in Taiwan provides citizens with an alternative way to achieve their educational goals. Each stage of formal schooling is closely connected with a tremendous array of supplementary institutions and programs which are either government or private-run, the former accounting for the majority. Supplementary education is classified into five categories: primary school, junior high school, senior high (vocational) school, junior college, and university continuing education. A graduation certificate or diploma is granted to the graduates below the junior college level and a degree is granted to the graduates from university continuing education. Table 5.3 shows that in the 2001–2002 academic year, 304,533 students enrolled in the supplementary schools at different levels and 14.47 people per 1,000 population attended these schools.

Table 5.3. Number of Supplementary Schools and Student Enrollment in Taiwan, 2001–2002

Total	Primary	Jr. High	Sr. High	Vocational	Jr. College	College & University	No. of Graduates in 1999	No. of Students Per 1,000 Population
No. of Supplementary Schools (unit: school)								
935	359	265	36	205	45	33		
No. of Students at Supplementary Schools (Unit: person)								
304,533	17,586	17,513	5,400	144,693	76,312	43,029	788,101	4.47

Source: Compiled by the author from: Ministry of Education (MOE) (ROC), *Education Statistical Indicators, Republic of China* (ROC), 2002, pp. 22–23.

funstional
↑ edu. → private
↑ edu. → sector

Contribution of

The expansion of ᶜ 1950 was made possible only through the active involvement of the private schools as in Korea. In Taiwan, this contribution by the private sector is particularly evident in senior high school education and higher education. There are many more private senior high schools and tertiary education institutions than those in the public sector. As table 5.4 indicates, in the 2002–2003 academic year there were 211 private senior high schools and senior vocational schools in all, which accommodated 45.1 percent of the total student enrollment in senior high and senior vocational schools. At the higher education level, private junior colleges and four-year universities combined accounted for 67.3 percent of the total number of higher education institutions and enrolled 77.5 percent of the total tertiary education student body. The private schools in Taiwan have made a great contribution to the educational expansion in the past several decades, especially impressive in light of the fact that the private schools in Taiwan have been less adequately funded than the public schools.

Universalization of Primary Education Prior to Economic Takeoff

One of the notable features of Taiwan's educational expansion is the high level of access to primary schooling prior to the region's economic takeoff. From figure 5.3 and table 5.5 it can be seen that by the mid-1960s the enrollment rate for primary education in Taiwan was universalized: 97.16 percent of the age-cohort attended primary education while the average enrollment in other economies of similar per capita income at that time was 73 percent. This expansion reserved a large pool of well-educated workforce for Taiwan's economic takeoff during the 1960s and 1970s.

As the expansion of primary education took priority in the early stage of growth and industrialization, proportionately much less was spent on secondary and tertiary education. These sectors therefore enrolled a relatively small proportion of the relevant age group. In the subsequent years, motivated both by changes in the economy and by the rising expectations of parents whose children were completing their primary schooling, first secondary and then tertiary education became the foci for expansion, as

Table 5.4.   Number of Public and Private Schools and Student Enrollment in Taiwan, 2002–2003

	Elementary School	*Jr. High School*	*Sr. High School*	*Sr. Vocational School*	*Jr. College*	*Four-year Univ.*
	Number of Public and Private Schools (Unit: school)					
Total	3,965	2,627	716	302	170	15	135
Public	3,615	2,597	704	166	95	3	50
Private	354	30	12	136	75	12	89
%	8.93	1.14	1.68	45.03	44.12	80.00	65.93
	Number of Students of Public and Private Schools (Unit: person)					
Total	4,716,155	1,918,034	956,823	383,509	339,627	347,247	770,915
Public	3,411,109	1,894,643	867,144	253,284	143,925	39,017	213,096
Private	1,305,050	23,391	89,679	130,225	195,706	308,230	557,819
%	27.67	1.22	9.37	33.96	57.62	88.76	72.36

Source: Computed and compiled by the author from: Ministry of Education (MOE) (ROC), *Educational Statistics of the Republic of China* (ROC), 2003, pp. 2–5 and 20–23.

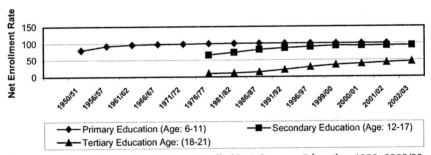

Figure 5.3.   Percentage of Age Group Enrolled in Taiwanese Education 1950–2002/03

Sources: Cited from table 5.5.

table 5.5 illustrates. An analysis of educational expenditure in Taiwan indicates that the expansion of secondary and tertiary education, which occurred on a broad scale in the 1970s and 1980s respectively, was accompanied by the remarkable growth of public expenditure on education in Taiwan. If 1952 is taken as a base year, then in 1991 the index of GNP was 27,999 while the index for educational expenditure in the same year was 100,102. In effect expenditure on education grew at a rate nearly four times as fast as the growth of GNP and by 1991 public expenditure on education amounted to approximately 5.5 percent of GNP.[5]

Table 5.5.   Percentage of Age Group Enrolled in Taiwanese Education, 1950–1951 to 2002–2003

School Year	Primary Education (Age: 6–11)	Secondary Education (Age: 12–17)	Tertiary Education Age: (18–21)
1950–1951	79.98		
1956–1957	92.33		
1961–1962	96.00		
1966–1967	97.16		
1971–1972	98.02		
1976–1977	99.42	65.73	9.97
1981–1982	99.76	72.96	11.47
1986–1987	99.87	81.50	14.24
1991–1992	99.9	86.17	20.98
1996–1997	99.94	89.57	29.07
1999–2000	99.92	92.56	35.43
2000–2001	99.94	92.19	38.7
2001–2002	99.95	92.92	42.51
2002–2003		93.74	45.68

Source: Compiled by the author from: Ministry of Education (MOE) (ROC), *Educational Statistics of the Republic of China* (ROC), 2003, pp. 34 and 38–39.

Balanced Gender Enrollment in Educational Expansion at All Levels

Unlike in many other developed and developing economies, in Taiwan the educational opportunities at all levels have been provided for male and female students relatively equally throughout the educational expansion. As table 5.6 shows, the provision and expansion of education has not been gender-specific. Both males and females at the different stages have benefited. Thus the discrepancy that once existed between male and female access was rapidly reduced. As seen from table 5.6, in the late 1970s the female enrollment rate of the age-group for primary education had reached the same percentage as for male students, while at secondary and tertiary levels the female enrollment rate of the age-group not only had caught up with but had also surpassed that of male students in the mid-1980s and the early 1990s, respectively.

Bias toward Vocational Education in Senior High Education

In Taiwan, there are two types of institutions for students above the junior high school level. These are the senior high and senior vocational schools,

Table 5.6.   Gender Percentage of Age Group Enrolled in Taiwanese Education, 1950–1951 to 2002–2003

School Year	Primary Education (Age: 6–11)			Secondary Education (Age: 12–17)			Tertiary Education Age: (18–21)		
	Average	Male	Female	Average	Male	Female	Average	Male	Female
1950–1951	79.98	93.44*	68.58*						
1956–1957	92.33	96.44	90.31						
1961–1962	96.00	97.54	94.34						
1966–1967	97.16	97.91	96.36						
1971–1972	98.02	98.26	97.77						
1976–1977	99.42	99.45	99.39	65.73	69.53	61.71	9.97	11.15	8.73
1981–1982	99.76	99.76	99.76	72.96	73.19	72.72	11.47	12.15	10.75
1986–1987	99.87	99.86	99.87	81.50	80.52	82.53	14.24	14.47	14.00
1991–1992	99.9	99.89	99.91	86.17	84.40	88.05	20.98	20.22	21.78
1996–1997	99.94	99.93	99.94	89.57	87.93	91.31	29.07	26.88	31.37
1999–2000	99.92	99.9	99.95	92.56	91.29	93.91	35.43	32.14	38.90
2000–2001	99.94	99.94	99.95	92.19	90.96	93.49	38.7	35.47	42.11
2001–2002	99.95	99.94	99.95	92.92	91.83	94.07	42.51	38.98	46.23
2002–2003				93.74	92.84	94.72	45.68	42.14	49.41

*indicates the data of 1951–1952.
Source: Compiled by the author from: Ministry of Education (MOE) (ROC), *Educational Statistics of the Republic of China* (ROC), 2003, pp. 34 and 38–39.

both of which take three years to complete. As in Korea, in Taiwan the provision of a large-scale program of technical and vocational education has been a central element in long-scale planning in the period following early industrialization. Before 1970, there were more students on what is termed the academic school track than on the vocational track. The Taiwanese government, following the adoption of a manpower development plan in 1966, decided to reverse this trend to meet the future needs of industry. This reversal was accomplished by the freezing of the student quota for academic high schools and the expansion of the quota for vocational high schools. Since the nine-year compulsory education program was launched in 1968, the vocational education has experienced rapid expansion. The year of 1971 was the turning point when more students were enrolled in the vocational track and by 1992 the ratio had shifted to 2:1 in favor of the vocational track. In recent years the enrollment in senior academic high schools has been increasing again and in 2002 students enrolled in the academic track outnumbered those enrolled in the vocational track. The ratio between senior high schools and senior vocational schools was 53.03 percent to 46.97 percent (See figure 5.4 and

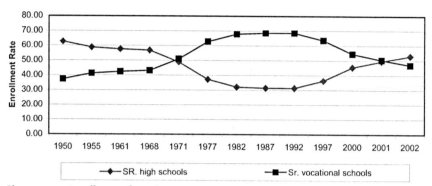

Figure 5.4.   Enrollment Share in Senior High Schools in Taiwan by Type, 1950–2002
Source: Cited from table 5.7.

table 5.7). The growth in enrollment in senior high schools is largely attributable to the expansion of higher education which attracts more graduates from senior high schools to further their academic pursuits through tertiary education.

School Curriculum and Changes at the Levels of Primary and Secondary Education

In Taiwan, the curriculum of primary and secondary schools is strongly controlled by the state, which results in a uniform national curriculum. Further, an established national system of assessment plays a critical role in selecting and allocating students through highly competitive and norm-referenced public examinations. The curriculum standards follow the goals and policies set by the Ministry of Education, which, in turn, follows governmental guidance regarding the education of the citizens. These standards may be adjusted in order to accommodate the needs of the changing society.

Since the implementation of a 9-year compulsory education system in the 1968 academic year, the curriculum for primary schools and junior high schools has frequently undergone revision (September 1993, October 1994). In the 1989 academic year, a system for the compilation of textbooks by bookstores, followed by screening and approval by the Ministry of Education, was established. The choice of elementary school text-

Table 5.7.   Enrollment Share in Taiwan, Senior Secondary Education by Type, 1950–2002

Year	Total	Sr. high schools		Sr. vocational schools	
		No.	*%*	*No.*	*%*
1950	30,092	18,866	62.69	11,226	37.31
1955	51,355	30,169	58.75	21,186	41.25
1961	108,656	62,548	57.57	46,108	42.43
1968	269,083	152,877	56.81	116,206	43.19
1971	389,767	190,798	48.95	198,969	51.05
1977	486,142	181,150	37.26	304,992	62.74
1982	581,273	187,015	32.17	394,258	67.83
1987	653,347	206,019	31.53	447,328	68.47
1992	730,597	229,876	31.46	500,721	68.54
1997	800,159	291,095	36.38	509,064	63.62
2000	783,955	356,589	45.49	427,366	54.51
2001	748,711	370,980	49.55	377,731	50.45
2002	723,136	383,509	53.03	339,629	46.97

Source: Computed and compiled from: Ministry of Education (MOE) (ROC), *Educational Statistics of the Republic of China* (ROC), 2003, pp. 20–23.

books has been opened to all of the versions reviewed and approved by the authorities since 1996.

Table 5.8 and table 5.9 show the subjects taught and the weekly teaching hour given in Taiwanese primary, junior high, and senior high schools. Readers will be impressed with the strong emphasis on the subjects of mathematics and science in the two tables: almost one-third of the teaching hours are allocated to these subjects at all primary, junior, and senior high school levels. In addition, the average school day is longer in Taiwan than in the United States. While most American students attend school for 180 days, Taiwanese students are in school for about 240 days. Further, youth of Taiwan devote about 50 percent more of their school days to academic-oriented activities.[6]

In recent years, a number of curriculum reforms have been under way. The Ministry of Education has been formulating the Curriculum Guidelines for Elementary and Junior High Schools. The goals include:

- Replacement of the separate subjects teaching approach with an integrated subject teaching approach, targeting 7 major subject areas,
- Concentrating on the 10 basic learning capabilities or skills,

Table 5.8.   Teaching Subjects and Weekly Teaching Hours in Taiwanese Elementary and Junior High Schools

School	Elementary School						Junior High School		
Grade	1	2	3	4	5	6	1	2	3
Civics & Ethics		2	2	2	2	2		2	2
Health Education							2		
Mandarin		10	9	9	9	9			
Chinese							5	5	5
English							3	3	1 + (1)
Mathematics		3	4	4	6	6	3	4	2 + (2)
Social Studies		2	3	3	3	3	1		
History							1	2	2
Geography							1	2	2
Natural Science		3	4	4	4	4	3	4	3 + (2)
Physical Education		2	3	3	3	3	2	2	2
Music		2	2	2	2	2	2	1	1
Fine Arts		2	3	3	3	3	2	1	1
Home Economic & Daily Technique							2	2	2
Computer								1	1
Elective Courses: Planting, Agricultural Products, Drawing, Abacus, Agriculture, Industry, Commerce, Home Economics, Marine Products, English, Mathematics, Music, Fine Arts, Second Foreign Language							1–2	2–3	2–5
Boy Scouts Training							1	1	1
Group Activities			1	1	1	1	2	2	2
Guidance Activities			1	1	1	1	1	1	1
Native Art Teaching Activities			1	1	1	1	1		
TOTAL		22–24	26	33	33	35	35	33–34	35–36	30 + (5)–33 + (5)

Notes:
1. The teaching hours of foreign language (English) and mathematics in junior high school are flexible in order to meet actual requirements.
2. One hour each week for weekly-meeting and extracurricular activities in junior high school are not included in this list. The figures in parentheses refer to individually teaching hour.
3. Since SY2001, 1st grade in elementary school has implemented the 1st–9th grade curriculum alignment.
Source: Ministry of Education (MOE) (ROC), *2001 Education the Republic of China* (ROC), 2002, p. 26.

Table 5.9.   Teaching Subjects and Weekly Teaching Hours in Taiwanese Senior High Schools

Grade	1		2		3	
Semester	*I*	*II*	*I*	*II*	*I*	*II*
Chinese	4	4	4	4	4	4
English	4	4	4	4	4	4
Civics			1	1	2	2
Three Principles of the People	2	2				
History	3	2	2	2		
Geography	2	3	2	2		
Mathematics	4	4	4	4		
Natural Science:						
Physics 1	2	(2)	3	3		
Chemistry 1	(2)	2	3	3		
Earth Science 1	2	(2)	2	2		
Biology 1	(2)	2	2	2		
Physical Education	2	2	2	2	2	2
Music	1	1	1	1		
Fine Arts	1	1	1	1		
Industrial Arts	1	1	1	1		
Home Economics	1	1	1	1		
Military Training (Military Training & Nursing for Girls)	2	2	2	2	1	1
Class Meeting	1	1	1	1	1	1
Group Activities	1	1	1	1	1	1
Elective Courses: Languages, Social Science, Mathematics, Natural Science, Home Economics, Industrial Arts, Arts, Fine Arts, Occupation, Cultivation, Physical Education	0–4	0–4	4–8	4–8	15–20	15–20
TOTAL	33–37	33–37	33–37	33–37	30–35	30–35

Notes: In the second year of senior high school, natural science is divided into four courses: Physics, Chemistry, Earth Science, and Biology. The student must select one course for at least two hours of weekly study.
Source: Ministry of Education (MOE) (ROC), *2001 Education the Republic of China* (ROC), 2002, p. 27.

- Instituting English instruction for all elementary school 5th-graders,
- Shortening school days to 200 days per year and 5 days per week.

High Quality of Taiwanese Students in Mathematics and Science

Due to Taiwan's special situation in the international setting, Taiwanese students are usually not included in the international mathematics and science achievement tests such as TIMSS or TIMSS-R as are Japanese and Korean students. As such there is not enough data available to compare the quality of Taiwanese students with their counterparts in other countries. However, American teachers and professors have been impressed with the fact that when Taiwanese students come to pursue their studies in U.S. schools and universities, they usually perform well and, more often than not, rise to the top of their classes in most subjects, particularly in science and mathematics.[7]

Harold Stevenson provides the following in his book *The Learning Gap*:[8] In 1980 and 1987, two international tests of mathematics were conducted to compare the mathematics achievement of U.S., Japanese, and Taiwanese first-grade and fifth-grade students. The purpose of these tests was to provide information about what students knew when they were just entering school as well as after several years of instruction. Students of three cities in these three nations and economies were selected: Sendai, Japan; Taipei, Taiwan; and Minneapolis, United States. In these two tests of mathematics achievement, for both grade levels in the studies, the scores of American students were far lower than those of their Taiwanese and Japanese peers.

Enrollment Distribution of Higher Education by Field of Study and Gender

As noted previously, centralization is one of the major features of Taiwan's higher education system. The government controls enrollment in each field and directs the development of higher education to meet the needs of society. In the 1950s and 1960s, the Taiwanese higher education structure was biased toward the humanities and social sciences rather than science and technology, because the economy in Taiwan was then still labor intensive. The Ministry of Education was influenced by a 1962 Stanford report, which suggested that in the 1960s there would be a surplus of graduates from the humanities and social sciences, but a shortage from S&T.[9] Since then, the Taiwanese government has been channeling students into such marketable fields as engineering, natural sciences, and—more recently—business. As figure 5.5 indicates, in the 2002–2003 academic year engineering, natural science, and math and computer science together accounted for 59 percent of the total enrollment of higher education at all levels in Taiwan, with engineering alone taking 33 percent.

Table 5.10 shows the distribution of gender and fields of study at different levels of higher education in Taiwan in the 2002–2003 academic year. At the level of junior college, male student enrollment dominated only engineering, accounting for 86.3 percent, while female student enrollment dominated most other fields. Male and female students each accounted for about half of the enrollment in agricultural science and math and computer science. But things were different at the four-year university level, where male enrollment dominated not just the areas of engineering (84.8 percent), but also math and computer science (67.1 percent). Male and female students each accounted for about half of the enrollment in natural science and agricultural science. The female students had larger percent-

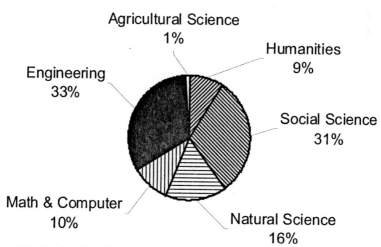

Figure 5.5. Tertiary Enrollment in Taiwan by Field of Study, 2002/2003
Source: Cited from table 5.10.

Table 5.10.   Taiwanese Tertiary Education Students by Field of Study and Gender, SY2002–2003

Total	Humanities	Social Sci.	Natural Sci.	Math & Computer Sci.	Engineering	Agricultural Sci.
		Junior College Students by Field of Study				
		Male				
159,377	7,747	27,843	6,574	17,743	97,221	2249
(45.9)	(25.1)	(25.7)	(11.8)	(49.9)	(86.3)	(51.9)
		Female				
187,870	23,141	80,517	48,951	17,805	15,375	2,081
(54.1)	(74.9)	(74.3)	(88.2)	(50.1)	(13.7)	(48.1)
		Total				
347,247	30,888	108,360	55,525	35,548	112,596	4,330
(100.0)	(8.9)	(31.2)	(16.0)	(10.2)	(32.4)	(1.3)
		Four-year University Students by Field of Study				
		Male				
381,320	37,410	92,451	37,747	49,841	154,605	9,266
(49.5)	(29.8)	(32.4)	(44.6)	(67.1)	(84.8)	(49.2)
		Female				
389,595	88,216	192,846	46,914	24,407	27,646	9,566
(50.5)	(70.2)	(67.6)	(55.4)	(32.9)	(15.2)	(50.8)
		Total				
770,915	125626	285,297	84,661	74,248	182,251	18,832
(100.0)	(16.3)	(37.0)	(11.0)	(9.6)	(23.6)	(2.4)
		Master's Students by Field of Study				
		Male				
65,272	9,530	16,876	6,350	6,840	23,839	1,837
(63.1)	(39.7)	(57.6)	(55.4)	(81.1)	(88.5)	(56.1)
		Female				
38,153	14,479	12,448	5,103	1,589	3,097	1,437
(36.9)	(60.3)	(42.4)	(44.6)	(18.9)	(11.5)	(43.9)
		Total				
103,425	24,009	29,324	11,453	8,429	26,936	3,274
(100.0)	(23.2)	(28.4)	(11.1)	(8.2)	(26.0)	(3.2)

Doctoral Students by Field of Study

Male						
14,203	1,374	1,874	2,583	1,329	6,378	665
(75.9)	(51.1)	(63.3)	(69.4)	(86.6)	(92.5)	(73.9)
Female						
4,502	1,317	1085	1,140	206	519	235
(24.1)	(48.9)	(36.7)	(30.6)	(13.4)	(7.5)	(26.1)
Total						
18,705	2,691	2,959	3,723	1,535	6,897	900
(100.0)	(14.4)	(15.8)	(19.9)	(8.2)	(36.9)	(4.8)

Notes:
1. Humanities includes education, fine and applied arts, humanities, and physical education. Social Science includes social and behavioral science, business administration, law and jurisprudence, home economics, service trades, and mass communication and documentation. Natural Science includes natural science and medical diagnostic treatment. Engineering includes craft and industry, engineering, architecture and town-planning, and transportation and communication. Agricultural Science includes agriculture, forestry, and fishery.
2. The figures in parentheses refer to percentage.
Source: Computed and compiled by the author from: Ministry of Education (MOE) (ROC), *Educational Statistics of the Republic of China* (ROC), 2003, pp. 110–11.

ages in humanities (70.2 percent) and social sciences (67.6 percent). At the graduate education level, male master's and doctoral students made up a larger percentage of the enrollment in all subjects except in the master's program of humanities where female students accounted for 60.3 percent. In the doctoral program of humanities, the proportion of female students constituted close to half of the enrollment (48.9 percent).

Doctoral Degrees Awarded to Taiwanese Students in Taiwan and in the United States

As in most other developing and newly industrializing economies (NIEs), graduate education in Taiwan, especially doctoral training, has been lagging behind the economy in terms of its rate and level of development. Graduate education requires a heavier investment than education at any other level. In addition to financial support, a higher development level of science and technology (S&T) is necessary to ensure the quality and standards of graduate education. Graduate education is closely linked with and conditioned by the development of the national economy. For example, before 1967, Taiwan had a per capita GNP of as low as about

US$260. There were no doctoral programs at Taiwanese universities, only 170 master's programs. However, when Taiwan had a per capita GNP of US$964 in 1975, 90 doctoral programs had already been created at Taiwanese universities, and 32 doctoral degrees were awarded in that year. Though doctoral education developed steadily in the following 25-year period—for example, in 1999, there were 790 doctoral programs nationwide, and 1,337 doctoral degrees were awarded (see table 5.11)—in comparison with some other developed nations, the establishment of doctoral training in Taiwan is still small and weak. As figure 5.6 shows, in the 2002–2003 academic year the enrollment of master's students and doctoral students accounted for only 8 percent and 2 percent, respectively, of total higher education enrollment in Taiwan. Despite its recent expansion, doctoral education in Taiwan is still far from satisfying the needs of economic development and the demands of young people for advanced studies.

A majority of Taiwanese international students go to the United States. Table 5.11 and figure 5.7 show that the total number of doctoral S&E degrees (6,744) awarded by U.S. universities to students from Taiwan is 1.5 times the number (4,543) awarded by Taiwanese universities in the same period from 1975 to 1999. The United States provides approximately 77 percent of Taiwanese students' doctoral degrees in natural science and engineering. However, Taiwan built up its advanced degree capability and expanded its doctoral-level training in the mid-1980s. The recent trend shows that the number of home-awarded doctoral degrees has been approaching the number awarded in the United States. In 1996, the number of U.S.-awarded doctoral S&E degrees decreased for the first

Table 5.11. Total Ph.D. Degrees Awarded in Taiwan and Ph.D. S&E Degrees Awarded in Taiwan and the United States, 1975–1999

	1975	1980	1985	1990	1995	1996	1997	1998	1999	Total
Total Ph.D's awarded in Taiwan	37	64	115	410	848	1,053	1,187	1,282	1,337	6,333
S&E Ph.D.'s awarded in Taiwan	21	30	109	312	650	783	839	907	892	4,543
S&E Ph.D.'s awarded in USA	NA	NA	743	1,012	1,240	1,149	995	871	734	6,744

Source: National Science Board (NSB), *Science and Engineering Indicators 2002* (Volume 2), pp. A2-72–A2-74.

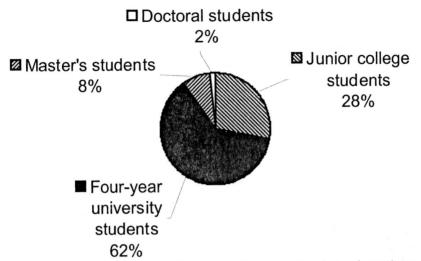

Figure 5.6. Distribution of Higher Education Enrollment in Taiwan by Level, 2002/2003

Source: Cited from table 5.10.

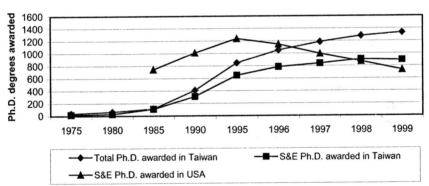

Figure 5.7. Total Ph.D. Degrees Awarded in Taiwan and Ph.D. S&E Degrees Awarded in Taiwan and the United States, 1975–1999

Source: Cited from table 5.11.

time, dropping from 1,240 in 1995 to 1,149 in 1996. Most remarkably, in 1998, for the first time, Taiwanese students earned more S&E doctoral degrees at Taiwanese universities than at universities in the United States (see table 5.11). A latest report shows that in the 2001–2002 academic year, 1,501 doctoral degrees were awarded by Taiwanese universities. Of them 1,285 were in S&E fields.[10]

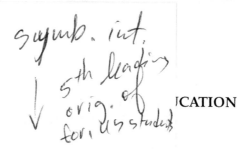

TAIWANI ICATION

The phenomena of study abroad and the international mobility of scientists and engineers are correlated. In Taiwan, these phenomena have been amplified by societal factors. It is a Chinese tradition that parents are respected and honored if they avail their children of advanced education or overseas study. Thus, the demand for higher education in Taiwan has been growing in the past 5 decades. However, due to the small higher education establishment, as well as political restrictions, there have been limited opportunities for higher and graduate study in Taiwan. Students therefore have traveled abroad to fulfill their own and their parents' ambitions. U.S. universities have been enrolling a huge majority of these students, making Taiwan the fifth leading nation of origin of international students in the United States from 1987 to 2003.

The steady annual increase of students from Taiwan between 1987 and 2003 is shown in figure 5.8. In the peak year of 1993–1994, 37,581 Taiwanese students were enrolled in 921 accredited colleges and universities in the United States. Since that year, trends in enrollment have shown a decline up until the most recent years. Taiwanese students are beginning to choose to study in Taiwan, as this economy has built a larger graduate education base that can accommodate more students. (Graduate students usually accounted for about two-thirds of the total Taiwanese international

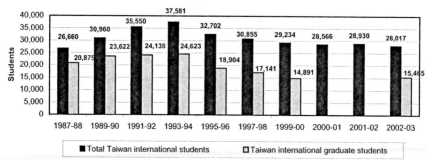

Figure 5.8. Enrollment of Taiwanese International Students in U.S. Universities, 1987/1988–2002/2003

Sources: Compiled by the author from: 1. National Science Board (NSB), *Science and Engineering Indicators 2002* (Volume 2), pp. A2-31–A2-32. 2. Institute of International Education (IIE), *Open Doors*, 2003.

students in the United States prior to the mid-1990s; since then, however, their share has reduced to slightly over half.)

As shown in table 4.21, like in Korea, a very important trend in Taiwan is that the efforts of the government to attract international students back home have been successful in comparison with the efforts of other Asian nations and economies, especially from the mid-1980s to the mid-1990s. As shown in table 4.21, of those Taiwanese international students who had earned doctoral S&E degrees in 1992–1993 only 36 percent were still working in the United States in 1997. Figure 5.9 shows the historical trends of Taiwanese students entering and leaving the United States in the period between 1971 and 1997. Until the 1990s, Taiwan had suffered a serious "brain drain" for almost 40 years. It was reported that, between 1950 and 1980, the Ministry of Education issued approvals to 63,061 college graduates to study abroad; only 7,240 of them returned. During this period, the brain drain due to students not returning from studying abroad reached as high as 90 percent. The brain drain slowed gradually in the 1980s: it decreased to 80 percent between 1981 and 1987.[11]

Only at the end of the 1980s did Taiwan start to benefit from its international students and their connections. A return flow of U.S.-trained scientists and engineers has occurred since the mid-1980s. A number of societal variables appear to account for this change. The most important variable is the economy. The statistics in figure 5.9 and figure 5.10 show

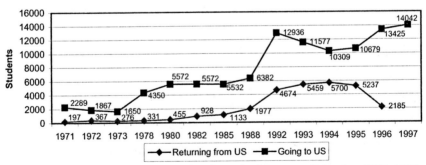

Figure 5.9. Taiwanese Students Entering the United States vs. Returning, 1971–1997

Sources:
1. Ministry of Education, *Educational Statistics of the ROC*, 1997, pp. 54, 56–57, 60.
2. Li, Chen-ching, "Returning Home after Studying in the USA: Reverse Brain Drain in Taiwan," *Cultural & Educational Digest*, 1995a, pp. 20–24.
3. *Cultural & Educational Digest*, Cultural Division of Taipei Economic and Cultural Representative Office in the United States, June 1998, p. 11.

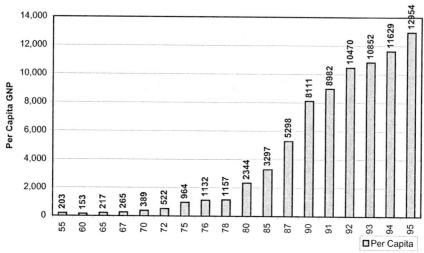

Figure 5.10.   Per Capita GNP in Taiwan, 1955–1995

Source: Li, Chen-ching, "Returning Home after Studying in the USA: Reverse Brain Drain in Taiwan," in *Cultural & Educational Digest,* Cultural Division of Taipei Economic and Cultural Representative Office in the United States, 1995a, pp. 20–24.

a close correlation between economic development and return flow. The strong increase of per capita GNP since the late 1980s put Taiwan in the group of NIEs. Rapid economic development has offered a great number of job opportunities for returning students with advanced degrees and professional expertise. The nationwide Ten Construction Projects Infrastructure Development, together with the establishment of the Hsinchu Science-Based Industrial Park in 1980, has opened many new avenues for young returned students to start new challenging careers.

The political situation is the second most important factor that has affected study abroad and the international mobility of scientists and engineers in Taiwan. As Taiwan's international status is unusual, its development has always been affected by the triangular relations among the People's Republic of China (PRC), the United States, and Taiwan itself. For example, in 1972, 367 Taiwanese students with advanced degrees returned home. However, the so-called "Nixon Shock"[12] of 1972 caused the number to drop from 367 to 276 the following year.[13] This political impact lingered for almost a decade, continuing even when former president Carter announced the normalization of relations between the United

States and the PRC in 1978: this was followed by an immediate decline in the number of returning students from 431 the prior year to 331 in that year. Only when the U.S. Congress enacted the Taiwan Relations Act in 1979 did the number of returning students gradually begin to rise. In 1987, coupled with an economic boom, Taiwan lifted martial law and certain other restrictions, and the number of returning students soared from 1,977 in 1988 to 4,674 in 1992. It later reached 5,700 in the peak year of 1994.

After 1995, the number of returning students dropped sharply to 2,185 in 1996. The reasons for this decline in returning students seem complex. There are four possible explanations. First, the job market in Taiwan for returning students is not as robust as it was before 1992. The returnees had to compete for fewer jobs. Second, the economy in the United States steadily improved in the late 1990s, providing more job opportunities. Third, the decline could be attributed to the military crisis on the Taiwan Strait in 1995 and 1996. Fourth, even worse, the Asian financial crisis in 1997 aggravated this decline. According to the recent reports, Taiwan is again experiencing a brain drain. This time, though, students are leaving primarily for Mainland China, specifically Suzhou and Shanghai.

At the same time as return flow increased, the Taiwanese government lifted restrictions governing students going overseas and allowed high school graduates to travel abroad to pursue undergraduate studies. As a result, the number of Taiwanese students abroad rose from 6,382 in 1988 to 12,936 in 1992. After that, as Taiwan increased its internal capacity for graduate education in science and engineering, more and more students decided to stay home for graduate studies instead of traveling abroad. The recent rise in Taiwanese students abroad is probably attributable to two factors. One is the growing number of graduates from junior colleges and high schools applying for undergraduate programs, or only for summer sessions, in U.S. universities. The other is the effect of unstable relations with Mainland China, especially during and after the military crisis on the Taiwan Strait in 1996.

Taiwan is a newly attractive center for both overseas Taiwanese students and foreign students

To increase its international involvement, Taiwan has also provided scholarships for international scholars, researchers, and students to spend time in Taiwan. Very few foreigners studied in Taiwan in the 1950s. Subsequently, Taiwan signed cultural agreements with other nations, offering scholarships, engaging in professor and student exchanges, mutually donating books and publications, all with the purpose of promoting international cultural exchange. As a result, a growing number of foreign students have come to Taiwan. The historical trend is shown in figure 5.11. In the 2002–2003 academic year, 7,331 foreign students were studying at Taiwanese colleges and universities. Most of them were enrolled in the fields of the humanities, social sciences, and languages. In the late 1990s, the Ministry of Education decided that, starting with the 1998–1999 academic year, it would provide a scholarship (with each person receiving about US$5,000 each month) to 20 foreign professors and researchers and 100 foreign students each year to encourage them to conduct research or study in Taiwan.[14]

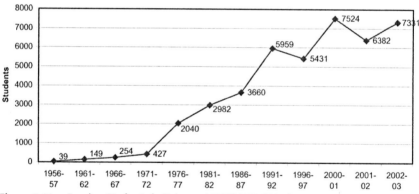

Figure 5.11.   Foreign Students in Taiwan, 1956/1957–2002/2003

Source: Compiled by the author from: Ministry of Education (MOE) (ROC), *Educational Statistics of the Republic of China* (ROC), 2003, pp. 50–61.

NOTES

1. Shun-fen Chen, 1997. "Taiwan," in *Asian Higher Education: An International Handbook and Reference Guide,* ed. Gerard A. Postiglione and Grace C. L. Mak, (Westport, CT: Greenwood Press), 345–58.

2. Ministry of Education (MOE) (ROC), *Education Statistics of the Republic of China, 2003 Edition,* (Taipei, Taiwan: MOE/ROC, Sept. 2003), 45.

3. Wing-wah Law. "The Role of the State in Higher Education Reform: Mainland China and Taiwan," *Comparative Education Review* 39, no. 3 (August 1995): 322–55.

4. Lu, Mu-lin, Vice Minister of Education of ROC, *Higher Education Reform in the Republic of China* delivered on Sept. 6, 2001 during his visit to Latvia, <http://140.111.1.22/english/index.htm> (23 Oct. 2002).

5. Paul Morris, "Asia's Four Little Tigers: a comparison of the role of education in their development," *Comparative Education, Vol. 32*, No. 1 (1996): 95–109.

6. Douglas C. Smith, Middle Education in the Middle Kingdom: The Chinese Junior High School in Modern Taiwan (Westport, CT: Praeger Publishers, 1997), 15.

7. Smith, *Middle Education in the Middle Kingdom*, 3–4.

8. Harold W. Stevenson and James W. Stigler, *The Learning Gap* (New York, NY: Summit Books, 1992), 33–38.

9. Wing-wah Law, "Fortress State, Cultural Continuities, and Economic Change: Higher Education in Mainland China and Taiwan," *Comparative Education* 32, no. 3 (1996): 385–86.

10. Ministry of Education (MOE) (ROC), *Education Statistics of the Republic of China, 2003 Edition*, (Taipei, Taiwan: MOE/ROC, Sept. 2003), 116–17.

11. Shun-fen Chen, "Taiwan," in *International Higher Education: An Encyclopedia*, Vol. 1, ed. Philip G. Altbach, (New York & London: Garland Publishing, Inc. 1991), 552.

12. Under the secret and careful arrangement of Dr. Henry Kissinger, late president Richard M. Nixon paid a visit to China in 1972 and signed the historic Shanghai Communique, stating that the United States acknowledged that there is only one China, and that Taiwan is part of China. The abrupt U.S. recognition of the PRC shocked the whole world—especially Taiwan—with an unpredictable political impact.

13. Chen-ching Li, "Returning Home after Studying in the USA: Reverse Brain Drain in Taiwan," *Cultural & Educational Digest* (Washington, DC: Cultural Division of Taipei Economic and Cultural Representative Office in the United States, 1995a), 20–24.

14. Cultural Division of Taipei Economic and Cultural Representative Office in the United States (CDTCRO), *Cultural and Educational Digest* (Washington, DC: CDTCRO, June 1998), 11.

Chapter Six

Profile of Chinese Education

Summary of findings: China has experienced two fundamental socioeconomic transformations in the past half-century: In the 1950s, China's semifeudal and semicolonial system transformed into socialism; then, in the late 1970s, China began to transform its planned economy into a market economy. Consequently the Chinese education system, affected by numerous political changes, has experienced a convoluted development process. Today, although China has moved back toward a Western concept of education, it still firmly abides by the centrally controlled model. The traditional reverence for education and the extensive training of high-level S&T talent are among China's strengths. The Chinese higher education system, which has undergone an unprecedented expansion in recent years, already exceeds the U.S. higher education system in terms of total student enrollment. China is a leading nation of origin of international students in a number of nations including the United States. With growing high-quality advanced education programs set up and its S&T capacity strengthened, China is destined to become an attractive center for both home-born brain and international talents.

OVERVIEW

Many Americans know China as a mysterious nation due to the sharp contrasts between the United States and China in terms of culture and sociopolitical system. China is the birthplace of Confucius, whose philosophy was introduced to many other Asian nations and played a significant role in shaping and developing these nations' civilizations and education systems, as we witnessed in Japan, Korea, and Taiwan. China keeps strongly alive the tradition of respecting education and honoring the teaching profession. Modern Chinese education was initiated only about one hundred years ago when the nation was undergoing dramatic changes. The Chinese education system has developed quite slowly due to the semifeudal and semicolonial nature of Chinese society before 1949, the date of the founding of the People's Republic of China (PRC).[1]

The Chinese education system, once heavily influenced by American and Japanese educators, came under Soviet hegemony in the period of 1949–1960s. Fortunately, in 1978, China started to implement the policy of reform and openness to the outside world. China increasingly turned to the West, especially the United States, as a source of technological knowledge and educational ideas. China is characterized by unique features such as its vast land, the world's largest population (over 1.2 billion people), large regional disparities in economic and cultural development, and the current efforts to shift from a planned economy to a market economy. After a half-century's development and reform, the Chinese education system has made remarkable achievements that attract the world's attention. The largest developing nation in the world, China today also runs the largest education system in the world.

This chapter focuses mainly on the status of Chinese education since 1978 when China started its policies of reform and openness to the outside world. Some attention will also be devoted to tracing the development since 1949. China's ambitious future development plans will be noted.

SCHOOL STRUCTURE, ADMINISTRATION, AND FINANCE IN CHINA

School Structure

The regular schooling structure in China includes preschool education, primary education, junior secondary education, senior secondary education, higher education, and postgraduate education. These levels are provided in a single-track 6-3-3-4 ladder which consists of six years of elementary school, three years each of junior and senior high school, and higher education. Higher education is characterized by a hierarchy of status, which is integrated into two basic institutions: four years of university or two–three years of junior college. The 9-year compulsory schooling consists of primary and junior secondary education: at present the 6 + 3 system, the 5 + 4 system, and the grade 1–9 integrated system exist side by side, with the 6 + 3 system predominating in most places. Primary school usually lasts for 5 or 6 years and junior secondary for 3 or 4 years.

The duration of the senior secondary school is 3 years. Senior secondary school is divided into two categories: regular senior high schools and specialized secondary schools which include technical schools and vocational schools. Junior colleges and technical and vocational colleges last for two to three years and their graduates are awarded certification upon successful completion of all the prescribed courses. The first degree level courses of full-time regular higher education institutions last 4 or 5 years, with some medical programs lasting for 7 or 8 years. There are two levels of graduate education: master's and doctoral. The duration of study of the former is 2–3 years while that of the latter is 3–4 years.

The graduates of primary schools are usually assigned to junior high schools on the basis of a "neighborhood school" principle while the graduates of junior high schools need to score well to be qualified to attend the "key-point senior high schools." These senior high schools are usually provided with better teachers, better equipment, and the better students in that region. As in Japan, Korea, and Taiwan, the university entrance examination is a central event in a student's life and for the society at large. One can imagine the ferocity of competition for university entrance in China, given that each year less than 10 percent of the college-age cohort in the world's most populous nation are able to enter colleges and universities. Many families frequently relocate in order to have access to good schools, or they turn to private tutors for supplementary teaching. China is now creating a new system of recruiting and selecting entrants for higher education institutions.

As in Japan, Korea, and Taiwan, apart from the regular school system in China there exists another parallel educational system—an adult education system that includes school equivalency programs of all types and levels. The curricula of various kinds of adult schools are designed in accordance with the principle of "same level, same standard." The duration of study of full-time secondary school for adults is usually the same as that of regular full-time secondary school. Part-time or spare-time programs usually last one year longer than those provided by regular schools of the same category. The first degree level programs provided by adult higher education institutions usually last 4–5 years **while the 2–3-year college programs for adults are diversified in form, ranging from 2–4 years in length of study.**

In recent years, education programs for adults at the various levels have developed rapidly, especially at the tertiary level. In 2001, total enrollment in adult institutions and programs reached 82,832,000, including 4,068,000 enrolled in primary schools for farmers, 4,227,000 in primary schools for adults, 69,977,000 in secondary schools for adults, and 4,560,000 in adult higher education institutions.[2]

Educational Administration

As we saw in Japan, Korea, and Taiwan, the Chinese education system is centrally controlled. Education in China was largely modeled after that in the Soviet Union in the early 1950s. Overall responsibility for all schools in China rests with the Ministry of Education, but the MOE is not involved in schools' day-to-day activities. The MOE's responsibilities include: enforcing the laws and decrees promulgated by the state, carrying out the principles and guidelines created by the state, formulating specific educational policies, drawing up overall plans for educational development, coordinating the efforts of various governmental departments in education, and drawing up a general scheme for and giving guidance related to the reform of China's educational structure.

A number of educational laws have been enacted and promulgated during the reform period of the past two decades. According to the law, the system of educational administration of China has a 4-tier structure comprised of the central government, provincial governments, city governments, and county governments. Education at the secondary school level or lower is administered by the local governments under the leadership of the MOE. Higher education is administered by the central government and by the provincial governments. Recent efforts have been made to strengthen the powers of the province-level governments. As the centrally planned economy gradually transforms into a more dynamic market economy, the Chinese central government will delegate more power to the local authorities and at the same time change its role from direct management to the provision of education policy guidance through supervision, coordination, evaluation and accreditation, and information services.

Education Finance

According to the education law of China, governmental allocation is the main source of educational finance, supplemented by funds raised through multiple channels. The central government and local governments divide responsibility in educational finance and management. For educational institutions under the jurisdiction of the central government, the funds needed are provided by state budgetary allocations; for institutions under the jurisdiction of local governments, the funds needed are provided by local budgets. For schools run by townships, village communities, or institutions, the funds needed are mainly provided by the sponsors of the school and are supplemented by governmental subsidies. For schools sponsored by social organizations (NGOs) or prominent personages, the funds needed are provided by the sponsors and are supplemented by tuition fees collected from students and donations. In addition to these sources of educational finance, taxes and fees levied by local governments at various levels for educational purposes are permitted according to the law. Schools of various types at different levels are encouraged to conduct work-study programs and to provide income-generating services to society so as to improve their financial situation and school facilities.

As the market economy system develops in China, cost sharing between the government and private individuals has been instituted at post-compulsory education levels; accordingly, tuition fees are collected from students as a certain percentage of the full education cost. As table 6.1 shows, at present, among the various sources of educational revenues, the tuition fees and miscellaneous fees paid by the students are gradually increasing and have become an important source of revenue second only to governmental budgetary allocations. In 2000, revenues from tuition and other fees totaled 46.4 billion yuan, accounting for 15.45 percent of total educational revenues, while the ratio of governmental budgetary contribution was about 54 percent. It is important to note that the ratio of non-

Chapter 6

Table 6.1. Sources of Educational Funds in China, 1996–2000 (Unit: billion yuan)

Year	1996 No.	1996 %	1997 No.	1997 %	1998 No.	1998 %	1999 No.	1999 %	2000 No.	2000 %
Total educational revenues	226	100.00	253	100.00	295	100.00	335	100.00	385	100.00
Governmental budgetary contribution	121	53.58	136	53.63	157	53.10	182	54.23	209	54.20
Taxes and fees levied by local gov.	24.0	10.61	26.8	10.58	27.9	9.46	28.2	8.42	28.4	7.38
Funds from organizations running and sponsoring schools	11.6	5.13	11.9	4.70	12.9	4.37	13.2	3.94	13.6	3.53
Income generated from school-factories, work-study, and social services	8.7	3.85	9.9	3.91	5.9	2.00	5.7	1.70	5.7	1.48
Funds from NGOs and citizens for running schools	2.6	1.15	3.0	1.18	4.8	1.63	6.3	1.88	8.6	2.23
Donations for running schools	18.8	8.31	17.1	6.75	14.2	4.82	12.6	3.76	11.4	2.96
Tuition and miscellaneous fees	26.1	11.54	32.6	12.88	37	12.55	46.4	13.85	59.5	15.46
Other educational funds	13.2	5.83	16.1	6.36	35.6	12.07	40.9	12.21	49.1	12.76

Source: Chen, Guoliang, Analysis of China's Educational Finance during the Ninth Five-year National Economical Development, China Education and Research Network: <http://www.edu.cn/20021111/3071941_1.shtml> (11 Nov. 2002).

governmental budgetary revenue[3] to total educational revenue increased. In 2000, this ratio reached 34.9 percent, over one third of the total educational revenue in China.

The Chinese government has taken a series of policy measures to ensure that students from poor families will not be deprived of access to education. Such measures include: a system of scholarships, a system of aiding study through part-time work, a system of granting subsidies to students with financial difficulties, a system of tuition reduction or tuition waiving, and a system of educational loans. The implementation of these measures has effectively ensured that students from poor families can pursue their studies to completion.

CHINESE EDUCATIONAL GROWTH AND ACHIEVEMENTS

The Chinese education system has progressed remarkably over the past half-century. Currently the average length of schooling for Chinese citizens is about 8 years. The student population totals 340 million, accounting for 27.5 percent of the total population of the country. By the end of 2001, there existed 1.35 million educational establishments of all types and levels, including 700,000 regular schools and 650,000 adult schools.[4]

Impressively, this development began from an extremely low education base. Before 1949, education in China was so underdeveloped that over 80 percent of the population was illiterate and the net enrollment ratio of the primary school-age cohort was only 20 percent. The following data will show a real picture of China's education system and its achievements in the past half-century, especially during the last two-odd decades when Chinese education has undergone numerous changes in accordance with the national economic, political, and social reforms.

Anti-illiteracy

In the old China of pre-1949 days, over 80 percent of China's total population, including 95 percent of the rural population and 98 percent of women, were unable to read or write.[5] Since the founding of the new China, more than 230 million illiterates have become neo-literates as the result of persistent efforts in literacy work. By 2001 the illiteracy rate of China's population had been reduced to under 6.72 percent, and the illiteracy rate among the 15–50 age group had declined to under 4.8 percent.[6]

Nine-year Compulsory Education

China began to implement its nine-year compulsory education in 1985; since then, great progress has been made in education. By 2002, the net enrollment ratio of primary school-age children had reached 98.8 percent (in contrast with about 20 percent in the pre-1949 days) and the gross enrollment ratio of junior high school-age children had reached 90 percent. There were 456,903 primary schools with a total enrollment of 121,567,100 and 97.02 percent of the primary school graduates continued their study in junior high schools. There were 65,645 junior high schools with a total enrollment of 66,874,300 and 58.3 percent of junior high school graduates continued their schooling in various types of schools at the upper secondary stage.[7] Thus, 9-year compulsory schooling has made a historic advance in China, and by the end of 2001 it had been universalized in areas inhabited by 85 percent of the country's population.[8]

Convoluted Development of Chinese Education in the Past Half-Century

As in many other nations, Chinese educational development has been affected by economic, demographic, and political changes. The curves in figure 6.1 and the data in table 6.2 reveal the convoluted development of Chinese education. Below, this development is summarized.

- Improving the education system was critical to the success of transforming China from an agricultural nation to an industrial nation. Shortly after they came to power in 1949, the leaders of the Communist Party of China immediately took action to restore and transform the schools. The return of the peace made it possible to enroll more students. As we see from table 6.2, enrollment in primary schools, junior high schools, senior high schools, and tertiary institutions increased by 109.5 percent, 168.0 percent, 105.3 percent, and 63.3 percent, respectively, from 1949 to 1952.

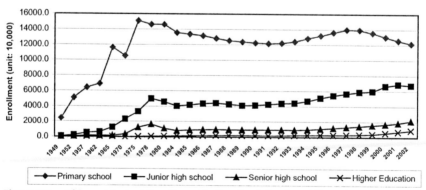

Figure 6.1.   Chinese Student Enrollment in Regular Schools at All Levels (1949–2002)
Source: Cited from table 6.2.

Table 6.2. Chinese Student Enrollment and Yearly Growth Rate of Regular Schools at All Levels (1949–2002)

	Total		Primary school		Junior high school		Senior high school		Higher Education	
Year	No. (unit: 10,000)	Annual Growth rate (%)	No. (unit: 10,000)	Annual Growth rate (%)	No. (unit: 10,000)	Annual Growth rate (%)	No. (unit: 10,000)	Annual Growth rate (%)	No. (unit: 10,000)	Annual Growth rate (%)
1949	2577.6		2439.1		83.2		43.6		11.7	
1952	5441.6	111.1	5110.0	109.5	223.0	168.0	89.5	105.3	19.1	63.3
1957	7178.3	31.9	6428.3	25.8	537.7	141.1	168.2	87.9	44.1	130.9
1962	7839.9	9.2	6923.9	7.7	645.6	20.1	187.4	1.0	83.0	88.2
1965	13120.1	67.4	11620.9	67.8	1246.3	162.0	185.5	−1.0	67.4	−18.8
1970	13181.0	0.4	10528.0	−9.4	2292.2	83.9	356.1	92.0	4.8	−92.9
1975	19681.0	49.3	15094.1	43.4	3302.4	44.1	1234.4	246.6	50.1	943.8
1978	21346.8	8.5	14624.0	−3.1	4995.2	51.3	1642.0	33.0	85.6	70.9
1980	20419.2	−4.4	14627.0	0.02	4583.7	−8.2	1094.1	−33.4	114.4	33.7
1984	18557.6	−9.1	13557.1	−7.3	4038.8	−11.9	822.1	−24.9	139.6	22.0
1985	18633.0	0.4	13370.2	−1.4	4194.3	3.9	898.2	9.3	170.3	22.0
1986	18692.2	0.3	13182.5	−1.4	4372.6	4.3	949.1	5.7	188.0	10.4
1987	18434.9	−1.4	12835.9	−2.6	4442.0	1.6	961.1	1.3	195.9	4.2
1988	17988.5	−2.4	12535.8	−2.3	4294.9	3.3	951.2	−1.0	206.6	5.5
1989	17635.3	−2.0	12373.1	−1.3	4120.2	−4.1	933.8	−1.8	208.2	0.8
1990	17553.1	−0.5	12241.4	−1.1	4163.7	1.1	941.7	0.9	206.3	−0.9
1991	17395.4	−0.9	12164.2	−0.1	4276.2	2.7	950.6	1.0	204.4	−0.9
1992	17774.1	2.2	12201.3	0.3	4408.7	3.1	945.7	−0.5	218.4	6.9
1993	18058.5	1.6	12421.2	1.8	4444.8	0.8	938.9	−0.7	253.6	16.1
1994	18809.5	4.8	12822.6	3.2	4722.3	6.2	984.7	4.9	279.9	10.4
1995	19533.6	3.9	13195.2	2.9	5106.1	8.1	1085.4	10.2	290.6	3.8
1996	20552.9	5.2	13615.0	3.2	5443.7	6.6	1192.1	9.8	302.1	4
1997	21308.0	3.7	13995.4	2.8	5679.7	4.3	1315.5	10.4	317.4	5.1
1998	21635.4	1.5	13953.8	0.3	5904.6	4.0	1436.1	9.2	340.9	7.4
1999	21519.6	−0.5	13548.0	−2.9	5993.0	1.5	1565.2	1.0	413.4	21.3
2000	21930.7	1.9	13013.0	−3.9	6670.8	11.3	1690.8	8.0	556.1	34.5
2001	22022.6	0.4	12543.0	−3.6	6897.5	3.4	1863.0	10.2	719.1	29.3
2002	21971.1	−0.2	12156.7	−3.1	6770.8	−1.8	2140.2	14.9	903.4	25.6

Note: Junior high school enrollment includes regular junior high schools and vocational secondary schools, senior high school enrollment includes regular senior high schools and specialized secondary schools while higher education enrollment includes only regular institution of higher education's two- and four-year undergraduate students.

Source: Computed and compiled by the author from:

1. MOE, China, *Educational Statistics Yearbook of China 1994*, People's Education Press, 1994, p. 5.

2. State Statistical Bureau, China, *China Statistical Yearbook 1995 and 2002*, China Statistical Publishing House, p. 587 of 1995 Edition and p. 673 of 2002 edition.

3. China.org.cn, *China: Facts and Figures 2002*, <http://www.china.org.cn/english/shuzi-en/en-shuzi/index.htm> (16 Dec. 2002).

4. MOE, China, *Educational Statistical Report*, Vol. 26, No. 1, February 27, 2003 <http://www.moe.edu.cn/stat/tjgongbao/report_2002.doc> (18 Nov. 2003).

- After the completion of the first five-year plan (1953–1958) for socioeconomic development, in 1958 the Chinese government launched the nationwide mass movement for development—the "Great Leap Forward." Higher education expanded dramatically. The number of higher education institutions increased from 229 in 1957 to 1,289 in 1960. More than 1,000 new universities and colleges were established within 3 years. The total enrollment increased from 44,181 in 1957 to 961,623 in 1960. Such a dramatic expansion caused severe problems related to low efficiency and poor quality. Therefore, in 1961, the Ministry of Education reduced the number of higher education institutions and consolidated small universities and colleges. After 3 years of adjustment, higher education enrollment was reduced to 674,000 in 1965. Affected both by the adjustment policy and by highly competitive entrance examinations for senior high schools during this period, enrollment in senior high schools was also reduced; enrollment in primary schools expanded due to the postwar baby boom.
- The Cultural Revolution, which lasted from 1966 to 1976, plunged China into turmoil, affecting every facet of Chinese society. But it was education, especially higher education, that suffered the most severe disruption and the most serious consequences. The national entrance examinations were abolished; many universities were shut down and not allowed to enroll students for more than 4 years. As table 6.2 indicates, in 1970 and 1975 only 48,000 and 500,000 students were enrolled in higher education institutions, respectively, and the duration of study was reduced from 4–6 years to 2–3 years. On the contrary, primary and secondary school enrollment increased dramatically during the Cultural Revolution. This was largely due to the late Chairman Mao's insistence on eradicating so-called social inequalities, which included canceling the entrance examinations at all school levels. The quality of instruction dropped precipitously because experienced teachers were humiliated and denied permission to teach and most textbooks were withdrawn and not replaced. According to official reports, 160 million young people were victimized by misguided education policies that reversed the past emphasis on academic achievement. Many of these young people are said to be barely literate.

- During the first years after the Cultural Revolution, driven by numerous nationwide reform policies, Chinese education, including nine-year compulsory education, experienced rapid expansion. Enrollment in senior high schools, however, grew relatively slowly during the period. In addition to the drop in birthrate, one probable factor is that the Chinese government had so emphasized nine-year compulsory education that fewer resources were allocated for the support of senior high schools.
- Total school enrollment declined during the period of 1990 to 1992 immediately after 1989's Tiananmen Square Incident.
- Since the mid-1990s, to meet the needs of economic and social development and the challenges of the rapid progress of world science and technology, China has formulated and implemented the strategy of revitalizing the nation through science and education and has placed the development of education as a strategic priority in the social modernization drive. With the universalization of primary education and junior secondary education reached in recent years, China has set its next goals: universalizing senior secondary education and transforming higher education from an elite model to mass higher education. As table 6.2 shows, between 1995 and 2002 the enrollment of senior high school increased by 97.2 percent, from 10,854,000 to 21,402,000. At the tertiary level, the period of 1999–2002 witnessed an unprecedented expansion in Chinese higher education in terms of absolute number. As seen from table 6.2, enrollment more than doubled within 4 years from 1998 to 2002, from 3,409,000 to 9,034,000. A specific discussion of Chinese higher education development projection and prediction occurs late in this chapter since this trend will have very important implications for American policymakers and educators.

Educational Finance Input

Since the mid-1990s, the dramatic expansion of the Chinese education system, and of higher education in particular, is mainly attributable to the growing educational financial input from the Chinese government. The data of table 6.3 indicate that during the period of 1991–2000 the Chinese government's financial allocation for education **grew by two digits** each

Table 6.3. Chinese Government Appropriation for Education, Annual Growth Rate and Percentage of GDP (1991–2001) (Unit: 10,000 yuan)

Year	1991	1992	1993	1994	1995
Government's Allocation for Education	6178286.0	7287505.8	8677618.3	11747395.6	14115233.3
Annual growth rate (%)		18.0	19.1	35.4	20.2
Percentage of GDP (%)		2.99	2.76	2.68	2.41

Year	1996	1997	1998	1999	2000	2001
Government's Allocation for Education	16717045.5	18625416.3	20324526.0	22871756.1	25626100.0	
Annual growth rate (%)	18.4	11.4	9.1	12.5	12.1	
Percentage of GDP (%)	2.44	2.49	2.55	2.79	2.87	3.19

Source: Collected and compiled by the author from:
1. MOE, China, *Educational Statistics Yearbook of China 2000*, People's Education Press, 2001, p. 348.
2. Chen, Guoliang, *Analysis of China's Educational Finance during the Ninth Five-year National Social and Economic Development*, China Education and Research Network: <http://www.edu.cn/20021111/3071941_1.shtml, 2002,11,11)>.

year except for 1998 due to the Asian financial crisis. Within the 10-year period, the government's financial allocation for education more than quadrupled, from 61,782.86 million yuan to 256,261.00 million yuan. In 2001 the government's allocation for education for the first time surpassed 3.0 percent of GDP, accounting for 3.19 percent of GDP. The goal of educational finance set by the Chinese government is to raise the level of public expenditure on education to 4 percent of GDP within a relatively short period.

Growing government investment in Chinese education in the last decade has fostered remarkable progress. As table 6.4 shows, apart from primary education and junior secondary education, which have been universalized, the gross enrollment ratio of both the senior secondary education age cohort and the higher education age cohort has increased very quickly, especially at the tertiary level. From 1990 to 2002, the gross

**Table 6.4.   Gross Enrollment Ratio of Regular Schools in China by Level (1990–2002)
(Unit: %)**

Year	Primary School Age 7–11	Jr. High School Age 12–14	Sr. High School Age 15–17	Higher Education Age 18–22
1990	111.0	66.7		3.4
1991	109.5	69.7		3.5
1992	109.4	71.8	26.0	3.9
1993	107.3	73.1	28.4	5.0
1994	108.7	73.8	30.7	6.0
1995	106.6	78.4	33.6	7.2
1996	105.7	82.4	38.0	8.3
1997	104.9	87.1	40.6	9.1
1998	104.3	87.3	40.7	9.8
1999	104.3	88.6	41.5	10.5
2000	104.6	88.6	42.8	11.5
2001	104.5	88.7	42.8	13.3
2002	107.5	90.0	42.8	15.0

Note: Junior high school enrollment includes regular junior high schools and vocational secondary schools, senior high school enrollment includes regular senior high schools and specialized secondary schools and higher education includes graduate and undergraduate education of regular higher education, military institutions, Radio/TV Universities, institutions authorized to administer examinations for students seeking formal academic qualifications, state-administered examinations for self-taught learners seeking tertiary qualifications and etc.

Source: Collected and compiled by the author from: 1. MOE, China, *Educational Statistics Yearbook of China 2000*, People's Education Press, 2001, p. 17.

2. MOE, China, *Educational Statistical Report*, Vol. 26, No. 1, February 27, 2003 <http://www.moe.edu.cn/stat/tjgongbao/report_2002.doc> (18 Nov. 2003).

enrollment ratio of the higher education age cohort increased from 3.4 percent to 15 percent. The year 2002 marked the beginning of the era when Chinese higher education entered the stage of mass higher education.

The rate of the graduates at different levels advancing to the next higher stage has also reflected the achievements in China. From table 6.5, we can see that the advancement rate of junior secondary education graduates and senior secondary education graduates to the next higher educational level have increased from 40.6 percent and 27.3 percent to 58.3 percent and 83.5 percent, respectively, between 1990 and 2002.

FEATURES AND CHANGES

Instruction and Curriculum

I will briefly introduce the teaching and curriculum in Chinese primary and secondary education. The teaching programs and the curricula

Table 6.5.   Promotion Rate of Regular Schools in China by Level and Type of
Graduates, 1990–2002 (Unit: %)

Year	Promotion Rate of Primary School Graduates	Promotion Rate of Jr. High School Graduates	Promotion Rate of Sr. High School Graduates
1990	74.6	40.6	27.3
1991	77.7	42.9	28.7
1992	79.7	43.6	34.9
1993	81.8	44.1	43.3
1994	86.6	47.8	46.7
1995	90.8	50.3	49.9
1996	92.6	49.8	51.0
1997	93.7	51.5	48.6
1998	94.3	50.7	46.1
1999	94.4	50.0	63.8
2000	94.9	51.1	73.2
2001	95.5	52.9	78.8
2002	97.0	58.3	83.5

Note: The advancement rate of senior high school graduates refers to the ratio between the number of regular (general) senior high school graduates and the number of regular higher education institution entrants.
Source: Collected and compiled by the author from:
1. MOE, China, Educational Statistics Yearbook of China 2000, People's Education Press, 2001, p. 17.
2. MOE, China, Educational Statistical Report, Vol. 26, No. 1, February 27, 2003 <http://www.moe.edu.cn/stat/tjgongbao/report_2002.doc> (18 Nov. 2003).

planned and designed by China's Ministry of Education are very demanding both in content and standards. A few examples will be provided to show the high quality of Chinese primary and secondary students in mathematics and science.

Teaching: The school year of primary and secondary schools is divided into two terms. The school year of primary schools comprises 38 weeks of teaching sessions with an additional week in reserve and 13 weeks for holidays and vacations. The school year of junior high schools comprises 39 weeks of teaching sessions with an additional week in reserve and 12 weeks for holidays and vacations. The school year of senior high schools comprises 40 weeks of teaching sessions with one or two weeks in reserve and 10 or 11 weeks for holidays and vacations. Formerly, five and a half days in a week were used for teaching in primary and secondary schools, but starting with the school year 1995–1996, a five-day week has been implemented in step with the five-day work week in China. There are 6–7 classes per day—30–33 classes per week. (Each class lasts for 45 minutes.) In addition to these curricular classes, there are always extracurricular activities such as sports, music, and social activities each week.

Curriculum: The objective of the curriculum of primary schools in China is to develop the students' abilities while enhancing their rudimentary knowledge of the Chinese language and arithmetic. Chinese lessons constitute about 40 percent of the total class periods (39 percent in six-year schools). The students are required to learn 3,000 Chinese characters. Arithmetic lessons account for about 25 percent of the total class periods, giving the students fundamental knowledge of quantitative relations and spatial forms and enabling them to do fundamental operations with integers, decimals, and fractions correctly and speedily, think logically, and soon have a certain understanding of space. The course in natural science is a combination of rudimentary physics, chemistry, astronomy, geography, biology, and **physiological hygiene**. This course enables the children to gain a certain understanding of nature and of how man explores, utilizes, and protects it. Science is usually offered to students in third grade and above, but this subject is offered to first and second graders where teachers are available. English, too, is usually offered to students in third grade and above, but it is offered to first and second graders where teachers are available.

In addition to the continuation of subjects offered at the elementary school level, the curriculum for Chinese general junior and senior high schools includes additional science subjects, such as physics, chemistry, and biology. As in Japan, Korea, and Taiwan, the curricula in Chinese secondary schools exhibits a strong bias toward mathematics, computer use, and science. More than one-third of the weekly teaching hours are devoted to these courses. To fully exploit available teaching capabilities and develop students' interests and special skills, many schools offer elective courses such as computer science, mapmaking, electronics, basic astronomy, oceanography, elementary medical science, formal logic, history of literature, theory of literature and art, ancient Chinese language, and a secondary foreign language. A number of schools conduct after-class lectures on science and technology. Subjects include astronavigation, fiber optics, bioengineering, lasers, new materials, new energy sources, and ocean development, to name a few. Most secondary schools also have organized recreational activities for the study of science and technology, art, and sports.

Since the early 1990s, several reforms have been made in the curriculum of primary and secondary education. In the fall of 1993, primary and junior high schools began to implement a new method, according to which subjects are divided into two categories: state-arranged subjects and locally-arranged subjects, with the latter determined by the province-level governments following the assessment of local realities and needs. Subjects taught in senior high schools are divided into the categories of obligatory and optional. According to the *Jiangnan Times* of February 13, 2003,[9] a significant reform of curriculum at the level of senior high school is underway in China. A new curriculum reform scheme for senior high schools will be released in the first half-year of 2003.

In China, throughout the course of primary and secondary education students are required to take examinations at the end of each semester, school year, or before graduation. The graduates of primary schools are usually recruited to nearby junior high schools without having to sit for entrance examinations. However, the graduates of junior high schools seeking to continue their education in any category of senior secondary school have to sit for and pass locally organized entrance examinations before admission. For students of senior high schools a system of locally unified school-leaving examinations has been instituted to assess the students' scholastic achievements. All students who successfully pass these leaving examinations are allowed to graduate.

High Quality of Chinese Students in Mathematics and Science

As previously mentioned in the discussion of education in Taiwan, China is not a developed country, so its students usually are not included in international mathematics and science achievement tests such as TIMSS or TIMSS-R. Therefore other data must be used to compare the quality of Chinese students with their counterparts in other countries.

It is useful to revisit an example Harold Stevenson provides in his book *The Learning Gap.*[10] In 1980, an international test of mathematics was conducted to compare the mathematics achievement of American, Japanese, and Taiwanese first-grade and fifth-grade students. In the follow-up test in 1987, China was also represented. The purpose of these tests was to give people information on what students knew when they were just entering school as well as after several years of instruction. Students of four cities in these four economies were selected: Sendai, Japan; Taipei, Taiwan; Minneapolis, America; and Beijing, China. In both tests of mathematics achievement, for both grade levels, the scores of American students were far lower than those of their Chinese and Japanese peers.

In the 1986–1995 period, Chinese secondary school students won 104 gold medals, 50 silver medals, and 26 bronze medals in the prestigious competition of the International Mathematics, Physics, Chemistry, Biology, and Information Olympiads.[11] In the past 8 years from 1995 to 2002, the Chinese secondary school student team ranked first in the International Mathematics Olympiad 6 times. From 1999–2002, China ranked first for 4 consecutive years.[12]

Enrollment Ratio of Regular Senior Secondary Education and Secondary Vocational/Technical Education

Beginning at the senior high school level, schools are being divided into regular or general schools and vocational or technical schools. Previously, regular senior high school graduates entered regular colleges and universities and vocational/technical school graduates received advanced vocational and technical education. As of recent years, however, graduates of both types of schools are eligible to apply for higher education institutions through unified entrance examinations.

The Chinese government has frequently shifted its emphasis between regular and vocational/technical education in the past half-century. According to the statistics shown in figure 6.2, prior to the mid-1960s more attention was paid to the secondary vocational/technical education. In 1965, secondary vocational/technical schools enrolled 4,980,400 students while regular senior high schools enrolled 1,308,000 students. The enrollment ratio between secondary vocational/technical schools and regular senior high schools was about 4:1. During the Cultural Revolution period, the secondary vocational/technical education shrank to skeleton size. In 1978, its student enrollment was only 889,000 in comparison with 15,531,000 students enrolled in regular senior high schools.

When the Cultural Revolution ended, vocational and technical educa-

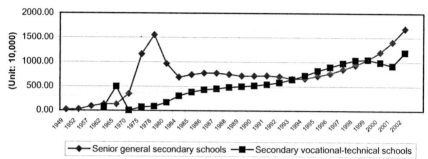

Senior general secondary schools — Secondary vocational-technical schools

Figure 6.2.   Enrollment Ratio of Regular Senior Secondary Education and Secondary Vocational/Technical Education in China, 1949–2002

Note: The secondary vocational/technical education includes all the regular specialized secondary schools and vocational schools.

1. MOE, China, Educational Statistics Yearbook of China 1994, People's Education Press, 1994, p. 5.
2. State Statistical Bureau, China, China Statistical Yearbook 1995 and 2002, China Statistical Publishing House, p. 587 of 1995 edition and p. 673 of 2002 edition.
3. MOE, Educational Statistical Report, Vol. 26, No. 1, February 27, 2003. http://www.moe.edu.cn/stat/tjgongbao/report_2002.doc (Nov. 18, 2003).

tion was the weakest link in the chain of China's education. The Chinese government started to restructure secondary education and vigorously promoted vocational and technical education. Beginning in the early 1980s, vocational and technical education began to catch up with regular secondary education in enrollment. After 1991 when the Chinese government made a public decision to vigorously expand vocational and technical education, and its enrollment expanded rapidly, in 1994 the enrollment of vocational and technical education reached 7,254,000 and outnumbered the enrollment (6,649,000) of regular senior high schools. Now all the companies and organizations that are engaged in highly specialized and technical work are required to hire graduates from vocational and technical schools ahead of those who have not received a qualification certificate.

Since 1999, when the Chinese government started to vigorously expand regular higher education, the enrollment of regular senior high schools has exceeded the enrollment of vocational and technical schools. By the end of 2002 there were 15,400 regular senior high schools with a total enrollment of 16,838,100 students. The gross enrollment ratio of the upper secondary age cohort reached 42.8 percent. There is space for 83.5 percent of upper secondary school graduates to continue their schooling in tertiary education.

Most recently, a major measure was made to expand senior high school education. In May 2003, China decided to allocate one billion yuan (US$121 million) in funding for planned increases in the enrollment of senior high school students, mainly in the central and western parts of the country. Sources with the State Development and Reform Commission said the revenue raised from treasury bonds would be used to finance construction of classrooms and laboratories with quality teaching resources for about 500 senior high schools across the country. The money would enable each senior high school in counties or cities with a large population to build 5,500 square meters in new rooms.

Each high school will be able to accommodate another 18 classes and enroll an additional 900 students after the expansion projects are completed by the end of 2003. About 450,000 more junior high school graduates are expected to be enrolled by senior high schools due to the investment.[13]

The Newly Emerging Private Schools in China

Before the twentieth century, almost all schooling in China was private. From 1949, when the Chinese Communist Party took power, until the early 1980s, private schools disappeared throughout the country.[14] It is unique to China that the educational development at all levels was made without any private education involved during the approximately 30-year period between 1949 and the early 1980s. Unlike Japan, Korea, and Taiwan, where private education has been making a great contribution to educational development, in China educational progress was made exclusively by the public education system during that period.

Private schools resurfaced in China after 1978 when the Chinese government embarked on its economic reforms for modernization, which thrust private ownership and competition into the state-planned economy. Private education has developed in the changing social and economic context of the reform era, catching national and international attention. The Chinese government now encourages non-state/private entities to set up and operate educational institutions at different levels. In 2002, according to the official report, there were over 61,200 non-state/private schools of various types and levels with a total enrollment of 11,159,700 students.[15] For more detailed information, see table 6.6. Thus, non-state/private

Table 6.6.   Private Institutions in China by Level, Type, and Enrollment (2001)

Kindergarten		Primary Education		General Secondary Education		Vocational/ Technical Education	
No. of Schools	Enrollment	No. of Schools	Enrollment	No. of Schools	Enrollment	No. of Schools	Enrollment
44,500	314,930	4,846	1,181,400	4,571	2,328,700	1,040	377,300

Higher Education Institutions (1)		Higher Education Institutions (2)		Higher Education Institutions (3)		Total	
No. of Schools	Enrollment	No. of Schools	Enrollment	No. of Schools	Enrollment	No. of Schools	Enrollment
37	72,000	157	258,000	1,202	1,113,040	56,200	9,074,100

Note:
(1) Refers to non-state/private HEIs which are authorized to award formal academic credentials.
(2) Refers to non-state/private HEIs which are authorized to administer examinations on a trial basis for students seeking formal academic qualifications.
(3) Refers to other non-state/private HEIs.
Source: Computed and compiled by the author from: MOE, PRC, *Education in China*, July 2002.

schools have become an important component of the education system in China and are expected to play a role in making senior secondary education universalized and higher education further expanded in the future.

Enrollment in China by Gender at all Levels of Schools

In the past 20-odd years, female enrollment in Chinese educational institutions at all levels has increased rapidly. The percentage of female students in the total student body increased from 43.0 percent in 1980 to 47.1 percent in 2001, as seen in table 6.7. The most remarkable growth rate of female enrollment can be seen at the secondary and tertiary education levels. During this 20-year period, the growth rate of female enrollment at the regular secondary schools increased from 39.6 percent to 46.5 percent; at the specialized secondary level, from 31.5 percent to 57.4 percent; at the vocational secondary school level, from 32.6 percent to 47.5 percent; and at the tertiary level, from 23.4 percent to 42.0 percent. In brief, the percentage of female enrollment in China at all education levels below tertiary education has exceeded the 45 percent which is considered the international standard for the normal ratio of female enrollment.

Table 6.7.   Enrollment in China by Gender at all Levels of School, 1980–2001
(Unit: 10,000)

	1980	1985	1990	1995	2000	2001
Grand Total	20419.2	18633.1	17553.1	19677.3	22087.9	22158.6
No. of Female Students	8778.3	8086.5	7880.8	9156.8	10339.6	10367.0
% of Female Students	43.0	43.4	44.9	46.5	47.1	47.1
Higher Education	114.4	170.3	206.3	290.6	556.1	719.1
No. of Female Students	26.8	51.1	69.5	102.9	227.9	302.3
% of Female Students	23.4	30.0	33.7	35.4	41.0	42.0
Specialized Secondary Schools	124.3	157.1	224.4	372.2	489.5	458
No. of Female Students	39.2	60.7	102	187.1	277.3	262.9
% of Female Students	31.5	38.6	45.4	50.3	56.6	57.4
Regular Secondary Schools	5508.1	7706.0	4586.0	5371.0	7368.9	7836.0
No. of Female Students	2180.1	1893.1	1920.1	2407.5	3402.4	3643.3
% of Female Students	39.6	40.2	41.9	44.8	46.2	46.5
Vocational Secondary Schools	45.4	229.5	295	448.3	503.2	466.4
No. of Female Students	14.8	95.4	133.7	218.2	237.4	221.7
% of Female Students	32.6	41.6	45.3	48.7	47.2	47.5
Primary Schools	14627.0	13370.2	12241.4	13195.2	13013.3	12543.5
No. of Female Students	6517.4	5986.2	5655.5	6241.1	6194.6	5936.8
% of Female Students	44.6	44.8	46.2	47.3	47.6	47.3

Source: Computed and compiled by the author from: State Statistical Bureau, China, *China Statistical Yearbook 2002*, China Statistical Publishing House, p. 673 and p. 680.

Chinese Higher Education Enrollment by Level

Four-year undergraduate education in China has been given priority in the past half-century. Junior college and graduate education has also been given consideration in the past 20 years since China began to restructure higher education to meet the changing demands for professionals. As figure 6.3 and table 6.8 show, four-year undergraduate education accounts for 58 percent of the total enrollment, while the junior college level accounts for 37 percent. The size of graduate education is smaller and accounts for only 5 percent.

Chinese Higher Education Enrollment by Field of Study

A distinguished feature of Chinese higher education is its strong bias toward natural science and engineering. The data in table 6.9 reveals that

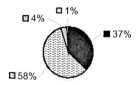

■ Junior College ▣ Four-year University ▨ Master's Degree Program ☐ Doctoral Degree Program

Figure 6.3.   Enrollment Distribution of Higher Education in China by Level, 2000

Source: Cited from table 6.8.

Table 6.8.   Enrollment Distribution of Higher Education in China by Level, 2000

Total		Junior College		Four-year University		Master's Degree Program		Doctoral Degree Program	
No.	%	No.	%	No.	%	No.	%	No.	%
5,861,337	100.0	2,160,719	36.9	3,400,181	58.0	233,144	4.0	67,293	1.1

Source: Computed and compiled by the author from:
1. State Statistical Bureau, China, *China Statistical Yearbook 2002*, China Statistical Publishing House, p. 675.
2. MOE, China, *Educational Statistics Yearbook of China 2000*, People's Education Press, 2001, pp. 40–41.

more than 45 percent of the students enrolled in higher education are majoring in natural science and engineering. At the graduate education level, the proportion of students enrolled in natural science and engineering is at **57 percent, with 54.6 percent in master's degree programs and 65.2 percent in doctoral degree programs**. At the undergraduate education level, the proportion of students enrolled in natural science and engineering is 44.6 percent, with 39.1 percent in junior colleges and 48.4 percent in four-year universities. As China has been, in recent years, transforming from a planned economy to a market economy, the ratio in subjects related to the economy has increased. Enrollment in management at the undergraduate education level and enrollment in economics at the master's degree level now account for 14.3 percent and 13.1 percent, respectively, the third largest proportion next to engineering and natural science.

Table 6.9. Chinese Regular Higher Education Enrollment by Field of Study (2001) (Unit: person)

	Total	Philosophy	Economics	Law	Education	Literature	History	Natural Sci.	Engineering	Agriculture	Medicine	Management
Junior Colleges (3 year)												
	2946914 (41.0)	397 (0.01)	137888 (4.7)	174602 (5.9)	232452 (7.9)	505282 (17.1)	16864 (0.6)	235986 (8.0)	917528 (31.1)	59443 (2.0)	168326 (5.7)	498146 (16.9)
Four-year Universities												
	4243744 (59.0)	4975 (0.1)	222000 (5.2)	213278 (5.0)	141998 (3.3)	554018 (13.1)	36504 (0.9)	480290 (11.3)	1573665 (37.1)	126579 (3.0)	361084 (8.5)	529353 (12.5)
Sub-total												
	7190658 (100.0)	5372 (0.1)	359888 (5.0)	387880 (5.4)	374450 (5.2)	1059300 (14.7)	53368 (0.7)	716276 (10.0)	2491193 (34.6)	186022 (2.6)	529410 (7.4)	1027499 (14.3)
Master's Degree Programs												
	233144 (77.6)	2918 (1.3)	30450 (13.1)	16401 (7.0)	6445 (2.8)	15159 (6.5)	3598 (1.5)	29177 (12.5)	98114 (42.1)	8409 (3.6)	22473 (9.6)	
Doctoral Degree Programs												
	67293 (22.4)	1089 (1.6)	4657 (6.9)	2484 (3.7)	970 (1.4)	2372 (3.5)	1383 (2.1)	12556 (18.7)	31284 (46.5)	2971 (4.4)	7527 (11.2)	
Sub-total												
	300437 (100.0)	4007 (1.3)	35107 (11.7)	18885 (6.3)	7415 (2.5)	17531 (5.8)	4981 (1.7)	41733 (13.9)	129398 (43.1)	11380 (3.8)	30000 (10.0)	
Grand Total												
	7491095 (100.0)	9379 (0.1)	394995 (5.3)	406765 (5.4)	381865 (5.1)	1076831 (14.4)	58349 (0.8)	758009 (10.1)	2620591 (35.0)	197402 (2.6)	559410 (7.5)	

Note:
1. The figures in parentheses refer to percentage.
2. Literature here includes Chinese language and foreign languages, and science of art. Education here includes science of physical culture and sports. Agriculture here includes forestry.
3. The data for master's degree and doctoral degree programs use the data of 2000.
Source: Computed and compiled by the author from:
1. State Statistical Bureau, China, *China Statistical Yearbook 2002*, China Statistical Publishing House, p. 675.
2. MOE, China, *Educational Statistics Yearbook of China 2000*, People's Education Press, 2001, pp. 40–41.

Chinese International Education at Home and Abroad

The Chinese government's decision to send thousands of students for overseas study represents a historical continuity rather than a radical departure in modern China's cultural policy. For over a century, with the sole exception of the period from 1967 to 1974, Chinese students have been studying abroad, frequently in large numbers. The returned Chinese international students have been playing an important role in knowledge transfer that is critical to the Chinese modernization drive.

Leading Home Country of International Students in a Number of Countries: In the past two decades from 1978 to 2001, about 458,000 Chinese students traveled to more than 103 nations and regions for overseas study, with the largest number traveling to the United States, according to a number of reports.[16] China is now the leading sender of international students to a number of nations, including the United States, Japan, Korea, Australia, Thailand, Malaysia, and Germany. The United States is the leading host country of Chinese international students.[17] From 1978 to 2000, more than half of Chinese international students were enrolled in U.S. universities. Figure 6.4 and table 6.10 clearly show the dramatically increasing enrollment and ratio of Chinese students among the total foreign students in U.S. universities from 1980 to 2003: the enrollment increased 23.4 times from 2,770 to 64,757 while the proportion rose from less than 0.9 percent to 11 percent. In comparison, the total number of foreign students in the United States increased from 311,880

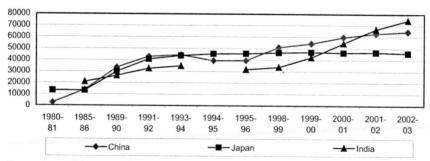

Figure 6.4. Chinese Students Enrolled in U.S. Universities in Comparison with Students from Japan and India: 1980/1981 to 2002/2003

Source: Cited from table 6.10.

Table 6.10. Chinese Students Enrolled in U.S. Universities in Comparison with Students from Japan and India: 1980/1981 to 2002/2003

	1980–1981		1985–1986		1989–1990		1991–1992		1993–1994		1994–1995	
	No.	%	No.	%	No.	%	No.	%	No.	%	No.	%
Total	311880	100	343780	100	386850	100	419590	100	449704	100	452635	100
China	2770	0.9	13980	4.1	33390	8.6	42940	10	44381	9.9	39403	8.7
Japan	13500	4.3	13360	3.9	29840	7.7	40700	9.7	43770	9.7	45276	10
India			21010*	6.1	26240	7.3	32530	7.8	34796	7.7		

	1995–1996		1998–1999		1999–2000		2001–2001		2001–2002		2002–2003	
	No.	%	No.	%	No.	%	No.	%	No.	%	No.	%
Total	453787	100	490933	100	514723	100	547867	100	582996	100	586323	100
China	39613	8.7	51001	10	54466	10.6	59939	10.9	63211	10.8	64757	11
Japan	45531	10	46406	9.9	46872	9.1	46497	8.5	46810	8	45960	7.8
India	31743	7	33818**	6.9	42337	8.2	54664	10	66836	11.5	74603	12.7

Note: The figure with * indicates the data of 1987–1988 academic year and that with ** refers to the data of 1997–1998 academic year.
Source: Computed and compiled by the author from:
1. U.S. Department of Education, Digest of Education Statistics 1996 and 1997, p. 450 and p. 456.
2. Institute of International Education (IIE), Open Doors, 1999, 2000, 2001, 2002, and 2003.
3. National Science Board (NSB), Science and Engineering Indicators 2002, pp. A2-31 and A2-32.

to 586,323 or by only 88 percent in the same period. Therefore, students from China became by far one of the fastest growing community on U.S. campuses. Although in 1994 and 1996 Chinese students comprised the second largest foreign student population in the United States after Japanese students, from 1989 to 1994 they led in total foreign student enrollment in the United States. The relative decline of Chinese students' enrollment after 1994 was due to the second reform tide of 1992, which led to more opportunities in both the job market and graduate studies at home. In the 1998/1999 to 2000/2001 academic years, however, Chinese students regained first place as the highest population of foreign students in the United States. Only in the past two academic years between 2001/ 2002 and 2002/2003, India surpassed China as the leading country of origin for international students in the United States.

Brain Drain: At least half of the Chinese overseas students are extending their stays or trying to seek permanent residency in foreign nations. According to incomplete statistics by the Chinese Embassy in the United States, in the past 20 years more than 160,000 Chinese students came to the United States to study, and by 1998 only 30,000 of them had returned home. According to data from the US National Science Foundation, for the period 1990–1996 the percentages of foreign S&E doctoral recipients planning to remain in the United States increased: over 68 percent planned to reside in the United States, and nearly 44 percent had firm offers to do so. The data in table 6.11 show that, in 1990, 41 percent of over 1,000 Chinese S&E doctoral recipients in U.S. universities had firm plans to remain in the United States. By 1996, about 56 percent of the over 3,000 Chinese S&E doctoral recipients from U.S. universities had firm plans to remain in the United States. The underlying cause for this shift is that a large number of Chinese students were granted permanent residence status in the United States in 1992 following China's response to student demonstrations.[18] The employers of these Chinese professionals and scholars range from academic institutions to government agencies to industrial companies to postdoctoral research programs. Given the scarcity of well-trained human resources in China and its ambitious economic development program, such a large outflow of high-level specialized personnel represents a severe brain drain problem for China.[19]

How to Turn Brain Drain into Brain Gain? Most Third World countries have experienced brain drain for a long time. However, the past 20 years saw some changes in this phenomenon. In some Asian countries and regions including China, the reverse flow of foreign-educated students has been making it possible to turn brain drain into brain gain. The phenomena of study abroad and the international mobility of China's scientists and engineers are correlated. Of the many factors affecting the movement of overseas students and scholars, the economy always plays a critical role. South Korea and Taiwan had a similar problem of brain drain before the mid-1980s. However, when their per capita GNP reached about US$4,000, their overseas students and scholars started to flow back home. Table 6.12 shows a recent study of foreign doctoral recipients working in the United States.[20] About 53 percent of the foreign students who earned S&E doctoral degrees in 1992 and 1993 were working in the United States in 1997. Stay rates differ by field of degree and country of origin, though. A great majority of 1992 and 1993 engineering doctoral recipients from India (83 percent) and China (92 percent) were working in the United States in 1997. In contrast, only 9 percent of South Koreans who completed engineering doctorates from U.S. universities in 1992 and 1993 were working in the United States in 1997.

Reverse Flow: What are the implications of the Korean and Taiwan cases for Mainland China? What inspiration will Mainland China draw

Table 6.11. Chinese Ph.D. Recipients from U.S. Universities Who Plan to Stay in the United States, (1990–1996)

All Fields

	1990				1991				1992				1993			
	Total Ph.D. recipients	Plan to stay in U.S.		Firm plans to stay in U.S.	Total Ph.D. recipients	Plan to stay in U.S.		Firm plans to stay in U.S.	Total Ph.D. recipients	Plan to stay in U.S.		Firm plans to stay in U.S.	Total Ph.D. recipients	Plan to stay in U.S.		Firm plans to stay in U.S.
		No.	%	No.	%		No.	%	No.	%		No.	%	No.	%	No.	%		No.	%	No.	%
	1,225	725	59	502	41	1,919	1,523	79	920	48	2,238	1,980	89	1,080	48	2,416	2,134	88	1,077	45

All Fields

	1994				1995				1996			
	Total Ph.D. recipients	Plan to stay in U.S.		Firm plans to stay in U.S.	Total Ph.D. recipients	Plan to stay in U.S.		Firm plans to stay in U.S.	Total Ph.D. recipients	Plan to stay in U.S.		Firm plans to stay in U.S.
		No.	%	No.	%		No.	%	No.	%		No.	%	No.	%
	2,772	2,548	92	1,223	44	2,979	2,744	92	1,341	45	3,201	2,896	91	1,788	56

Source: NSB, Science and Engineering Indicators 1998, NSF, 1998 (NSB 98-1), pp. A-89–A-90.

Table 6.12. Asian Foreign Students Earning Doctoral S&E Degrees in 1992/1993 Who Were Working in the United States in 1997, by Place of Origin

Nation of Origin	Foreign Doctoral Recipients	Percent (%) Working in U.S. in 1997
S&E Fields, Total	16,391	53%
Taiwan	2,149	36%
Korea	2,056	9%
China (PRC)	4,010	92%
Japan	214	21%
India	1,549	83%

Source: Johnson, Jean, *Collaboration in S&T Information Exchange between the United States and China*, paper presented at CIES 2000 Conference, San Antonio, Texas, March 7–11, 2000.

from Korea's and Taiwan's experience? There is already a distinct change in the rate of Chinese students planning to remain and return in the past 6–7 years. In contrast to the higher percentage of Chinese students planning to remain in the United States in the period between the early and mid-1990s (see table 6.11), a study made in 1999 shows a counter trend.[21] According to the study, the percentage of Chinese students in the United States planning to return increased: of the 1,045 Chinese students questioned, 21.2 percent had plans to go home within 5 years, 36.5 percent had plans to go home within 5–10 years, 22.9 percent had plans to go home after 10 years, and only 19.4 percent had plans to remain. In contrast to previous cohorts, over 80 percent had plans to return in the future. This is very encouraging progress for China.

Currently, China has a per capita GDP of about US$1,000, and a number of foreign-educated Chinese students have already returned home, as indicated in figure 6.5. According to official reports, from 1990 to 1998

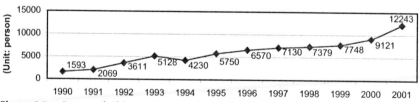

Figure 6.5.   Returned Chinese students (1990–2001)

Source: State Statistical Bureau, China, *China Statistical Yearbook 2002*, China Statistical Publishing House, p. 675.

the returnees increased by 13 percent each year, from 1,593 in 1990 to 7,379 in 1998.[22] And the number of returnees more than doubled between 1998 and 2002, from 7,379 in 1998 to 18,000 in 2002.[23]

If China continues to reform its economic structure, relying on scientific and technological progress in its transition to a market economy, the demand for high-level specialized personnel will be even higher. Considering China's vast land, rich physical resources, and large population as well as its uneven development level from region to region, it seems likely that when China reaches a per capita GDP of about US$1,500–2,000, the nation will turn brain drain to brain gain and benefit from the reverse flow of overseas Chinese students and scholars. But, to turn this possibility into reality there will need to be an improvement of the political environment and of the legal system.

Main Host Country of Foreign Students: From 1978 to 2001, China received large numbers of international students. During the past two decades an aggregate number of nearly 456 thousand foreign students from 170 countries in the world have traveled to China to study at different levels, including bachelor's, master's, and doctoral programs as well as short-term programs. Over 86,000 foreign students were present in 2002 alone, 72 times as many as the figure (1,200) in 1978 who were studying in China.[24] Of the 4,569 foreign students sponsored by the Chinese government in 1997, 4.9 percent were enrolled in doctoral programs, 14.5 percent in master's degree programs, and 33 percent in bachelor's degree programs. In addition, in the same year, there were 39,035 self-financed students, of which 2 percent were pursuing doctoral degrees, 4.6 percent master's degrees, 28 percent bachelor's degrees, and 0.3 percent short-term diplomas.[25]

In addition to the foreign students in China, there are also growing numbers of students from the overseas regions of Hong Kong, Macao, and Taiwan traveling to study in Mainland China. During the ten-year period from 1988 to 1997, 403 students from these three regions were enrolled in Chinese universities. Most of them were graduate students.[26] The recent trend is that more students from Taiwan come to Mainland China to pursue advanced studies. In 2001, 1,078 Taiwanese students were enrolled in Mainland Chinese universities. In 2002, the applicants for graduate studies had doubled from the figure of the previous year, reaching 1,369.[27]

Projections for Chinese Higher and Graduate Education

Projections for Higher Education Expansion: To meet both the demands on national economic development and the high pressure placed on the government by young people and parents for higher education opportunities, from 1998 to 2003 the Chinese higher education system has experienced unprecedented expansion in terms of absolute number, as mentioned previously. The number of new students enrolled in colleges and universities of both regular and adult higher education rose from 2.15 million in 1998 to 2.85 million in 1999, to 3.90 million in 2000, to 4.81 million in 2001, to 5.63 million in 2002, and to 6.29 million in 2003. All the entrants, enrollments, and graduates have been tripled in the past five years (see table 6.13). In 2003, total postsecondary enrollment reached 19 million. Overall gross enrollment rates reached about 17 percent of the age cohort in 2003. China successfully changed its higher education from elite to mass higher education. And the Chinese Government is planning to continue the expansion of higher education in 2004 and the total post-secondary enrollment will surpass 20 million.

What do the unprecedented expansion and the current scale of Chinese higher education mean? What implication is there for U.S. policymakers and educators? Just as Chinese educational policy-makers always take developed nations, especially the United States, as the major reference point in planning Chinese educational development, the United States stands to gain from comparing the world's two largest higher education systems. Figure 6.6 shows the enrollment and the number of graduates in both Chinese and U.S. higher education in 2002 and in the 2000/2001 academic year. After four consecutive years of rapid expansion, from 1999 to 2002, Chinese higher education enrollment reached 15.13 million in 2002, approaching the U.S. figure of 2000: 15.31 million. However, higher education graduates in China in 2002 outnumbered those in U.S. higher education in the 2000/2001 academic year: 2,593,000 to 2,416,645.[28] In China, almost all students who register in regular higher education institutions are full-time students in contrast with less than 60 percent of U.S. higher education students who study as full-time students. In the Chinese system, students tend to complete their studies within the prescribed time span. Thus, although the United States has more students enrolled in higher education, China can produce more graduates than the United States each year. As indicated in table 6.13, the overall Chinese

Table 6.13. **Chinese Higher Education Expansion since 1998 (unit: 10,000)**

	Regular HEIs					
	Entrants		Enrollment		Graduates	
Year	No.	Growth Rate %	No.	Growth Rate %	No.	Growth Rate %
1998	108.4		340.9		83.0	
1999	159.7	47.3	413.4	21.3	84.8	2.2
2000	220.6	38.1	556.1	34.5	95.0	12
2001	268.3	21.6	719.1	29.3	103.6	9.1
2002	320.5	19.5	903.4	25.6	133.7	29.1
2003	382.2	19.3	1,108.6	22.7	187.8	40.5
2004	410.0*	7.7*				

	Adult HEIs					
	Entrants		Enrollment		Graduates	
Year	No.	Growth Rate %	No.	Growth Rate %	No.	Growth Rate %
1998	100.14		282.22			
1999	115.8	15.6	305.5	8.3	88.8	
2000	156.2	34.9	353.6	15.8	88.0	-0.9
2001	195.9	25.5	456.0	28.9	93.1	5.8
2002	222.3	13.5	559.2	22.6	117.5	26.2
2003	220.0*		726.3*	29.9*		
2004	220.0**					

	Graduate Programs					
	Entrants		Enrollment		Graduates	
Year	No.	Growth Rate %	No.	Growth Rate %	No.	Growth Rate %
1998	7.3		19.9		4.7	
1999	9.2	26.0	23.4	17.6	5.5	17
2000	12.8	39.1	30.1	28.6	5.9	7.3
2001	16.5	28.9	39.3	30.6	6.8	15.3
2002	20.3	23.0	50.1	27.5	8.1	19.1
2003	26.9	32.5	65.1	29.9	11.1	37
2004	33.0**	22.7**				

	Grand Total					
	Entrants		Enrollment		Graduates	
Year	No.	Growth Rate %	No.	Growth Rate %	No.	Growth Rate %
1998	215.8		643.0		87.7	
1999	284.7	31.9	742.2	13.9	179.1	
2000	389.6	36.9	939.9	26.6	188.9	5.5
2001	480.7	23.4	1,214.4	29.2	203.5	7.7
2002	563.1	17.1	1,512.7	24.6	259.3	27.4
2003	629.1	11.7	1,900.0	25.6		
2004	750.0**	19.2**				

(*) figures estimated and (**) figures projected by Ministry of Education.
Source: Computed and compiled by the author from:
1. State Statistical Bureau, China, *China Statistical Yearbook 2002*, China Statistical Publishing House, pp 673–675 and 681.
2. MOE, China, *Educational Statistics Yearbook of China 2000*, People's Education Press, 2001, pp 100–101.
3. Ministry of Education (MOE) (PRC), *Statistical Report of National Education Development in 1998, 1999, 2000 and 2001*.
4. MOE, China, *Educational Statistical Report*, Vol. 26, No. 1, February 27, 2003 <http://www.moe.edu.cn/stat/tjgongbao/report_2002.doc> (18 Nov. 2003).
5. Lu, Ruo, *Nearly 3.97 Million People Registered for the 2003 National Entrance Examination to the Adult Higher Education*, China Education and Research Network. http://www.edu.cn/20031117/3094452.shtml (2004, 2, 8).
6. Zhou, Ji, Minister of Education. Speech at 2004 Educational Workshop held on December, 25, 2003. http://www.moe.edu.cn/edoas/website18/info3380.htm (2004, 4, 6).
7. Zhou, Ji, Minister of Education, *Looking Back and Forward to the Educational Reform and Development of the Period of 2003–2004*. January 6, 2004, China Education and Research Network. http://www.edu.cn/20040106/3096913.shtml (2004, 4, 8).

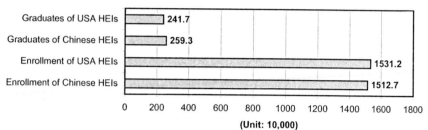

Figure 6.6.   Comparison of Chinese and U.S. Higher Education Scale (2002 and 2000/2001)

Notes:
1. Data for the enrollment of U.S. higher education are from the year of 2000 and the data for its graduates are from 2000/2001 academic year. The data for both enrollment and graduates of Chinese higher education are from 2002.
2. The graduates of USA HEIs include the recipients of all the associate's degrees, bachelor's degrees, master's degrees, doctoral degrees, and first professional degrees conferred in the 2000–2001 academic year while the graduates of Chinese HEIs include all graduates from junior colleges and above in 2002.
Source: Computed and compiled by the author from:
1. Table 6.13
2. U.S. Department of Education, *Digest of Education Statistics 2002.*

postsecondary education enrollment had reached 19 million in 2003, outnumbering the enrollment figure in the United States for the same year.

The objective of the ambitious Chinese plan is to raise postsecondary education enrollment to 16 million, equal to the figure in the United States, by 2005, and to change Chinese higher education from elite to mass higher education. I am confident that this aim will be achieved ahead of schedule given the current momentum in Chinese higher education development.

The Chinese long-term goal is to have 25 million students, and 23–25 percent of the age cohort, enrolled in higher education by 2010; to have 42 million students and 40 percent of the age cohort in gross enrollment by 2020; and to reach 50 percent in gross enrollment of the college age cohort by 2030–2035, thereby making Chinese higher education universalized.

Projections of Graduate Education Expansion: Though the capacity of the United States' higher education system may be surpassed by that of China's education system, the United States currently leads in the conferring of graduate degrees. In 2001 China awarded 85,932 graduate degrees while the United States awarded 593,087 in the 2000/2001 academic year,[29] seven times as many. China has a long way to go to catch up with the United States. My following research findings made in 1997 predict the future trends of Chinese graduate education's development.

Trends of Graduate Expansion: 1995–2020

Graduate enrollment is mainly affected by the growth rate of both the national economy and the relevant age cohort. But, in China, to a great extent it is affected by public policy—by whether enrollment quotas are set to restrict growth, or whether enrollment is left to be driven by demand. My projection here is mainly based on the first two factors: the growth rate of the economy and of the relevant age group.

The demand for high-level educated personnel depends, to a large extent, on how fast the economy grows. As mentioned above, according to the ninth five-year plan (1996–2000) for national economic and social development and the long-term goal for the year 2010, the Chinese government's goal for GDP in 2000 is to quadruple that of 1980, and its goal for GDP in 2010 is to double that of 2000. This plan entails an average annual growth rate of 8 percent between 1995 and 2000, and over 7 percent between 2000 and 2010. Given the momentum of China's historical growth rate in the period between 1978 and 1994, it is realistic to expect the GDP to continue to grow at an annual average of 7 to 9 percent in real terms over the next 25 years. Table 6.15 provides the estimation of GDP per capita based on three scenarios of average annual GDP growth rate: (a) slow growth at 7 percent; (b) medium growth at 8 percent; and (c) fast growth at 9 percent. According to these projections, China's GDP per capita would be $600–$700 by 2000; $1,100–$1,600 by 2010; and $2,100–$3,500 by 2020. In other words, in five years' time, China would be on its way to becoming a lower-middle-income country and in 15 years' time it would be poised to join the league of upper-middle-income countries.[30]

The population of possible graduate students in China is here referred to as the 25–29 age cohort. There are two reasons for choosing this age group: first, the average age of all the master's degree recipients in the period between 1991 and 1994 is 27.5 years (see table 6.14). Given the current system of Chinese graduate education, the time span for master's studies is between 2.5 and 3 years. This means that when a student enters graduate school, he or she is usually around 25 years old. Although the average age of doctoral degree recipients in this period is 31 years, the real average time span for doctoral studies in China is around 3.5 years,[31] meaning that when a student enters a doctoral program he or she is usually around 27.5 years old. The ratio of annually awarded master's degrees to doctoral degrees is 10.5:1.

Table 6.14.   Average Age of Recipients of Doctoral and Master's Degrees Awarded for Full-Time Studies, 1991–1994

(Number in person)				
	Doctoral Degree		Master's Degree	
Year	Total	Average Age	Total Age	Average
1991	2,519	31	29,112	27
1992	2,503	31	23,572	27
1993	2,082	31	23,029	28
1994	3,523	32	24,780	28

Source: Data of Academic Degrees and Graduate Education Statistics to 1991–1994, China Archives Press, 1995.

The second reason I choose to consider the 25–29 age cohort as possible graduate students is that I have to base my research on the statistical data currently available. The population of 25- to 29-year-olds in China is projected by the World Bank to decline gradually from 1994 to around 2005, when the generation born after the implementation of the one-child policy in 1979 comes of age. The size of the 25–29 age cohort is projected to fluctuate between 90 million at the lowest point in 2010 and 115 million at the highest in 2015, and then to go down to the lower point of 99 million in 2020.

The projected graduate enrollment is based on two different enrollment growth rates (see table 6.15):

Gradual Growth. If graduate enrollment is to follow the historical average annual undergraduate enrollment growth rate of 7.6 percent up to 2020, China would reach an enrollment ratio of 0.15 percent by 2000, 0.43 percent by 2010, and 0.81 percent by 2020. This growth rate lags behind the historical GDP growth rates but keeps pace with the undergraduate enrollment rate if the latter still follows its own previous growth rate over the next 25 years. If both undergraduate and graduate enrollments grow at the same rate of 7.6 percent in the future 25 years' time, the ratio between them will be at the 1994 level: 100:4.57.

Fast Growth. If graduate enrollment growth is to catch up with the historical average annual GDP growth rate of 9.8 percent, the enrollment ratio would reach 0.19 percent by 2000, 0.64 percent in 2010, and 1.47 percent in 2020. Although the total enrollment by 2020 would be 1,455,000, the enrollment ratio would still only be 1.47 percent by then. However, this enrollment could be considered enormous because, if 25–30 percent of these students graduate annually, the graduate degrees

Table 6.15. Expansion Trends for Graduate Education, 1995–2020 (in Constant 1994 Yuan)

	1994	2000	2010	2020
GDP Per Capita in Yuan				
Slow Growth (r = 7%)	3,800	5,400	9,900	18,300
Medium Growth (r = 8%)	3,800	5,700	11,500	23,300
Fast Growth (r = 9%)	3,800	6,000	13,300	29,600
In Dollars (8.5 Yuan = $1)				
Slow Growth (r = 7%)	447	630	1,200	2,200
Medium Growth (r = 8%)	447	670	1,300	2,700
Fast Growth (r = 9%)	447	710	1,600	3,500
Country Income Level	Low	Becoming Lower-Middle	Lower-Middle	Becoming Upper-Middle
Enrollment Ratio (%)				
r = 7.6%	0.11	0.15	0.43	0.81
r = 9.8%	0.11	0.19	0.64	1.47
Enrollment (Thousand Students)				
r = 7.6%	128	186	387	805
r = 9.8%	128	224	571	1,455

Note: The numbers are rounded.
Sources: Computed and compiled by the author from:
1. China Statistical Yearbook 1995, China Statistical Publishing House, 1995, p. 62. .
2. The World Bank Report No. 15573-CHA, pp. 61–62 and pp. 148–51.

awarded annually would number around 400,000. This volume of annually awarded graduate degrees would be similar to that in today's U.S., where advanced degrees awarded annually number about 300,000 master's degrees, 35,000 doctoral degrees, and 70,000 first-professional degrees.[32]

Projection of GDP: To estimate the amount of public resources available in the future, projections are made for three scenarios of average annual GDP growth rates between 1995 and 2020: 7 percent, 8 percent, and 9 percent, respectively. The reason for choosing these average annual growth rates is as follows—7 and 8 percent fall within the Chinese government's own target, and 9 percent is close to the historical growth rate of 9.8 percent between 1978 and 1994. The projected GDP then forms the basis for the projection of the Chinese government expenditure on higher education.

Projection of Government Expenditure on Higher Education: The projection of government expenditure on higher education assumes that future government expenditure remains at 12.9 percent of GDP (the ratio in 1994), and that the government expenditure on higher education is about 2.6 percent of total government spending (the ratio in 1992). The reason for choosing the 1992 ratio instead of the 1994 ratio is because government expenditure on higher education in 1994 increased considerably from the previous years, and this level might conflict with the objective of deficit reduction. The projection is based on the pessimistic assumptions that the future growth of revenue remains unchanged and that the future growth of public spending on higher education will be constrained by the need to reduce the consolidated government deficit. Using these ratios for projection, total government expenditure on higher education would increase from about Y19 billion to Y79 billion (in constant 1994 prices), if the GDP grows at 7 percent per year between 1994 and 2020; it would increase to Y100 billion if the GDP grows at 8 percent; and it would increase to Y128 billion if the GDP grows at 9 percent.[33]

The above predictions, formulated in 1997, are rather conservative. In 1999, the Chinese government decided to vigorously expand its graduate education. Table 6.16 shows that in the period from 1999 to 2003, the enrollment growth rate in graduate education has been much higher than

Table 6.16.   Chinese Graduate Education Expansion since 1998 (Unit: 10,000)

	Entrants		Enrollment		Graduates	
Year	No.	Growth Rate %	No.	Growth Rate %	No.	Growth Rate %
1998	7.3		19.9		4.7	
1999	9.2	26.0	23.4	17.6	5.5	17
2000	12.8	39.1	30.1	28.6	5.9	7.3
2001	16.5	28.9	39.3	30.6	6.8	15.3
2002	20.3	23.0	50.1	27.5	8.1	19.1
2003	26.9	32.5	65.1	29.9	11.1	37
2004	33.0**	22.7**				

Note: The figure with ** is projected by Ministry of Education.
Source: Computed and compiled by the author from:
1. Zhou, Ji, Vice Minister of Education, "Speech," in *Xiaoxiang Morning News*, Changsha, China, October 12, 2002.
2. State Statistical Bureau, China, *China Statistical Yearbook 2002*, China Statistical Publishing House, p 675.
3. MOE, China, *Educational Statistical Report*, Vol. 26, No. 1, February 27, 2003 <http://www.moe.edu.cn/stat/tjgongbao/report_2002.doc> (18 Nov. 2003).
4. Jing Wu, "China Planning to Admit 330,000 New Graduate Students Next Year," *China Scholars Abroad*, Nov. 18, 2003 <http://www.chisa.edu.cn/newchisa/web/1/2003-11-18/news_13176.asp> (19 Nov. 2003).
5. Ministry of Education (MOE) (PRC), *Statistical Report of National Education Development in 2002 and 2003*.
6. Zhou, Ji, Minister of Education. Speech at 2004 Educational Workshop held on December 25, 2003. http://www.moe.edu.cn/edoas/website18/info3380.htm (2004, 4, 6).
7. Zhou, Ji, Minister of Education, *Looking Back and Forward to the Educational Reform and Development of the Period of 2003–2004*. January 6, 2004, China Education and Research Network. http://www.edu.cn/20040106/3096913.shtml (2004, 4, 8).

the fast growth rate of 9.8 percent predicted in 1997. The real enrollment growth rate was 17.6 percent in 1999, 28.6 percent in 2000, 30.6 percent in 2001, 27.5 percent in 2002, and 29.9 percent in 2003. The average annual growth rate reached as high as 26.8 percent in the past 5 year period. Graduate enrollment in China had already passed half a million in 2002. The Ministry of Education has planned to raise the graduate enrollment up to one million by 2005.[34]

In 2000, the number of graduate students enrolled in U.S. universities was 1,850,000 in contrast with the figure of 501,000 graduate students enrolled in Chinese universities in 2002. Based on these numbers, people might doubt the correctness of my prediction that China will catch up with the United States within 20 years in producing the same number of graduate degrees. I would like to support my prediction by giving two more points: First, since the majority of graduate students in China study on a full-time basis, it is possible for them to complete their studies within the prescribed time span. This is why the United States has greater enrollment in higher education but produces fewer graduates than China. Secondly, it is important to consider the recent expansion momentum in graduate degrees production in China, as indicated in figure 6.7 and table 6.17: from 1998 to 2001, graduate degrees conferred in China increased by 75 percent, from 49,175 to 85,932. I am convinced China will also realize its goal within fewer than 20 years.

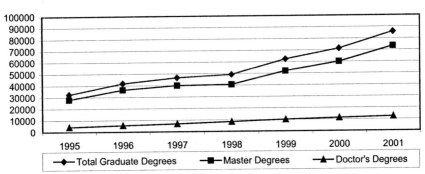

Figure 6.7. Graduate Degrees Awarded in China (1995–2001)

Source: Cited from table 6.17.

Table 6.17. Graduate Degrees Awarded and Growth Rate in China, 1995–2001 (Unit: person)

Year	Total Graduate Degrees No.	Growth Rate %	Master's Degrees No.	Growth Rate %	Doctoral Degrees No.	Growth Rate %
1995	32,489		28,125		4,364	
1996	41,883	28.9	36,305	29.1	5,578	27.8
1997	46,743	11.6	39,950	10.0	6,793	21.8
1998	49,175	5.2	40,657	1.8	8,518	25.4
1999	62,406	26.9	52,246	28.5	10,160	19.3
2000	71,464	14.5	60,081	15.0	11,383	12
2001	85,932	20.3	73,467	22.3	12,465	9.5

Source: Computed and compiled by the author from: Academic Degrees Committee under the State Council, China, June 2002 <http://www.moe.edu.cn/moe-dept/xueweiban/2> (18 Nov. 2003).

NOTES

1. Ministry of Education (MOE) (PRC), A Brief Account of Education in the People's Republic of China (November 2000): 1.

2. China.org.cn, *China: Facts and Figures 2002*, available at <http://www.china.org.cn/english/shuzi-en/en-shuzi/index.htm> (15 Dec. 2002).

3. This nongovernmental budgetary revenue includes income generated from school-factories, work-study and social services; funds of NGOs and citizens for running schools; donations and fundraising for running schools; tuition and miscellaneous fees and other educational funds.

4. Ministry of Education (MOE) (PRC), *Education in China* (July 2002): 8.

5. Robert F. Arnove, "A Comparison of the Chinese and Indian Education Systems," *Comparative Education Review*, Vol. 28, No. 3 (1984): 378–401.

6. Ministry of Education (MOE) (PRC), *Education in China* (July 2002): 9.

7. Ministry of Education (MOE) (PRC), *Educational Statistical Report*, Vol. 26, No. 1, February 27, 2003 <http://www.moe.edu.cn/stat/tjgongbao/report_2002.doc> (18 Nov. 2003).

8. Ministry of Education (MOE) (PRC), *Education in China* (July 2002): 8–9.

9. Jiangnan Times, *Reform Curriculum for Senior High Schools will be finalized: Increase Proportion of Selected Courses and Adopt Credit System*, February 13, 2003, available at <http://www.china.org.cn/chinese/EDU-c/275934.htm> (20 Feb. 2003).

10. Harold W. Stevenson and James W. Stigler, *The Learning Gap* (New York, NY: Summit Books, 1992), 33.

11. Ministry of Education (MOE) (PRC), *Basic Education in China* (1996): 16.

12. International Mathematics Olympiad (IMO), *Unofficial Country Rankings—IMO,* 2002, Web: available at <http://imo.math.ca/results/TCBY.html> (17 Dec. 2002).

13. Xinhua News Agency, *China to Expand Senior High School Education,* May 20, 2003, available at <http://www.china.org.cn/english/2003/May/65039.htm> (2 June 2003).

14. Jing Lin, *Social Transformation and Private Education in China* (Westport, CT: Praeger Publishers, 1999), xiii.

15. Ministry of Education (MOE) (PRC), *Educational Statistical Report,* Vol. 26, No. 1, February 27, 2003 <http://www.moe.edu.cn/stat/tjgongbao/report_2002.doc> (18 Nov. 2003).

16. china.org.cn, 10/10/02, available at <www.china.org.cn> (16 Oct. 2002).

17. Wang Fang, "Over Ten Thousand Chinese Overseas Students in Malaysia," *Huasheng Newspaper,* June 12, 2003 <http://www.chisa.edu.cn/newchisa/web/2/2003-06-12/news_2233.asp> (18 June 2003). And Xinhua News Agency, *Mainland China is the Top Leading Sender of International Students to Germany,* September 12, 2003, available at <http://www.china.org.cn/english/2003/May/65039.htm> (13 Sept. 2003).

18. National Science Board (NSB), *Science and Engineering Indicators—1998,* (Arlington, VA: National Science Foundation, 1998).

19. Xiaonan Cao, "Debating 'Brain Drain' in the Context of Globalization," *Compare,* Vol. 26, no. 3 (1996): 269–85.

20. Jean Johnson, "Collaboration in S&T Information Exchange between the United States and China" (paper presented at CIES 2000 Conference, San Antonio, Texas, March 7–11, 2000).

21. Pichang Wang, "The Study of the Latest Trends of Overseas Chinese Students," *China Scholars Abroad,* Vol. 132, No. 2 (2001): 8–15.

22. *Newsweekly,* July 31, 2000, available at <http://www.china.org.cn/chinese/9837.htm> (5 Aug. 2000).

23. China Scholars Abroad, December 4, 2003, available at <http://www.chisa.edu.cn/newchisa/web/1/2003-12-04/news_14109.asp> (4 Dec. 2003).

24. China.com, January 3, 2002 <http://edu.china.com/zh_cn/1055/2002 0103/10184476.html> (30 Nov. 2002); Ministry of Education (MOE) (PRC), *Education in China* (July 2002): 18, and Rui Feng, "One-third of Foreign Students Choosing Universities in Beijing for Study," *Beijing Evening,* December 13, 2003 <http://www.china.org.cn/chinese/kuaixun/460769.htm> (13 Dec. 2003).

25. China Scholars Abroad, May 6, 1998, available at <www.chisa.edu.cn> (7 July 1998).

26. China Scholars Abroad, May 6, 1998, available at <www.chisa.edu.cn> (7 July 1998).

27. Chinese World Journal, April 14, 2002, available at <www.chineseworld .com/publish/today/11_0900.4w/m/4wms(020415)13_tb.htm> (4 April 2002).

28. U.S. Department of Education, Digest of Education Statistics 2002.

29. Note: The graduate degrees awarded in China include master's and doctoral degrees and the graduate degrees awarded in America include master's, doctoral, and first professional degrees.

Source: 1. Academic Degrees Committee under the State Council, China, June 2002 <http://www.moe.edu.cn/moe-dept/xueweiban/2> (10 Nov. 2003).

2. U.S. Department of Education, *Digest of Education Statistics 2002.*

30. The World Bank's definition of country income level is as follows: low-income countries are those with a GNP per capita of $695 or less; lower-middle-income countries are those with a GNP per capita between $696 and $2,784, and upper-middle-income countries are those with a GNP per capita between $2,784 and $8,626 (World Development Report 1995).

31. See Data of Academic Degrees and Graduate Education Statistics to 1991, 1992, 1993, and 1994, (China Archives Publishing House, 1995).

32. These data are cited from Patricia J. Gumport, "Graduate Education and Organized Research in the United States," in *The Research Foundations of Graduate Education: Germany, Britain, France, United States, Japan,* ed. Burton R. Clark, (Berkeley and Los Angeles, CA: University of California Press, 1993), 225.

33. World Bank, *China: Higher Education Reform,* Report No. 15573-CHA (Washington, DC: 1996).

34. Ji Zhou, Vice Minister of Education (China), "Speech," *Xiaoxiang Morning News* (Changsha, China: 12 Oct. 2002).

Chapter Seven

Profile of Indian Education

Summary of findings: The education system in India is noteworthy for the diversification of its education structures among different states, joint responsibility between the central and state governments, free educational provision to all, and the overproduction of graduates at the higher education level. India is currently the leading provider of international students to U.S. higher education, but this trend may decline, as India becomes a more attractive source for higher education and an attractive employer for the brightest science and technology students from India and other nations.

OVERVIEW

Unfortunately, for India information on certain variables is very hard to assemble. The data and statistics I have collected so far are rather limited, fragmentary, and out-of-date in comparison with those for Japan, Korea, Taiwan, and Mainland China. One of my Indian friends from whom I had requested data responded to me in disappointment: "I am trying for the statistics you have requested but usually data in India is hard to come by even though we are supposed to be the IT savvy country of the globe!" So we will have to proceed relying on the information and data that are available and hope this chapter may serve as a foundation for a more focused case study in the future as more data becomes available. Thus, I can only provide a very general overview of Indian education.

India is home to 17 percent of the world's total population accommodated in an area which comprises 2.4 percent of the world's total area. In comparison with 2,820 languages in the entire world, as many as 325 languages are effectively used in India alone. Local dialects change in India almost after every 8–10 km. The country has witnessed phenomenal educational development—both in quantitative and qualitative terms, since independence. However, the national goals of universal elementary education and total eradication of illiteracy have still remained elusive. The government is committed to achieving these national goals and has been steadily increasing the budgetary allocation for education. The country has also made significant strides in higher and technical education.

Unlike the previous case studies of Japan, Korea, Taiwan, and Mainland China whose education systems are generally viewed as centralized, controlled education systems, the Indian education system is inherited from the pre-independence British colonial model that is characterized by concurrent responsibility between central and state governments. India has some features similar to China's, such as vast land, an immense population (India is the world's second most populous nation with about 1 billion people), a splendid ancient civilization, great reverence and love for education, and great social diversity. But India also has many unique features based on differences in classes, castes, religion, regions, and languages. These regional, cultural, and linguistic variations are reflected in the educational structures and organization that serve the nation. As a result, education varies from state to state with only the slightest uniformity between states and Union Territories (UTs). The foregoing discussion will attempt to indicate the commonalities that can be found in education in India.

SCHOOL STRUCTURE, ADMINISTRATION, AND FINANCE IN INDIA

Structure and Level of School

A uniform structure of school education, the 10 + 2 system, has been adopted by all the states and UTs of India. However, within the states and the UTs there remain variations in the number of classes constituting the primary, upper primary, high and higher secondary school stages, age for admission to class I, language of instruction, public examinations, teaching of Hindi and English, number of working days in a year, academic session, vacation periods, fee structure, and years of compulsory education.

Stages of School Education: The primary stage consists of classes I–V, i.e., of five years duration, in 20 states/UTs and the primary stage consists of classes I–IV, i.e., of four years duration, in the remaining states/UTs.

The middle stage of education comprises classes VI–VIII in 18 states/UTs, classes V–VII in 12 states/UTs, classes VI–VII in 3 states/UTs, and in Nagaland classes V–VIII constitute the upper primary stage.

The secondary stage consists of classes IX–X in 19 states/UTs; the high school stage comprises classes VIII to X in 13 States/UTs. However, the higher secondary/senior secondary stage of school comprising classes XI–XII (10 + 2 pattern) is available in all the states/UTs although in some states/UTs these classes are attached to universities/colleges.

Age Restriction for Admission: The minimum age for admission to class I of the primary school stage is generally 5 + or 6 + years. In 22 states/UTs the minimum age for admission to class I is 5 + years and in 7 states/UTs the minimum age for admission is 6 + years. There is no age restriction in the case of Mizoram. In Gujarat, the minimum age for admission is 5 + years (voluntary) and 6 + years (compulsory). In Lakshadweep, the minimum age for admission is 5 ½ years.

Compulsory Education: Compulsory education has been enforced in 4 states/UTs at the primary stage of education while in 8 states/UTs there is compulsory education covering the entire elementary stage of education. As many as 20 states/UTs had not introduced any measure of compulsion by the year 1997–1998.

Free Education: A majority of states and UTs have introduced free education in classes I–XII of their schools.

Higher Education Qualifications—Degree Structure: There are three principle levels of qualifications within the higher education system in India. These are: the bachelor's/undergraduate level, the master's/postgraduate level, and the doctoral/predoctoral level.

Diploma courses are also available at the undergraduate and postgraduate levels. The duration of study at the undergraduate level varies between one to three years. Postgraduate diplomas are normally awarded after one year's study.

Bachelor's degrees in arts, commerce, and sciences are awarded after three years of higher education (following 12 years of primary and secondary education). In certain regions honors and special courses are available. These are not necessarily longer in duration but indicate greater depth of study. Bachelor's degrees in the professional fields of agriculture, dentistry, engineering, pharmacy, technology, and veterinary medicine generally require four years of study while bachelor's degrees in architecture and medicine require five and five and a half years respectively. Bachelor's degrees are also offered in education, journalism, and librarianship; these are second degrees. The bachelor's degree course of study in law can be taken either as a five-year course granting an integrated degree or as a three-year course granting a second degree.

The master's degree program is normally of two-year duration. It may be purely coursework-based or may require a research thesis. Admission to postgraduate programs in engineering and technology is granted on the basis of a Graduate Aptitude Test in Engineering or a Combined Medical Test.

A predoctoral program—Master of Philosophy (M.Phil.) is taken after completion of the Master's Degree. This may be research-based or may also include course work. A Ph.D. is awarded two years after the M.Phil. or three years after the Master's degree. Students who are expected to write a substantial thesis based on original research generally take longer.

In conformity with the National Policy on Education, 1986, vocationalization at the first degree level was introduced in 1994–1995 to provide career orientation. A university or college may introduce one to three vocational courses in 35 identified subjects.

Educational Administration

Before 1976, education in India was exclusively the responsibility of the states. The central government was concerned only with certain areas such as the coordination and determination of standards in technical and higher education, etc. In 1976, through a constitutional amendment, education became a joint responsibility of the central and state governments. Decisions regarding the organization and structure of education remain largely the concern of the states. The central government, however, has a clear responsibility regarding the quality and character of education. In addition to policy formulation, the Department of Education, as a component of the Ministry of Human Resource Development, shares with the states the responsibility for educational planning. The Ministry of Human Resource Development is accountable to the Cabinet Ministry, which is headed by the prime minister.

The Department of Education is the principal body for education policy formulation and planning in India. The Central Advisory Board of Education (CABE), set up during the pre-independence period in 1935, continues to play a lead role in the evolution and monitoring of educational policies and programs, the most notable of which are the National Policy on Education (NPE), 1986, Program of Action (POA), 1986, and a revised NPE and POA (1992).

At the state level, the state ministries of education are supported by state departments, directorates, or secretariats of education, which are accountable to the chief ministries of the state. State departments of education typically share progress reports with the national Department of Education through forums and consultative meetings. Responsibilities for education in India are concurrent not only for national and state bodies but also for state and intermediate bodies. While the recent constitutional amendments and accompanying state legislation delegate responsibility for primary education to locally elected bodies at the district, subdistrict, and village levels, by tradition and under administrative orders state-level bodies have been assigned a variety of technical, personnel, and quality control responsibilities exercised at all levels. At the village level individuals rather than institutions are typically assigned responsibility. The complexity of the system and the potential overlap in authority make successful administration a major challenge.

The central government is responsible for major policies relating to higher education in the nation. It provides grants to the University Grants Commission (UGC) and establishes central universities in the nation. The central government is also responsible for the declaration of educational institutions "deemed to be universities" based on the recommendation of the UGC. Presently India has 16 central universities; the remaining universities function under the state acts. The total number of universities and colleges in India in 2000 were 221 and 10,555, respectively.[1]

State governments are responsible for the establishment of state universities and colleges, and provide plan grants for their development and nonplan grants for their maintenance. The coordination and cooperation between the union and the states is brought about in the field of education through the Central Advisory Board of Education (CABE).

The tier of government managing various schools, by level, along with percentages from 1973–1974 and 2001–2002 are given in table 7.1. In 1973–1974 central government-run primary schools comprised 54.51 percent of the total public primary schools in India. In 1978–1979, 1986–1987, and 1993–1994 a large percentage of public primary schools were managed by local bodies but the trend again shifted in 1996–1997 and

Table 7.1. Percentage of Public Primary, Upper Primary, and High/Higher Secondary Schools under Management of the Central Government and Local Bodies in India

Primary Schools			
Year	Government	Local Body (LB)	Govt. + LB
1973–74	54.51	45.49	100
1978–79	41.45	58.55	100
1986–87	44.45	55.55	100
1993–94	48.46	51.54	100
1996–97	52.13	47.87	100
2001–02*	52.12	47.88	100
Upper Primary Schools			
1973–74	65.38	34.62	100
1978–79	51.34	48.66	100
1986–87	56.97	43.03	100
1993–94	57.82	42.18	100
1996–97	61.94	38.06	100
2001–02*	61.99	38.01	100
High/Higher Secondary Schools			
1973–74	70.99	29.01	100
1978–79	77.75	22.25	100
1986–87	82.9	17.1	100
1993–94	80.26	19.74	100
1996–97	85.25	14.75	100
2001–02*	85.18	14.82	100

Note: * Provisional.
Source: Computed and compiled by the author from the Department of Education, India, Website: http://www.education.nic.in/htmlweb/edusta.htm#INTRODUCTION, 11-02-2003.

2001–2002 in which the percentage of central government-run primary schools was greater than that of primary schools run by local bodies. The central government continued to manage a majority of upper primary schools and high/higher secondary schools, the percentage of upper primary schools managed by the central government ranging from 65.38 percent to 61.99 percent from 1973–1974 to 2001–2002 and the percentage of central government-managed high/higher secondary schools ranging from 70.99 to 85.18 during the same period.

Education Finance

The National Policy on Education, 1986, and the Program of Action, 1992, envisage that free and compulsory education of satisfactory quality should be provided to all children up to the age of 14 years before the commencement of the twenty-first century. The general impression given is that Indian households spend little on education, including higher education, and that higher education is provided by the government almost free to everybody. So the central government and state governments take concurrent responsibilities in educational finance. Correspondingly, the share of every other sector has declined: the share of student fees, the only contribution from the students and their parents, declined from 20.39 percent in 1950–1951 to 3.82 percent in 1991–1992, and the share of other sources such as endowments, donations, etc., remained more or less stable at about 2–4 percent. Other potential sources are rarely considered reliable sources of funds for education in India. From the data in table 7.2 we can see that the percentage borne by the states/UTs in 1967–1997 was much higher than that borne by the central government. The reason is that maintenance and development of primary and secondary education (except for the central schools all over the nation) is entirely with the state governments' mandate, barring a few centrally-sponsored initiatives.

In addition to the funds from the governments at different levels, there are also funds from nongovernment sources including tuition fees and endowments as shown in table 7.3. But the funds from governments account for the majority, 93.44 percent in 1991–1992, while the funds from other sources account for only 6.56 percent.

Table 7.2. **Percentage of Expenditure on Education in Total Budget (All India) 1967–1997**

Year	State/Union Territory	Central Govmt.	Total
1967–68	19.8	1.6	11.9
1970–71	21.4	2.6	13.9
1975–76	22.7	2.1	13.6
1980–81	20.6	1.6	11.6
1981–82	20	1.5	11.3
1982–83	21.3	1.3	10.8
1983–84	20.8	1.5	11.4
1984–85	20.5	1.6	11.2
1990–91	21.2	2.2	11.7
1991–92	19.4	2.1	11
1992–93	19.6	1.9	11
1993–94	19.3	1.9	10.7
1994–95	19	2.1	10.8
1995–96	19.2	2.5	11.1
1996–97	19.6	2.8	11.2

Source: Department of Education, India, Website: http://www.education.nic.in/htmlweb/top, 12-20-2002.

Table 7.3. **Percentage Distribution of Total Income (Recurring and Non-Recurring) of All Educational Institutions by Source (All India)**

Year	Central Government Funds	Local Body Funds	University Funds	Total Funds	Fees	Endowment & Other Sources	Total
1950–51	57.06	10.93	—	67.99	20.39	11.62	100
1960–61	67.97	6.53	—	74.5	17.14	8.35	100
1970–71	75.65	4.34	1.36	81.35	12.81	5.85	100
1980–81	81.7	4.71	1.37	87.78	8.2	4.03	100
1983–84	81.51	5.61	1.61	88.73	7.5	3.78	100
1987–88	85.94	6.79	0.01	92.42	4.17	3.09	100
1988–89*	83.08	6.72	0.04	89.84	6.08	4.08	100
1989–90**	83.51	9.89	0.01	93.41	3.55	3.04	100
1990–91**	87.87	6.22	0.01	94.1	3.53	2.37	100
1991–92**	86.35	7.08	0.01	93.44	3.82	2.74	100

* Excludes affiliated institutions of higher education.
** School Education only.
Source: Department of Education, India, Website: http://www.education.nic.in/htmlweb/top, 12-20-2002.

INDIAN EDUCATIONAL GROWTH AND ACHIEVEMENTS

Similar to China's case, India started to develop its education and science from an extremely low base when India declared independence in 1947. Over the past half-century, India has built up one of the world's largest education systems and made remarkable achievements in educational development. It is difficult to believe that prior to 1947, 84 percent of India's adult population was illiterate (75 percent of male individuals and 92 percent of female individuals) and only 25 percent of the school age population (ages 6–17) was in school. The following data shows a picture of India's education system and its achievements in the past half-century.[2]

Anti-illiteracy

At independence the literacy rate was 18.33 percent (male literacy was at 27.16 percent and female literacy rate was at 8.86 percent). It was only in 1991 that India crossed the halfway mark, achieving a literacy rate of 52.21 percent. The male literacy rate was 64.1 percent and the female literacy rate was 39.3 percent. In 2001, the literacy rate reached 65.4 percent. Figure 7.1 and table 7.4 show an average decadal growth rate of 9.4 percent from 1951 to 2001. A jump of 13.2 points was reflected between 1991 and 2001.

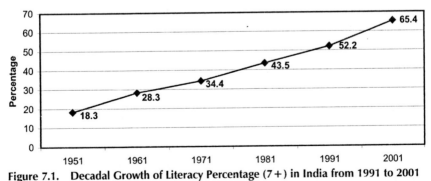

Figure 7.1.   Decadal Growth of Literacy Percentage (7 +) in India from 1991 to 2001

Source: Department of Education, India, http://www.education.nic.in/htmlweb/edusta_pt3.htm#Literacy, 11-01-03/

Table 7.4.   Literacy Percentage and Percentage Decadal Growth Rate in India
(1951–2001)

Year	Literacy Percentage	Percentage Decadal Growth
1951	18.3	
1961	28.3	10
1971	34.4	6.1
1981	43.5	9.1
1991	52.2	8.7
2001	65.4	13.2

Source: Department of Education, India, http://www.education.nic.in/htmlweb/edusta_pt3.htm#Literacy, 11-01-03.

Eight-Year Compulsory Education

Since independence, the Indian governments at different levels have been paying great attention to universalization of elementary education. The Indian national policy on education envisages that free and compulsory education of satisfactory quality should be provided to all children up to the age of 14 years old. In the year 2000, as a result of the efforts made by the central government and state governments, 94 percent of the country's rural population had primary schools within one km and 84 percent had upper primary schools within three km. The enrollment of children of 6–14 years of age in primary and upper primary schools has increased steadily since independence to finally reach 89.7 percent and 58.5 percent gross enrollment rates in 1998, respectively, and the total gross enrollment of elementary schools reached 78.6 percent as shown in table 7.5. Significant improvements have been made in the enrollment of girls, whose ratio accounted for 70 percent of total girls of age 1–14 years in 1998; and the number of primary and upper primary schools have increased from 22.3 million in 1950–1951 to 148.3 million in 1997–1998, an increase of 6.7 times.

Educational Growth

After examining the data in figures 7.2 and 7.3 and tables 7.6 and 7.7, one is definitely impressed with the enormous education system and the fast and steady development at all education levels in India over the past half-century. The Indian government has been persistently making a

Table 7.5. Compulsory Enrollment and Ratio by Stages and Gender (1950–1998)

Year	Primary Level (Class I–V) Age 6–11 years				Middle Level (Class VI–VIII) Age 11–14 years				Total Gross Enrollment & Ratio (%) (Class I–VIII) Ages 6–14			
	No.*	Gross Enrol. (%)			No.*	Gross Enrol. (%)			Total No.*	Gross Enrol. (%)		
		Primary Level I–V	Boys I–V	Girls I–V		Middle Level VI–VIII	Boys VI–VIII	Girls VI–VIII		Elementary I–VIII	Boys I–VIII	Girls I–VIII
1950–51	19.2	42.6	60.6	24.8	3.1	12.7	20.6	4.6	22.3	32.1	46.4	17.7
1960–61	35.0	62.4	82.6	41.4	6.7	22.5	33.2	11.3	41.7	48.7	65.2	30.9
1968–69	54.4				12.5							
1979–80	71.6				19.3							
1989–90	97.4				32.2							
1991–92	101.6	100.2	113	86.9	34.5	61.35	75.1	49.6	136.1	87.7	101.2	73.2
1992–93	105.4	84.6	95	73.5	38.7	67.5	72.5	48.94	144.1	77.75	87.7	65.7
1993–94	108.2	81.9	90	73.1	39.9	54.2	62.1	45.4	148.1	72.3	80.23	63.7
1994–95	109.0	104	115	92.6	40.2	67.2	79	55	149.2	90.7	101.8	78.8
1995–96	109.8	104.3	115	93.3	41.0	67.6	79.5	55	150.8	90.9	101.8	79.3
1996–97	110.4	90.6	98.7	81.9	41.1	62.4	70.9	52.8	151.5	80.7	88.85	71.8
1997–98	108.8	89.7	97.7	81.2	39.5	58.5	66.5	49.5	148.3	78.6	86.4	70

Note: * Unit: million persons.
Source: Computed and compiled by the author from: 1.RRTD, 2000, p 82.
2. Department of Education, India, Website: available at <http://www.education.nic.in/htmlweb/edusta.htm> (20 Dec. 2002).

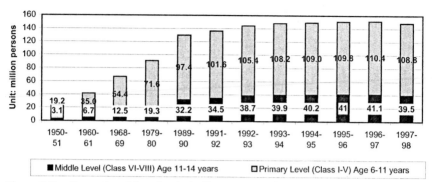

Figure 7.2.   Elementary Education in India: Progress of Enrollment (1950–1998)
Source: Compiled by the author from: RRTD, 2000, p. 82.

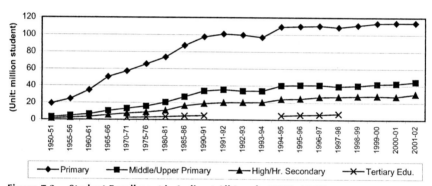

Figure 7.3.   Student Enrollment in India at All Levels (1950–2002)
Sources: Computed and compiled by the author from:
1. Department of Education, India, Website: http://www.education.nic.in/htmlweb/edusta.htm, 10-15-02.
2. Department of Education, India, Website: http://www.education.nic.in/htmlweb/edusta.htm#INTRO-DUCTION, 11-02-2003.
3. Institute for Statistics, UNESCO, Website, 2002.
4. RRTD, India, 2000, p. 97.

heavy investment in education, which is considered to be the stimulus both to national economic development and to social democratization.

Growth of Educational Institutions: There has been a considerable increase in the spread of educational institutions during the period from 1950–1951 to 2001–2002. This is evident from table 7.6. During this period the number of primary schools increased by 3 times, while the upper primary schools and higher secondary schools increased by 16 and 18 times respectively. The number of colleges for general education and

Table 7.6. Growth of Recognized Educational Institutions in India from 1950–1951 to 2001–2002

Years	Primary	Upper Primary	High/Hr. Sec/ Inter/Pre. Jr. Colleges	Colleges for General Education	Colleges for Professional Education (Eng., Tech., Arch., Medical & Education Colleges)	Universities/ Deemed Univ./Inst. Of National Importance
1950–51	209671	13596	7416	370	208	27
1955–56	278135	21730	10838	466	218	31
1960–61	330399	49663	17329	967	852	45
1965–66	391064	75798	27614	1536	770	64
1970–71	408378	90621	37051	2285	992	82
1975–76	454270	106571	43054	3667	3276	101
1980–81	494503	118555	51573	3421	3542	110
1985–86	528872	134846	65837	4067	1533	126
1990–91	560935	151456	79796	4862	886	184
1991–92	566744	155926	82576	5058	950	196
1992–93	571248	158498	84608	5334	989	207
1993–94	570455	162804	89226	5639	1125	213
1994–95	586810	168772	94946	6089	1230	219
1995–96	593410	174145	99274	6569	1354	226
1996–97	603646	180293	103241	6759	1770	228
1997–98	619222	185961	107140	7199	2075	229
1998–99*	626737	190166	112438	7494	2113	237
1999–2000*	641695	198004	116820	7782	2124	244
2000–2001*	638738	206269	126047	7929	2223	254
2001–2002*	664041	219626	133492	8737	2409	272

Note: * Provisional.
Source: Department of Education, India, Website: http://www.education.nic.in/htmlweb/edusta.htm# INTRODUCTION, 11-02-2003.

professional education increased by about 24 and 12 times respectively while the number of universities increased by 10 times during the period.

Growth of Enrollment: According to the data in figure 7.3 and table 7.7, total student enrollment increased by 8 times during the period of 1950–2002, from 23.8 million in 1950–1951 to 189.2 million in 2001–2002. During the same time, the enrollment at primary, middle/upper primary and high/higher secondary levels increased by 5.9 times, 14.5 times, and 20.3 times, respectively, rising from 19.2 million, 3.1 million, and 1.5 million in 1950–1951 to 113.9 million, 44.8 million, and 30.5 million in 2001–2002, respectively. At the tertiary level, within about 30 years between 1970–2000, student enrollment almost tripled, from 2.5 million in 1970 to 7.1 million in 2000.

It is well-known that, in terms of size and scale, India has the world's second largest education system, after China's. India also had the largest

Chapter 7

Table 7.7.   Student Enrollment and Ratio in India by Level (1950–2002)
(Unit: million)

	Total	Primary		Middle/Upper Primary		High/Hr. Secondary		Tertiary Education	
Year	No.	No.	%	No.	%	No.	%	No.	%
1950–51	23.8	19.2	80.7	3.1	13.0	1.5	6.3		
1955–56	32	24.6	76.9	4.8	15.0	2.6	8.1		
1960–61	45.1	35	77.6	6.7	14.9	3.4	7.5		
1965–66	66.7	50.5	75.7	10.5	15.7	5.7	8.5		
1970–71	80.4	57	70.9	13.3	16.5	7.6	9.5	2.5	3.1
1975–76	93.5	65.6	70.2	16	17.1	8.9	9.5	3	3.2
1980–81	109.1	73.8	67.6	20.7	19.0	11	10.1	3.6	3.3
1985–86	135.5	87.4	64.5	27.1	20.0	16.5	12.2	4.5	3.3
1990–91	155.5	97.4	62.6	34	21.9	19.1	12.3	5	3.2
1991–92	156.9	100.9	64.3	35.6	22.7	20.4	13.0		
1992–93	154.2	99.6	64.6	34.1	22.1	20.5	13.3		
1993–94	151.8	97	63.9	34.1	22.5	20.7	13.6		
1994–95	178.7	109.1	61.1	40.3	22.6	24.4	13.7	4.9	2.7
1995–96	181.4	109.8	60.5	41	22.6	24.9	13.7	5.7	3.1
1996–97	184.5	110.4	59.8	41	22.2	27	14.6	6.1	3.3
1997–98	182.5	108.7	59.6	39.5	21.6	27.24	14.9	7.1**	3.9
1998–99*	179	110.9	61.96	40.3	22.51	27.8	15.53		
1999–00*	183.9	113.6	61.77	42.1	22.89	28.2	15.33		
2000–01*	184.2	113.8	61.78	42.8	23.24	27.6	14.98		
2001–02*	189.2	113.9	60.20	44.8	23.68	30.5	16.12		

Note: * Provisional.
** indicates the data of 2000.
Source: Computed and compiled by the author from:
1. Department of Education, India, Website: http://www.education.nic.in/htmlweb/edusta.htm, 10-15-02.
2. Department of Education, India, Website: http://www.education.nic.in/htmlweb/edusta.htm#INTRODUCTION, 11-02-2003.
3. Institute for Statistics, UNESCO, Website, 2002.
4. RRTD, India, 2000, p 97.

higher education system in the world, only surpassed by China in very recent years. The highly developed higher education system in India in the past decades has made India the third largest scientific community in the world. Table 7.7 shows that the ratio at the secondary and tertiary levels has steadily increased in the past half-century and that secondary and tertiary education made up 16.12 percent and 3.9 percent, respectively, of total student enrollment in 2001–2002 and 2000.

Gross Enrollment Ratios: Gross Enrollment Ratio (GER) is defined as the percentage of the enrollment in the primary (classes I–V) and upper primary (classes VI–VIII) and/or elementary I–VIII to the estimated child population in the age groups 6 to below 11 years and 11 to below 14 and/ or 6 to below 14 years respectively. Enrollment in these stages includes underage and overage children. Hence the total percentage may be more than 100 percent in some cases as seen in table 7.8. During the period 1950–2002, the total gross enrollment ratios for the age group 6 to below 11 years increased by 53.7 percentage points, from 42.6 percent to 96.3 percent; for the age group 11 to below 14 years increased by 47.5 percentage points, from 12.7 percent to 60.2 percent; for the age group 6 to below 14 years increased by 50.3 percentage points, from 32.1 percent to 82.4 percent. Within each category, the gross enrollment ratios for girl students increased much more greatly than that for boy students.

Gross Dropout Rates: The Gross Dropout Rate represents the percentage of students who drop out from a given grade or cycle or level of education in a given school year. The rates of dropout have decreased from 64.9 percent in 1960–1961 to 39.0 percent in 2001–2002 in primary classes. The rate of dropouts which was 78.3 percent in 1960–1961 and has come down to 54.6 percent in 2001–2002 in the upper primary

Table 7.8.   Gross Enrollment Ratios in India from 1950 to 2002 (GER)

Year	Primary (I–V)			Upper Primary (VI–VIII)			Elementary (I–VIII)		
	Boys	Girls	Total	Boys	Girls	Total	Boys	Girls	Total
1950–51	60.6	24.8	42.6	20.6	4.6	12.7	46.4	17.7	32.1
1960–61	82.6	41.4	62.4	33.2	11.3	22.5	65.2	30.9	48.7
1970–71	95.5	60.5	78.6	46.5	20.8	33.4	75.5	44.4	61.9
1980–81	95.8	64.1	80.5	54.3	28.6	41.9	82.2	52.1	67.5
1990–91	114	85.5	100.1	76.6	47	62.1	100	70.8	86
1991–92	112.8	86.9	100.2	75.1	49.6	61.4	101.2	73.2	87.7
1992–93	95	73.5	84.6	72.5	48.9	67.5	87.7	65.7	77.2
1993–94	90	73.1	81.9	62.1	45.4	54.2	80.2	63.7	72.3
1994–95	96.6	78.2	87.7	68.9	50	60	87.2	68.8	78.4
1995–96	97.1	79.4	88.6	67.8	49.8	59.3	86.9	69.4	78.5
1996–97	97	80.1	88.8	65.8	49.2	58	85.9	69.4	78
1997–98	99.3	82.2	91.1	66.3	49.7	58.5	87.4	70.7	79.4
1998–99*	100.9	82.9	92.1	65.3	49.1	57.6	87.6	70.6	79.4
1999–00*	104.1	85.2	94.9	67.2	49.7	58.8	90.1	72	81.3
2000–01*	104.9	85.9	95.7	66.7	49.9	58.6	90.3	72.4	81.6
2001–02*	105.3	86.9	96.3	67.8	52.1	60.2	90.7	73.6	82.4

Note: * Provisional.
Source: Department of Education, India, Website: http://www.education.nic.in/htmlweb/edusta.htm# INTRODUCTION, 11-02-2003.

classes. Similarly, the rate of dropouts which was 82.5 percent in 1980–
1981 has decreased to 66.0 percent in 2001–2002 in the secondary
classes, implying an improvement in retention rates as is evident from
table 7.9.

Educational Finance Input

The steady development of the Indian education system, higher education
in particular, in the past half-century has been attributed to the growing
educational finance input from the government. The data of table 7.10
indicate that during the period of 1951–2002, the total public expenditure
on education in India increased by 1,306 times, from 64.46 crore in 1951–
1952 to 84,179.46 crore in 2001–2002. In 1951–1952 the expenditure on
the education sector was slightly less than 1 percent of the GDP. The
expenditure on education as a percentage of GDP shows an irregular rise
and fall. It rose to 2.33 percent in 1972–1973 but in 1973–1974 declined
to 2.15 percent. It increased to 3.07 percent in 1979–1980 and decreased
to 2.83 percent in 1981–1982. Continuing to rise and fall slightly, it has
reached a level of 4.02 percent in 2001–2002. Similarly, the expenditure

Table 7.9. Dropout Rates at Primary, Elementary, and Secondary Stages in India from
1960 to 2002

	1960–1961	1970–1971	1980–1981	1990–1991	1992–1993	1999–2000*	2001–2002*
			Classes I–V				
Boys	61.7	64.5	56.2	40.1	43.8	38.7	38.4
Girls	70.9	70.9	62.5	46	46.7	42.3	39.9
Total	64.9	67	58.7	42.6	45	40.3	39
			Classes I–VIII				
Boys	75	74.6	68	59.1	58.2	52	52.9
Girls	85	83.4	79.4	65.1	65.2	58	56.9
Total	78.3	77.9	72.7	60.9	61.1	54.5	54.6
			Classes I–X				
Boys	N.A.	N.A.	79.8	67.5	70	66.6	64.2
Girls	N.A.	N.A.	86.6	76.9	77.3	70.6	68.6
Total	N.A.	N.A.	82.5	71.3	72.9	68.3	66

Note: * Provisional.
Source: Department of Education, India, Website: http://www.education.nic.in/htmlweb/edusta.htm#
INTRODUCTION, 11-02-2003.

Table 7.10. Public Expenditure on Education in India from 1951 to 2002 (in crore)

Year	Govt. expenditure on education (Trg. & Rev.) by education and other Depts. (center + state)	Total Govt. expenditure on all sectors (Rev.)	GDP at current prices (at factor cost) base year 1993–1994	% of Expenditure on Education to Expenditure on all sectors	% of Education Expenditure to GDP
1951–52	64.46	814.13	10080	7.92	0.64
1952–53	72.26	857.67	9941	8.43	0.73
1953–54	80.06	908.2	10824	8.82	0.74
1954–55	95.82	973.74	10168	9.84	0.94
1955–56	118.39	1111.26	10332	10.65	1.15
1956–57	132.88	1158.01	12334	11.47	1.08
1957–58	150.26	1416.62	12610	10.61	1.19
1958–59	173.78	1594.36	14106	10.9	1.23
1959–60	207.59	1770.06	14816	11.73	1.4
1960–61	239.56	1997.93	16220	11.99	1.48
1961–62	260.3	2225.4	17116	11.7	1.52
1962–63	278.76	2942.67	18302	9.47	1.52
1963–64	313.93	3488.97	20916	9	1.5
1964–65	369.29	3844.91	24436	9.6	1.51
1965–66	432.61	4404.82	25586	9.82	1.69
1966–67	487.83	5100.24	29123	9.56	1.68
1967–68	593.14	5619.77	34225	10.55	1.73
1968–69	649.13	6922.07	36092	9.38	1.8
1969–70	760.23	7908.07	39691	9.61	1.92
1970–71	892.36	8787.12	42222	10.16	2.11
1971–72	1011.07	10610.89	44923	9.53	2.25
1972–73	1150.43	11863.56	49415	9.7	2.33
1973–74	1300.72	12884.48	60560	10.1	2.15
1974–75	1570.67	14625.03	71283	10.74	2.2
1975–76	1849.47	17958.99	75709	10.3	2.44
1976–77	2039.09	20482.83	81381	9.96	2.51
1977–78	2630.6	22666.31	92881	11.61	2.83
1978–79	2994.69	26134.84	99823	11.46	3
1979–80	3347.57	30915.39	108927	10.83	3.07
1980–81	3884.2	36398.39	130178	10.67	2.98
1981–82	4435.29	33667.31	152056	13.17	2.92
1982–83	5509.17	43996.18	169525	12.52	3.25
1983–84	6229.53	61889.25	198630	10.07	3.14
1984–85	7455.88	69025.45	222705	10.8	3.35
1985–86	8713.02	67091.41	249547	12.99	3.49
1986–87	9479.13	80454.66	278258	11.78	3.41
1987–88	11798.35	92518.38	315993	12.75	3.73
1988–89	14069.82	107543.75	378491	13.08	3.72
1989–90	17192.5	126045.97	438020	13.64	3.93
1990–91	19615.85	146711.53	510954	13.37	3.84
1991–92	22393.69	170370.38	589086	13.14	3.8
1992–93	25030.3	190327.45	673221	13.15	3.72
1993–94	28279.69	218535.15	781345	12.94	3.62
1994–95	32606.22	251691.92	917058	12.95	3.56
1995–96	38178.09	286194.55	1073271	13.34	3.56
1996–97	43896.48	329389.92	1243546	13.33	3.53
1997–98	48552.14	380728.45	1390148	12.75	3.49
1998–99	61578.91	439768.11	1598127	14	3.85
1999–00	74816.09	512519.33	1761932	14.6	4.25
2000–01	82486.43	572160.14	1917724P	14.42	4.3
2001–02	84179.46(R.E)	639048.06	2094013Q	13.17	4.02

Note: A crore is 10,000,000.
Source: Department of Education, India, Website: http://www.education.nic.in/htmlweb/edusta.htm# INTRODUCTION, 11-02-2003.

on education and training as a percentage of total expenditure on all sectors has increased during the last five decades from 7.92 percent in 1951–1952 to 13.17 percent in 2001–2002, i.e., by 5.25 percentage points. This translates to an annual average growth of 0.11 percent during the period from 1951–1952 to 2001–2002.

FEATURE AND CHANGES

Non-Formal Education

The non-formal education system in India is similar to that in Japan, Korea, and Taiwan only in name, and different in essence. The government of India, Department of Education, has been running, since 1979–1980, a program of Non-Formal Education (NFE) for children of the 6–14 age-group who remain outside the formal system due to various reasons. These students include dropouts of the formal schools, children from habitations without schools, working children, children who assist in performing domestic chores like fetching fuel, fodder, water, attending to siblings, grazing cattle, etc., and girls who are unable to attend formal schools. Though the focus of the scheme is on ten educationally backwards states, it also covers urban slums and hilly, tribal, and desert areas. The program is in operation in 25 states/UTs. Under this program assistance is given to states/UTs in the ratio of 60:40 and 90:10 for running coeducational and girls' centers respectively. Some assistance is given to voluntary agencies for running NFE centers and undertaking experimental and innovative projects. In 2000, 297,000 NFE-sanctioned centers were in operation, catering to about 7.425 million children. Of the total number of centers about 117,000 centers were exclusively for girls.

Role of Private Sector

India has a long tradition of private schools that goes back to the days of missionary activity. Some of the existing private schools operate under religious auspices or are conducted by independent groups and associations. In current India's mixed economy, where the contribution of the private sector has been significant in general, the contribution of the private sector to higher education has not been encouraging.[3] There are no private universities in India, but a large number of private colleges, which form about three-fourths of the total number of colleges. According to the statistics of the World Bank (1997),[4] in India, "at all levels, some private schools—about 40 percent of urban primary schools and more than half of all secondary schools in 1987 were private—offer a first-class education to those who can afford the fees."

Private schools are of two types: privately managed but publicly funded schools familiarly known as government-"aided" schools, and privately managed and funded schools, known as "unaided" schools. A substantial number of private schools belong to the former category, and they receive government aid to meet almost the whole recurrent expenditure. Hence strictly from the point of view of finances, such private schools do not have any significant role.[5] Pure or "unaided" private schools do provide financial relief to the government in providing education, but at huge and long-term economic and noneconomic cost to the society.

The contribution of private agencies, as indicated in table 7.11, has been relatively small though increasing over the years. The highest percentage of private primary schools was in the year 2001–2002 (9.08 percent). The percentage of primary aided schools has been slowly decreasing over the years while the percentage of unaided schools has been increasing. The private upper primary schools (aided and unaided) had a percentage share of 21 percent to 25 percent over the years between 1973–1974 and 2001–2002. On the contrary, during this period, the majority of high/higher secondary schools were under private management. The ratio of private-managed to government-managed high and higher secondary schools varied from 63:37 in 1973–1974; 61:39 in 1978–1979; 55:45 in 1986–1987; 53:47 in 1993–1994; 54:46 in 1996–1997; and 58:42 in 2001–2002.

However, a declining trend in the privately managed schools is observed while the government's share in the management of secondary and higher secondary schools increased to 38.96 percent in 1996–1997 then slightly decreased to 36.16 percent in 2001–2002. Further, the share of private aided high/higher secondary schools receiving annual grants from the government is declining while the percentage of private unaided schools is increasing.

From the demand side, private colleges have been growing in number essentially due to the existence of an excess of demand over supply, par-

Chapter 7

Table 7.11. Percentage of Primary, Upper Primary, and High/Higher Secondary Schools of Different Management and Types In India

		Primary Schools			
Year	Govt.	Local Body (LB)	Govt. + LB	Private Aided	Private Unaided
1973–74	50.88	42.47	93.34	5.01	1.64
1978–79	38.96	55.03	93.99	4.42	1.59
1986–87	41.37	51.71	93.08	4.34	2.57
1993–94	44.63	47.47	92.1	3.78	4.12
1996–97	47.78	43.88	91.66	3.34	5
2001–02*	47.45	43.47	90.92	3.07	6.01
		Upper Primary Schools			
1973–74	50.71	26.86	77.57	17.75	4.67
1978–79	40.31	38.13	78.44	16.9	4.66
1986–87	42.79	32.33	75.12	16.3	8.58
1993–94	45.94	33.51	79.45	9.53	11.02
1996–97	46.41	29.13	75.54	10.25	14.2
2001–02*	47.36	29.05	76.41	7.81	15.77
		High/Higher Secondary Schools			
1973–74	26.54	10.85	37.39	57.02	5.59
1978–79	30.44	8.71	39.15	57.3	3.55
1986–87	37.49	7.73	45.22	44.79	9.99
1993–94	37.76	9.29	47.05	37.78	15.17
1996–97	38.96	6.74	45.7	36.2	18.1
2001–02*	36.16	6.29	42.45	33.99	23.56

Note: * Provisional.
Source: Department of Education, India, Website: http://www.education.nic.in/htmlweb/edusta.htm# INTRODUCTION, 11-02-2003.

ticularly among the upper classes and of those who fail to get admission into government colleges for higher education. According to **Tilak**,[6] these institutions are rarely regarded as being superior in terms of quality, unlike in the case of private primary and secondary schools where the "Chivas Regal effect" also offers an explanation for their growth. From the point of view of supply, motives of profit, influence, and political power explain the growth of these private colleges.

Instruction and Curriculum of Indian Primary and Secondary Education

Due to limited data, I can cover only briefly the instruction and curriculum of Indian primary and secondary education.

Language of Instruction: Mother tongue or regional language is the language of instruction at the primary stage of education in most of the states/UTs. Facilities for studying in a medium other than regional language vary considerably in different states and UTs.

Teaching of Hindi: The teaching of Hindi is compulsory in most of the non-Hindi-speaking states/UTs, though the classes (grade levels) from which the teaching of Hindi is compulsory differ from state to state. The teaching of Hindi is not compulsory in the states of Tamil Nadu and Tripura, and in the Karaikal region of Pondicherry.

Teaching of English: The teaching of English is compulsory in all the states/UTs, except Bihar. However, the classes in which the teaching of English is compulsory differ from state to state. It is compulsory in classes VI–X in most of the states/UTs.

Public Examinations: In all the states/UTs public examinations are conducted at the end of X and XII classes by the respective state boards of secondary and higher secondary education. The minimum age for the secondary school examination varies from 14 + to 16 + years in 19 states/UTS. In Mizoram, the minimum age for secondary school examination is 13 + years. Other states/UTs either do not have an age restriction **or have not prescribed one.** The minimum age for higher secondary school examination varies from 16 + to 18 + years in 13 states/UTs. In other states/UTs, either there is no age restriction prescribed or, if it exists, **it has not been indicated.** In some of the states/UTs, the first public examination is conducted at the middle stage of education.

Number of Working Days: The number of working days of primary and secondary education in a year is generally more than 200 days in all the states/UTs. The academic session begins in different months of the year in the different states and UTs. In most of the states, the long vacation periods occur in the summer season, while in some of the hilly states these vacation periods fall in the winter months.

Curriculum: Elementary schools are primarily state-supported but are administered by local government units. The elementary school curriculum defines the subjects to be taught and gives general guidance on the frequency and duration of instruction. Sometimes it is accompanied by a syllabus that specifies more precisely what is to be taught and what is to be assessed. In most states in India, the curriculum is embodied in textbooks. Responsibility for curriculum development in primary education resides with the states, although the National Council of Educational

Research and Training (NCERT) provides model materials that can be adapted at state and district levels.

To bring primary education standards into line with children's developmental capabilities, the Department of Education has established a minimum level of learning (MLL) for language, mathematics, and social and environmental studies in each of the five primary grades. The standards are expressed as competency statements for curriculum domains and grade level. Although neither states nor districts are obligated to adopt them, MLL standards have been widely disseminated, and model textbooks have been developed to support them. The standards provide a target of achievements to be attained by all students.[7]

At the secondary school level, in addition to language, the curriculum includes courses in the humanities, science, technology, commerce, agriculture, fine arts, and home economics. Much of the secondary curriculum is college preparatory and is dominated by university matriculation examinations. In an attempt to make secondary education more relevant to non-university-bound students, 2,000 multipurpose high schools have been established since 1962 to offer technical, commercial, and craft education as well as liberal arts preparation.[8]

In 1984–1985, a pilot project on Computer Literacy and Studies in Schools (CLASS) was initiated in collaboration with the Department of Electronics. The broad objectives of the pilot project included demystification of computers and provided "hands-on" experience. The project was continued up to 1992–1993 on an ad hoc basis and funds in the range of Rs 4 to 5 million were provided on a year-to-year basis. 2,598 schools were covered by 1992–1993. The program has been modified and is being implemented as a centrally-sponsored initiative since 1993–1994. To be eligible for assistance under the modified program, the following conditions are to be satisfied by the states/UTs: (a) The coverage of the program for new schools will be restricted to senior secondary schools; (b) In selected schools, instruction in Computer Literacy will be compulsory for all students of classes XI and XII and will be part of the school time-table with the evaluation in the subject taking place with/without formal examination and; (c) infrastructure such as a pukka room with electricity and other fittings will have to be constructed in the school to be covered under the project by the concerned state government, before taking up the project.

To improve the quality of science education and to promote scientific curiosity, a centrally-sponsored program, Improvement of Science Education in Schools, was initiated during 1987–1988. This program provides science materials to upper primary schools; upgrades and strengthens science laboratories in secondary/senior secondary schools; supplies books on science-related subjects to secondary and senior secondary schools; and trains science and mathematics teachers. One of the most important components of this program is the participation of Indian students at the primary and secondary levels in the International Mathematical Olympiad (IMO), International Physics Olympiad (IPO), and International Chemistry Olympiad (IChO).[9]

Vocational Education

Vocational schools are also making progress in India. The National Policy on Education (NPE), 1986, accords high priority to the vocationalization of education at the secondary stage. The NPE as revised in 1992 aimed at diverting 10 percent of the students at the +2 level to the vocational stream by 1995 and 25 percent by 2000. Accordingly, a centrally-sponsored program of Vocationalization of Secondary Education was launched in February 1998. Under this program, substantial financial assistance is provided to states/UTs for the introduction of vocational courses in classes XI and XII of the school system. By 2000, all states/UTs except Lakshadweep had joined the program. In all, 18,719 vocational courses had been sanctioned in 6,486 schools all over the nation, thereby creating the capacity for the diversion of about 935,000 students to the vocational stream, which comprises 11 percent of enrollment at the +2 stage.

About 150 vocational courses have been introduced, most falling into one of six major areas: agriculture, business and commerce, engineering and technology, health and paramedical, home economics, and humanities. 94 vocational courses are sanctioned under the Apprenticeship Act. Collaborative arrangements have been made with national and regional organizations and agencies. Under the program, 75 voluntary organizations have been provided assistance for conducting innovative, non-formal programs of vocational education. In addition, a centrally-sponsored program of prevocational education was launched in 1993–1994 with the objective of imparting simple marketable skills to the students of classes IX and X. By 2000, assistance had been provided to 11 states/UTs for the introduction of pre-vocational courses in 652 schools.[10]

Percentage of Female Enrollment in India at all Levels of Education

India's government has made efforts to reduce gender disparities in education through various initiatives since independence, especially after the adoption of the National Policy on Education (NPE), 1996. The NPE is committed to "a well conceived edge in favor of women." It recognizes that the education of women is possibly the most crucial condition for the participation of girls and women in the developmental process. Through various preferential programs and policies, the participation of girls at all stages of education has been increasing steadily over time, as may be seen from table 7.12. During the period of 1950–1951 and 1997–1998, the female ratio of total enrollment increased from 28.1 percent to 43.6 per-

Table 7.12.   Percentage of Female Enrollment to Total Enrollment by Stages (1950–1998)

Year	Primary I–V	Middle VI–VIII	Sec./Hr. Sec./10 + 2/Intermediate	Hr. Education (Degree & above level)
1950–51	28.1	16.1	13.3	10
1955–56	30.5	20.8	15.4	14.6
1960–61	32.6	23.9	20.5	16
1965–66	36.2	26.7	22	20.4
1970–71	37.4	29.3	25	20
1975–76	38.1	31.3	26.9	23.2
1980–81	38.6	32.9	29.6	26.7
1985–86	40.3	35.6	30.3	33
1990–91	41.5	36.7	32.9	33.3
1991–92	41.9	38.2	33.8	32.3
1992–93	42.6	38.8	33.9	33.2
1993–94	42.7	39.1	34.3	33.5
1994–95	42.8	38.9	34.4	34
1995–96	43.2	39	35.3	37.2
1996–97	43.4	39.8	36.2	38.2
1997–98	43.6	40.1	37.1	34.8

Source: Department of Education, India, Website: <http://www.education.nic.in/htmlweb/edusta.htm>, 2002,10.22.

cent at primary I–V level, from 16.1 percent to 40.1 percent at middle VI–VIII level, from 13.3 percent to 37.1 percent at secondary/higher secondary/10 + 2 level, and from 10 percent to 34.8 percent at the tertiary level. In view of the fact that 92 percent of India's adult female population was illiterate before independence in 1947, these achievements are remarkable. However, the female percentages still fall below 45 percent of the total, which is considered an international standard for the normal ratio of female enrollment.

Incomplete Picture of Current Indian Higher Education

One of the simplest indicators of the success of higher education in India is its rapid growth—both in terms of size and diversification. India had the largest higher educational system in the world until very recently it was surpassed by China. Unfortunately, the data and statistics I need for analysis are very limited, fragmentary, and out-of-date. Through my efforts, I have managed the following three tables and our brief analysis will be based on the data of these three tables.

Table 7.13 shows the total enrollment in higher education (general) in India by faculty, gender, and level from 1971 to 1998. At all three levels of doctorate/research, postgraduation, and graduation, enrollment is largely concentrated in arts. Over 50 percent of students and close to 60 percent of female students are enrolled in the arts. In Indian society, the choice of most women entering higher education remains confined to arts, humanities, and other subjects considered feminine. Men have greater enrollment in all subjects at all three levels except the arts at the graduate level where female enrollment takes the lead.

The ratio between doctorate/research, postgraduation, and graduation in total enrollment was 1:12:128.5 in 1998; the ratio within men's enrollment was 1:10.2:113.9 and that within women's enrollment was 1:16.1:164.4 at the same time.

As the incomplete statistics in table 7.14 reveal, in professional education the largest student population was enrolled in engineering and technology while the second choice of students was education, whose graduation level was the only place where female student enrollment took

Table 7.13. Total Enrollment in Higher Education (General) in India by Faculty, Gender, and Level (All India) (1971–1998)

Total Enrollment in Higher Education (General) by Faculty and Level

Faculty	Doctorate/Research				Postgraduation				Graduation			
	1971	1981	1991	1998	1971	1981	1991	1998	1971	1981	1991	1998
Arts	10119* (97.50)	13003 (53.34)	#	#	90970 (62.88)	160673 (63.17)	202831 (57.26)	287161 (60.15)	764387 (51.23)	1016036 (49.76)	1534348 (46.70)	2790889 (54.34)
Science	**	10403 (42.68)	#	#	37806 (26.13)	52809 (20.76)	71891 (20.30)	113476 (23.77)	495285 (33.19)	489415 (23.97)	756896 (23.03)	1142724 (22.25)
Commerce	259 (2.50)	971 (3.98)	#	#	15890 (10.99)	40879 (16.07)	79494 (22.44)	76791 (16.08)	232404 (17.66)	536217 (26.27)	994532 (30.27)	1202570 (23.41)
Total	10378 (100.00)	24377 (100.00)	27815 (100.00)	39968 (100.00)	144666 (100.00)	254361 (100.00)	354216 (100.00)	477434 (100.00)	1492046 (100.00)	447359 (100.00)	3285776 (100.00)	5136183 (100.00)

Enrollment of Men in Higher Education (General) by Faculty and Level

Faculty	Doctorate/Research				Postgraduation				Graduation			
	1971	1981	1991	1998	1971	1981	1991	1998	1971	1981	1991	1998
Arts	7658* (96.66)	8194 (48.76)	#	#	60179 (57.05)	101910 (57.64)	125935 (52.93)	163439 (56.65)	508634 (44.70)	633745 (44.07)	918955 (42.81)	163919 (51.00)
Science	**	7790 (46.35)	#	#	29713 (28.17)	37255 (21.07)	47542 (19.98)	69464 (24.08)	403266 (35.44)	353052 (24.55)	475861 (22.17)	739033 (24.04)

	Doctorate/Research				Postgraduation				Graduation			
	1971	1981	1991	1998	1971	1981	1991	1998	1971	1981	1991	1998
Commerce	256 (3.36)	821 (4.89)	#	#	15598 (14.78)	37638 (21.29)	64451 (27.09)	55605 (19.27)	225912 (18.86)	451223 (31.38)	751596 (35.02)	832659 (25.96)
Total	7914 (100.00)	16805 (100.00)	18696 (100.00)	28169 (100.00)	105490 (100.00)	176803 (100.00)	237928 (100.00)	288508 (100.00)	1137812 (100.00)	1438020 (100.00)	2146412 (100.00)	3207611 (100.00)

Enrollment of Women in Higher Education (General) by Faculty and Level

Faculty	Doctorate/Research				Postgraduation				Graduation			
	1971	1981	1991	1998	1971	1981	1991	1998	1971	1981	1991	1998
Arts	2461* (99.88)	4809 (63.51)	#	#	30791 (78.60)	58763 (75.77)	76896 (66.12)	123722 (65.49)	255753 (72.19)	382291 (63.33)	615393 (54.01)	1154970 (59.89)
Science	**	2613 (34.51)	#	#	8093 (20.66)	15554 (20.05)	24349 (20.94)	44012 (23.29)	92019 (25.98)	136353 (22.59)	281035 (24.67)	403691 (20.93)
Commerce	3 (0.12)	150 (1.98)	#	#	292 (0.74)	3241 (4.18)	15043 (12.94)	21192 (11.22)	6492 (18.33)	84994 (14.08)	242936 (21.32)	369911 (19.18)
Total	9598 (100.00)	7572 (100.00)	9129 (100.00)	11729 (100.00)	39176 (100.00)	77558 (100.00)	116288 (100.00)	188926 (100.00)	354264 (100.00)	603648 (100.00)	1139364 (100.00)	1928572 (100.00)

Note: + Figures relate to 1989–1990;
** Note separately available;
# Breakup of Arts, Science, and Commerce is not available.
Figures in brackets are percentages in relation to total.
Source: Department of Education, India, Website: http://www.education.nic.in/htmlweb/iamr2.htm#top, 2002,10,22.

Table 7.14.   Total Higher Education Enrollment in India in Selected Fields of Study and Years by Levels and Gender (1971–1998)

Enrollment in Engineering/Technology/Architecture by Levels and Gender

Level	1971		1981		1986		1991		1998	
	Boys	Girls	Boys	Girls	Boys	Girls	Boys	Girls	Boys	Girls
Doctorate	878	45	1995	169	2207	405	NA	NA	NA	NA
Postgraduate	6704	186	10792	567	11229	1271	NA	NA	NA	NA
Graduate	84025	820	111064	4982	169388	13061	215081	26287	285137	57968
Total	91607	1051	123851	5678	182824	14737	NA	NA	NA	NA

Enrollment in Medicine* by Levels and Gender

Level	1971		1981		1985		1987	
	Boys	Girls	Boys	Girls	Boys	Girls	Boys	Girls
Doctorate	392	106	338	118	348	156	488	234
Postgraduate	5517	1872	11930	3129	14782	4061	14844	4344
Graduate	66296	16764	81197	24712	80524	33736	82259	37805
Total	72205	18742	93465	27959	95654	37953	97591	42383

Enrollment in Agriculture and Forestry by Levels and Gender

Level	1971		1981		1985		1987	
	Boys	Girls	Boys	Girls	Boys	Girls	Boys	Girls
Doctorate	896	25	2030	119	1842	176	1991	232
Postgraduate	3975	106	6773	432	6711	717	6997	887
Graduate	20063	46	30140	1085	30105	1741	32750	2243
Total	24934	177	38943	1636	38658	2634	41738	3362

Enrollment in Education (Teacher's Training) by Levels and Gender

Level	1971		1981		1986		1991		1998	
	Boys	Girls	Boys	Girls	Boys	Girls	Boys	Girls	Boys	Girls
Doctorate	112	43	404	194	658	393	NA	NA	NA	NA
Postgraduate	2042	1068	3185	3465	3818	3121	NA	NA	NA	NA
Graduate	34798	21234	36340	31509	44604	35772	51453	40764	64416	48857
Total	39652	22345	39929	35168	49080	39286	NA	NA	NA	NA

Enrollment in Veterinary Science by Levels and Gender

Level	1971		1981		1985		1987	
	Boys	Girls	Boys	Girls	Boys	Girls	Boys	Girls
Doctorate	129	1	334	6	404	6	333	11
Postgraduate	691	7	1091	22	1180	51	1228	84
Graduate	5019	60	5650	224	6695	490	7071	632
Total	5839	68	7075	252	8279	547	8632	727

Enrollment in Others by Levels and Gender

Level	1971 Boys	Girls	1981 Boys	Girls	1985 Boys	Girls	1987 Boys	Girls
Doctorate	527	64	621	169	802	263	1062	420
Postgraduate	8941	1649	18173	4147	18377	4462	18612	4987
Graduate	86228	6558	190515	35513	211014	30835	212047	35872
Total	95696	8271	209309	39829	230193	35560	231721	41279

Note: Medicine includes Allopathy, Homeopathy, Ayurveda, and Unani.
Source: Department of Education, India, Website: http://www.education.nic.in/htmlweb/iamr2.htm#top, 2002,10,22.

the lead in 1986. The male students dominated all other professional subjects at all levels.

Table 7.15 indicates the progress of production of degrees and diplomas in higher education in India in selected courses from 1951 to 1997. Here we can see that natural science attracts the largest student body while engineering has the second largest student population over the period as indicated in table 7.15. As Sureshchandra Shukla commented in 1991,[11] "In India's open and democratic polity, the government has found it useful to expand the humanities and social sciences as a safety valve to avoid excessive expense on higher education as a whole. Over the decades the proportion of students enrolled for commerce has risen from about 14 to 20 percent, and in humanities/social sciences has remained steady at 40 percent. Enrollment in natural sciences, as a fraction of total enrollment in higher education, has fallen from a little under 30 percent to 20 percent in 1985–1986 even though the absolute enrollment in the sciences has risen almost six times to over 700,000, out of a total of 3,500,000."

INDIAN INTERNATIONAL EDUCATION AND PROFESSIONAL MIGRATION ABROAD

Today, the 20 million strong overseas population of Indian expatriates spreads across various countries and regions of the world. They are, however, concentrated in a few selected nations and regions, including the United States, the United Kingdom, Canada, Australia, and South Africa. Around 1.7 million Indian expatriates are in the United States, comprising a small 0.6 percent of the total U.S. population of 280 million, but enjoy-

Table 7.15. Progress of Production of Degrees and Diplomas in Higher Education in India in Selected Courses (1951–1997)

| | Engineering | | | | Agriculture | | Veterinary | |
| | Degree | Diploma | | | | | | |
Year	Level	Level	Medical	Dental	B.Sc.	M.Sc.	B.V.Sc.	M.V.Sc.
1951	2893	2626	1557	14	1041	192	100	
1961	7026	10349	3387	140	2608	610	857	
1971	18223	17699	10407	478	5280	1159	1031	226
1981	19012	35487	12170	501	5986	1620	1349	360
1986	29291	50390	12490*	567	8381	2543	1249	417
1987	30078	56560	12640*	677	5532	2567	1360	535
1988	33864	56229	13396*	660	6403	2334	1415	415
1989	37615	60125	12492*	821	6557	2762	1219	508
1990	41464	63794	13500*	1280*				
1991	44724	65325	14300*	1500*				
1992	44144	63888	14500*	1460*				
1996	60749**	95283**	NA	2065				
1997	59311	91266	NA	2186				

Selected Paramedical Courses

| | Natural Science | | Nurses | | Auxiliary Nurse- | |
| | | | (Diploma/ | | Midwives (Health | Heal |
Year	B.Sc.	M.Sc.	Certificate)	Midwives	Workers Female)	Visitors
1951	11193	1856				
1961	26157	6598	2851	2277	2083	315
1971	100773	14964	6257	5416	5104	479
1981	125030	21339	7256	6541	4264	483
1986	112936	28489	8208	6687	11208	1505
1987	125535	30141	8992	7681	10981	1196
1988	126575	29042	10092	8682	15538	663
1989	128988	29997	9859	8799	13230	999
1990			11032	9366	12377	1185
1991			10753	7852	10890	754
1992			11686	7893	9390	508
1996			11437	6256	6541	475
1997						

* Corrected to account for nonresponding institutions.
** Estimated.
Source: Department of Education, India, Website: http://www.education.nic.in/htmlweb/iamr4.htm#top, 2002,10,02.

ing the distinction of being one of the highest-earning, best-educated, and fastest-growing ethnic groups. Indian-Americans' high levels of literacy, economic success, knowledge of English, and experience with democracy in their home country has eased their transition in the country of their abode and adoption.[12]

Leading Nation of Origin of International Students in the United States

India has a long history of sending numerous students to industrialized countries for overseas study since independence. As its large higher education system kept producing more graduates than its domestic economy could absorb in the past decades, a great number of Indian students chose to go abroad for further study after they graduated from universities and colleges. In the early days, the designated nations for Indian international students included the United Kingdom, Canada, and the United States. Since the early 1970s, the United States has been the major host nation for Indian international students and, according to the statistics of the NSF, India has been among the leading nations of origin of international students in the United States. Figure 7.4 indicates a growing trend of Indian international students living in the United States during the period from 1987–2003. Since the mid-1980s, the number of Indian international students in the United States has steadily been growing except for a slight decline during the mid-1990s. It is worth noting that between 1997 and 2003 the number of Indian students in the United States more than doubled, from 33,818 in 1997–1998 to 74,603 in 2002–2003. Of particular note, India surpassed China as the first leading nation of origin of international students in the United States for the first time ever, with a 22 percent increase in U.S. enrollment in 2002. India's 74,603 students now represent 12.7 percent of the total number of international students in the United States.

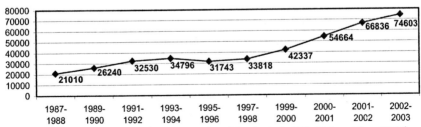

Figure 7.4.   Enrollment of Indian International Students in U.S. Universities, 1987/ 1988–2002/2003

Source:
1. National Science Board (NSB), *Science and Engineering Indicators 2002*, pp. A2-31 and A2-32.
2. Institute of International Education (IIE), Open Doors, 2001, 2002, and 2003.

Advanced Level and S&E Bias: In addition to its fast growth and large size, the Indian body of international students shares other features with that of China. The majority of Indian international students, more than 70 percent, as table 7.16 shows, are pursuing their studies at the graduate level. In addition, more than 75 percent of them are registered in the S&E fields, particularly in engineering, which accounts for more than 40 percent over the period observed.

Brain Drain

The surveys made by the US NSF from 1990 to 1999 reveal that the percentages of Indian international S&E doctoral recipients planning to remain and firmly planning to remain in the United States has remained steady: over 80 percent planned to locate in the United States, and more than half had firm offers to do so.[13] Table 7.17 provides the results of the survey made by the US NSF on the planned stay rate of Indian international S&E doctoral recipients in the United States from 1990 to 1997.

Table 6.12 in chapter 6 shows a recent study of foreign doctoral recipients working in the United States.[14] About 53 percent of the foreign students who earned S&E doctoral degrees in 1992 and 1993 were working

Table 7.16. Enrollment of Indian International Students in U.S. Universities by Field and Academic Year: 1987–1988 to 2002–2003

Year	Total Indian students	Indian graduate students	Percentage distribution of Indian international graduate students across selected field groupings (%)							
			S&E	Social Sci.	Physical & Life Science	Math & Computer Science	Agriculture	Engineering	Other Sci.	Non-S&E
1987–1988	21,010	15,547	75.4	6.8	13.6	12.8	1.6	37.5	3.1	24.6
1989–1990	26,240	19,811	77.3	6.1	12.2	16.3	1.6	38.7	2.4	22.7
1991–1992	32,530	25,536	78.8	4.7	10.4	16.9	1.6	43.2	2.0	21.2
1993–1994	34,796	27,533	79.5	4.5	10.1	17.0	1.6	43.8	2.5	20.5
1995–1996	31,743	23,593	79.5	4.2	10.4	17.7	2.8	41.3	3.1	20.5
1997–1998	33,818	25,128	76.9	4.1	9.2	17.9	1.5	41.6	2.6	23.1
1999–2000	42,337	30,533	NA	NA	NA	NA	NA	NA	NA	NA
2000–2001	54,664									
2001–2002	66,836									
2002–2003	74,603									

Source:
1. National Science Board (NSB), *Science and Engineering Indicators 2002*, pp. A2-31 and A2-32.
2. Institute of International Education (IIE), Open Doors, 2001, 2002 and 2003.

Table 7.17. Indian Ph.D. Recipients from U.S. Universities with Plans to Stay in the United States (1990–1997)

Year	Total Ph.D. recipients	Plan to stay in U.S. No.	Plan to stay in U.S. %	Firm plans to stay in U.S. No.	Firm plans to stay in U.S. %
1990	881	586	67	470	53
1991	924	689	75	518	56
1992	1,072	880	82	609	57
1993	1,139	920	81	577	51
All fields					
1994	1,289	1,049	81	662	51
1995	1,425	1,179	83	746	52
1996	1,500	1,264	84	882	59
1997	1,382	1,131	82	839	61
All fields					

Source: Compiled from NSB, Science and Engineering Indicators 2000, NSF, 2000, vols. 1 & 2, tables 4–42.

in the United States in 1997. Stay rates differ by field of the degrees and nation of origin, though. The large majority of 1992 and 1993 engineering doctoral recipients from India (83 percent) were working in the United States in 1997. In contrast, only 9 percent of South Koreans who completed engineering doctorates from U.S. universities in 1992 and 1993 were working in the United States in 1997.

If Korea and Taiwan are currently benefiting from "brain gain," India suffers from "brain drain." According to research conducted by Binod Khadria in 1998,[15] few Indian international students want to return permanently. Most of the returnees are being driven away by continuing economic recession and job cuts in the United States rather than attracted by any developmental progress in the state of the Indian economy. Most would like to work in India for a short period of 4 to 12 weeks on summer or winter holidays.

Brain Drain through Immigration and Employment: What should be particularly noted is that India has been experiencing brain drain not only through overseas study, but also, in large degree, via professional immigration and employment. This might be one of India's distinguishing features. Table 7.18 presents trends in immigration from India to the United States, Canada, and the United Kingdom over the period 1950 through 1990. It shows that Indian professional immigrants to the United States outnumbered those to the United Kingdom in the 1970s, and those to Canada outnumbered those to the United Kingdom in the 1980s. Indian immigration constituted a minuscule proportion of total immigration from all nations to the United States and Canada during 1950s, registered rapid increases during the next two decades, and then stabilized at over 3.5 percent in the United States[16] and about 6 percent in Canada during the 1980s. This was in sharp contrast to the United Kingdom where the proportion was halved from 20 percent in the 1960s to 10 percent in the 1980s. It is now generally accepted that the United States absorbed between 80 and 90 percent of Indian professional, technical, and related personnel permanently settling abroad, numbering an average of between 4,000 and 6,000 persons every year.[17]

The above-mentioned average figure of Indian professionals who had immigrated into the United States only reflects the situation of the early 1990s. In recent years, as the statistics of the U.S. Immigration and Naturalization Services show, this figure has significantly increased. In 1998,

Table 7.18. Trends in Immigration from India to Selected Industrialized Nations, 1951–1990

Year	USA	Canada	UK	Year	USA	Canada	UK
1951	109	120	n.a.	1971	14,310	5,313	6,900
1952	123	126	n.a.	1972	16,926	5,049	7,600
1953	104	169	n.a.	1973	13,124	9,433	6,240
1954	144	208	n.a.	1974	12,779	12,731	6,650
1955	194	224	n.a.	1975	15,773	10,106	10,200
1956	185	254	n.a.	1976	17,487	6,637	11,020
1957	196	186	n.a.	1977	18,613	5,514	7,340
1958	323	325	n.a.	1978	20,753	5,112	9,890
1959	351	585	n.a.	1979	19,708	4,517	9,270
1960	391	505	n.a.	1980	22,607	8,491	7,930
1961	421	568	n.a.	1981	21,522	8,263	6,590
1962	545	529	2,900	1982	21,738	7,792	5,410
1963	1,173	737	15,500	1983	25,451	7,051	5,380
1964	634	1,154	13,000	1984	24,964	5,513	5,140
1965	582	2,241	17,100	1985	26,026	4,038	5,500
1966	2,458	2,233	16,700	1986	26,227	6,970	4,210
1967	4,642	3,966	19,100	1987	27,803	9,747	4,610
1968	4,692	3,229	23,100	1988	26,268	10,432	5,020
1969	5,963	5,395	11,000	1989	31,175	8,836	4,580
1970	10,114	5,670	7,200	1990	30,667	10,662	5,040

Note:
1. Data on immigration are reported by nation of birth for the United States; by nation of last permanent residence for Canada; and by nation of nationality for the United Kingdom.
2. Information on immigration from India to the United Kingdom is not available for the period before 1 July 1962 because, until then, Commonwealth citizens were not subject to immigration control.
3. n.a.: not available.
Source: Khadria, Binod, "Divides of Development-Underdevelopment Relationship in Higher Education and the Policy for Brain Drain," in Shukla, Sureshchandra and Kaul, Rekha (ed.), *Education, Development and Underdevelopment*, Sage Publications, 1998, p. 179.

of the total immigrated professional and technical personnel under the category of employment-based preference[18] who were admitted into the United States, 8,694 were from India, accounting for 11.2 percent of the total number (77,517). In 1999, this figure was 5,025, accounting for 8.8 percent of the total number (56,817), and in 2000, this figure jumped to 15,381, accounting for 14.4 percent of the total number (107,024).[19] Of the total 136,787 H1B visas issued specifically to foreign professionals to work in the United States in 2000, 60,757 were granted to Indians, accounting for 44.4 percent of the total H1B visas issued that year.[20]

Over the past decades brain drain, a steady outflow of some of India's cream of highly-skilled professionals and the highly-educated—the "knowledge workers"—to the developed countries of the West, mainly to the United States, eventually has led to the formation of an Indian "scientific diaspora." The Indian Ministry of External Affairs (MEA) cites a recently estimated figure that 38 percent of doctors, 12 percent of scientists, 36 percent of NASA employees, 36 percent of Microsoft employees, 28 percent of IBM employees, and 17 percent of Intel employees in the United States are Indian—a sign of the success of Indians abroad.[21]

The statistics in table 7.19 give further evidence of the relative large share of the Indian diaspora among S&E faculty in U.S. higher education. In 1977 the faculty members of Indian origin accounted for 3.1 percent of the total faculty members, 15.3 percent of the total foreign faculty members, and 23.2 percent of the total faculty members of Asian origin in U.S. higher education, respectively.

Measures to Attract Indian Diaspora Back Home: Currently, the Indian diaspora numbers over 20 million expatriates spread across the world and the Indian scientific diaspora is a subset of this large set. Since India achieved independence in 1947, overseas Indians have been interacting with India to seek their roots and to explore new avenues and sectors for mutually beneficial relationships in fields ranging from investment and the transfer of skills and technology to outright philanthropy and charitable works. This trend has become more marked in the last decade as the Indian economy has opened up, giving rise to a new range of opportunities for the emerging generations. In order to attract more Indian emigrants back home, in 2000, the Indian government set up a "High Level Committee (HLC) on the Indian Diaspora," whose mandate is to recommend policy options for strategies, programs, and forms

Table 7.19. Indian Emigrants as Percentage of S&E Faculty in U.S. Higher Education, 1997

Total S&E		U.S. Origin		Foreign origin		Asian origin			Indian origin			
No.	%	No.	% of total faculty	No.	% of total	No.	% of total	% of foreign	No.	% of total	% of foreign	% of Asian
224707	100	179689	80	45009	20	23559	10.5	52.3	6876	3.1	15.3	23.2

Note: Data includes first job of postsecondary teaching at four-year colleges and universities in the U.S.; does not include faculty in two-year or community colleges, or those who teach as a secondary job.

Source: Computed and compiled by the author from NSB, *Science and Engineering Indicators 2000*, vols. 1 and 2, tables 4-46 to 4-48.

of organization. The Committee, in its report submitted to the Prime Minister of India in January 2002, emphasizes that members of the diaspora are generally motivated to do something for India, and need help to do so. Within the Committee, a group of experts on the role of expatriates in science and technology made 13 specific recommendations, including: establishing a central database of expatriate scientists; setting up high-tech joint ventures; a system for accommodating visiting high-skilled and postdoctoral Indians in expatriate laboratories; and coordinating expatriates' cooperation on technology transfer.[22]

One concrete effort made by the Indian government to strengthen the link of the expatriates of Indian descent including Indian-born naturalized American citizens with India was the creation of the PIO-Card. Recently, the Government of India has, through official notification, introduced the PIO-Card for those persons of Indian origin who have obtained foreign citizenships by surrendering their Indian citizenship. The PIO scheme was promoted by the Ministry of Home Affairs in the Gazette of India dated 30 March, 1999. The main features of the scheme are: Excepting for those who now hold citizenship of Pakistan, Bangladesh, and other nations that may be specified from time to time, anytime holders of Indian passports in the past; the children, grandchildren, and great-grandchildren of those who were born in India and were permanently resident in India as defined in the Government of India Act, 1935, and other territories that became part of India thereafter; and spouses of citizens of India or PIO as per the criteria of the PIO-Card scheme, are all entitled to apply, by paying a fee of US$1,000 (inclusive of nonrefundable processing fee of US$250), and get the PIO-Card with validity of 20 years, terminable prematurely along with the passport. The card extends the facility of visa waiver for entering India; and exemption from the requirement of registration for stays in India up to 180 days. The introduction of the PIO-Card is welcome among the Indian diaspora because it helps those persons of Indian origin keep their contact with their home nation with ease.

NOTES

1. Research, Reference and Training Division (RRTD), *India 2000: A Reference Annual,* (Ministry of Information and Broadcasting Government of India, 2000), 97.

2. Robert F. Arnove, "A Comparison of the Chinese and Indian Education Systems," *Comparative Education Review 28*, no. 3 (1984): 378–83.

3. Jandhyala B. G. Tilak, "Financing Higher education in India," in *Higher Education Reform in India: Experience and Perspectives*, ed. Philip G. Altbach and Suma Chitnis, (New Delhi, India: Sage Publications India Pvt Ltd., 1993): 66.

4. World Bank, *Primary Education in India*, the International Bank for Reconstruction and Development/the World Bank, 1997.

5. Tilak, "Financing Higher education in India," 66.

6. Tilak, "Financing Higher education in India," 67.

7. World Bank, *Primary Education in India*, the International Bank for Reconstruction and Development/the World Bank, 1997.

8. Jasper J. Valent and Gerald L. Gutek, *Education and Society in India and Thailand* (Washington, DC: University Press of America, 1977), 143.

9. Research, Reference and Training Division (RRTD), *India 2000: A Reference Annual,* (Ministry of Information and Broadcasting Government of India, 2000), 95.

10. Research, Reference and Training Division (RRTD), *India 2000: A Reference Annual,* (Ministry of Information and Broadcasting Government of India, 2000), 91.

11. Sureshchandra Shukla, "India," in *International Higher Education: An Encyclopedia*, ed. Philip G. Altbach, Vol. 1 (New York, NY: Garland Publishing, Inc., 1991), 473–74.

12. Binod Khadria, "Case-Study of the Indian Scientific Diaspora," in *Scientific Diasporas: How Can Developing Countries Benefit from Their Expatriates and Engineers?* IRD Editions, Institut de Reccarche Pour le Development, Paris, 2003.

13. National Science Board (NSB), *Science and Engineering Indicators—2002*, Vol. 1 (Arlington, VA: National Science Foundation, 2002), 2–34.

14. Jean Johnson, "Collaboration in S&T Information Exchange between the United States and China" (paper presented at CIES 2000 Conference, San Antonio, Texas, March 7–11, 2000).

15. Binod Khadria, "Divides of Development-Underdevelopment Relationship in Higher Education and the Policy for Brain Drain," in *Education, Development and Underdevelopment*, eds. Sureshchandra Shukla and Rekha Kaul, (New Delhi, India: Sage Publications India Pvt Ltd., 1998), 183.

16. It was after the U.S. Immigration and Nationality Act Amendments of 1965, that gradually, over the 1970s onwards, large numbers of Indian migrants in various categories of knowledge occupations and skills (doctors, engineers, architects, teachers, nurses, etc.) were absorbed into the U.S. labor market.

17. Khadria, "Divides of Development-Underdevelopment Relationship in Higher Education and the Policy for Brain Drain," in *Education, Development and Underdevelopment,* eds. Sureshchandra Shukla and Rekha Kaul, (New Delhi, India: Sage Publications India Pvt Ltd., 1998), 178.

18. The employment-based preferences consist of five categories: priority workers; professionals with advanced degrees or aliens with exceptional ability; skilled workers, professionals (without advanced degrees), and needed unskilled workers; special immigrants (e.g., ministers, religious workers, and employees of the U.S. government abroad); and employment creation immigrants or "investors."

19. Immigration and Naturalization Services (INS), *1998, 1999 and 2000 Statistical Yearbook.*

20. Immigration and Naturalization Services (INS), *2000 Statistical Yearbook.*

21. Binod Khadria, "Case-Study of the Indian Scientific Diaspora," in *Scientific Diasporas: How Can Developing Countries Benefit from Their Expatriates and Engineers?* Vol. 2, ed. Institut de Recearche Pour le Development (Paris, France: IRD Editions, 2003).

22. Khadria, "Case-Study of the Indian Scientific Diaspora."

Chapter Eight

Conclusion

The comprehensive picture of K–12 education, higher education, and international education in Japan, Korea, Taiwan, China, and India, which has been shown in this book, might impress people with the different patterns of their development history, their remarkable achievements, as well as their future trends. Within about a half-century since World War II, education at all levels in these five Asian nations and economies has experienced a substantial development that has attracted worldwide attention, especially from the United States. This book has provided a description of K–12 education, higher education, and international education in Japan, Korea, Taiwan, China, and India and has introduced comparisons with the United States. I will in conclusion summarize some common features of these five Asian nations and economies and highlight implications for the United States in its education reform.

DEPENDENCE, INDEPENDENCE, AND INTERDEPENDENCE

The development approach and the world-system approach are helpful in explaining the features that these five nations and economies have been developing over the past half-century and in guiding the discussion of comparisons with and implications for the United States.

The development approach views education as an aspect and function of national development. All of the five nations and economies view education as an integral part of their whole national development and assume

229

great responsibility for the advancement of education. The centralized administration in Japan, Korea, Taiwan, and China controls all aspects of education, including educational growth, structure, quantity, quality, standards, appointments, finance, curricula, teaching, etc. so as to make education serve the nation's social and economic development. (The administration of education in India is centralized to a lesser degree.)

All five nations and economies have undergone the painful experience in the not-so-distant past of having been either colonized, semicolonized, or occupied by foreign powers. Therefore these nations and economies have gained a strong desire to be independent of outside control. Accordingly, they have implemented the policy of training educational and scientific talents to ensure self-reliance. The typical example is India, which has recently produced many more high-level specialized personnel than was domestically demanded in the past decades.

Before beginning the comparative discussion of these five nations and economies and the United States, I will consider the world-system approach, which views national educational phenomena as reflections of external or international processes, primarily of an economic nature. World-system analysts usually divide nations into two categories: the metropolitan countries with advanced civilization (in the areas of science and technology, industry, education, etc.) and those with underdeveloped civilization. The former nations have greater influence on the latter and, in turn, the latter have greater dependence on the former.

As economic globalization driven largely by information technology has become entrenched, more and more nations have integrated themselves into the international economic community. Within these new international contexts, there is no longer a unidirectional dependence of one nation on another. In today's world, there is no exception for any country, even the United States, the world's superpower.

It is true that, in the past half-century since World War II, many developing and developed nations and economies, including these five Asian economies examined, have been, in varying degree, reliant on the United States for knowledge, capital, technology, and goods for their national development. I want to emphasize here that the United States has also been gaining from new knowledge discovered abroad and from increases in foreign economic development. U.S. industry has been increasingly relying on R&D performed abroad. The United States also relies heavily on other nations for its scientific and technical talents. Japan, Korea, Taiwan, China, and India are the five leading nations and economies in sending scientific and technical talents to the United States.

The following statistics will show how much the United States relies on other regions, particularly these five Asian economies, for foreign scientists and engineers:

• Figure 8.1 shows the professional immigration from these five Asian economies to the United States from 1998 to 2000. In 1998, of the total immigrated professional and technical personnel under the category of employment-based preference[1] who were admitted into the United States, 24,486 came from these five Asian economies examined, accounting for 31.6 percent. In 1999, this figure was 14,166, accounting for 28.5 percent. In 2000, this figure jumped to 39,170, accounting for 36.6 percent.

• U.S. industry has turned to foreign workers on H1B visas to fill a gap in needed labor—as many as 195,000 per year. In 2000 alone, the H1B holders from the five Asian economies examined accounted for 60 percent (44.4 percent came from India).[2]

• According to the NSF's report (2002), in 1999, 27 percent of doctorate-holders in S&E in the American workforce were foreign-born. The lowest percentage of foreign-born doctorate-holders was in psychology (7.6 percent), and the highest percentage was in civil engineering (51.5 percent). Almost one-fifth (19.9 percent) of those with master's degrees in S&E were foreign-born. Even at the bachelor's degree level,

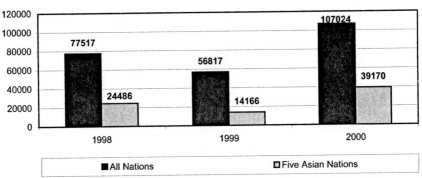

Figure 8.1.   Professional Immigration to the United States from Five Asian Nations and from All Nations, 1998–2000

Source: Computed and compiled by the author from: U.S. Immigration and Naturalization Services (INS), *1998, 1999, and 2000 Statistical Yearbook.*

9.9 percent of those with S&E degrees were foreign-born; the largest percentages of degrees were in chemistry (14.9 percent), computer sciences (15.2 percent), and engineering (14.6 percent).

- Also in 1999, of the total foreign-born U.S. residents with S&E highest degrees, 35 percent came from the five Asian economies examined, while 45 percent of the total foreign-born U.S. residents with S&E doctorates came from the five Asian economies examined (see Figure 8.2 and Figure 8.3).

- For the years 1988–1996, Chinese students earned 7.5 percent of all S&E doctorates in U.S. universities—16,550 of 219,643. Chinese doctoral recipients made up the highest percentage (more than 9.8 percent) in the natural sciences and engineering, 13 percent of the physical sciences, and 15 percent of mathematics. More than 8 percent of them worked as university research assistants or teaching assistants. During the same period, more than 5,000 Chinese scientists and engineers were offered the appointment of postdoctoral researcher, the highest number from any country by 2001.[3]

- Aside from the contribution to the U.S. S&E workforce through professional immigration and employment visas, these five Asian economies keep sending more foreign students to the United States for study and

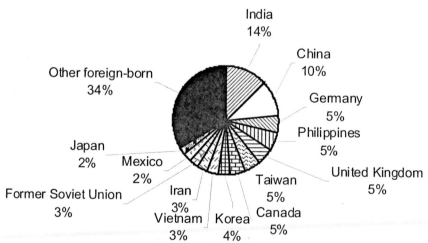

Figure 8.2.   Foreign-Born U.S. Residents with S&E Highest Degrees, by Place of Birth, 1999

Source: Compiled by the author from: National Science Board (NSB), *Science and Engineering Indicators 2002*, Vol. 2, p. A3-169.

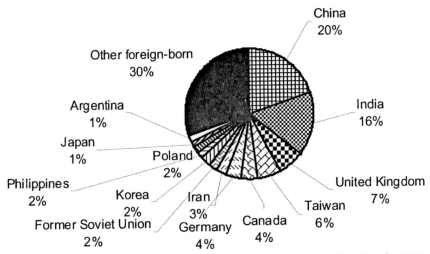

Figure 8.3. Foreign-Born U.S. Residents with S&E Doctorates, by Place of Birth, 1999

Source: Compiled by the author from: National Science Board (NSB), *Science and Engineering Indicators 2002*, Vol. 2, p. A3-167.

research than do any other nations in the world. Many of these students remain in the United States after they complete their study. Table 8.1 shows that Asian students constituted 56.7 percent of all foreign students enrolled in U.S. universities in 2002–2003 and that India, China, Japan, Korea, and Taiwan were the five leading regions whose students combined accounted for 45.1 percent of the entire foreign student population in the United States. The only change is in the rank order: India surpassed China and became first in the 2001–2002 academic year and Korea replaced Japan as the third in the same year.

From the above-indicated statistics, it is clear that the United States has benefited and continues to benefit greatly from this international flow of knowledge and personnel. The question must be asked, if these foreign scientists and engineers are less available some day in the future, who is going to fill the gap they leave? In fact, this time has come much earlier than we expected. There are signs that the days of the U.S. brain gain are dated. The data in Table 8.2 clearly shows that the 2002–2003 academic year increase of only 0.6 percent in international enrollment in U.S. colleges and universities was the smallest increase since the 1995–1996 academic year, and follows five consecutive years of steady growth. Of the top 20 sending countries, fourteen countries experienced a decrease in

Table 8.1. Five Top Leading Places of Origin, 2000–2001 to 2002–2003

Rank	Place of Origin	2000–2001	% of U.S. Foreign Student Total	Place of Origin	2001–2002	% of U.S. Foreign Student Total	Place of Origin	2002–2003	% of U.S. Foreign Student Total
	World Total	547867		World Total	582996		World Total	586323	
1	China	59939	10.9	India	66836	11.5	India	74603	12.7
2	India	54664	10	China	63211	10.8	China	64757	11
3	Japan	46497	8.5	Korea	49046	8.4	Korea	51519	8.8
4	Korea	45685	8.3	Japan	46810	8.0	Japan	45960	7.8
5	Taiwan	28566	5.2	Taiwan	28930	5.0	Taiwan	28017	4.8
Sub-total		235351	43.0		254833	43.7		264856	45.1

Source: Collected and compiled by the author from: Institute of International Education (IIE), *Open Doors*, 2001, 2002 and 2003.

Table 8.2. Percentage Changes of International Student Enrollment in the United States by Leading Places of Origin, 2001–2002 and 2002–2003

Rank	Place of Origin	2001–2002	2002–2003	2002–2003 % Change
	World Total	582,996	586,323	0.6
1	India	66,836	74,603	11.6
2	China	63,211	64,757	2.4
3	Korea	49,046	51,519	5
4	Japan	46,810	45,960	−1.8
5	Taiwan	28,930	28,017	−3.2
6	Canada	26,514	26,513	0
7	Mexico	12,518	12,801	2.3
8	Turkey	12,091	11,601	−4.1
9	Indonesia	11,614	10,432	−10.2
10	Thailand	11,606	9,982	−14
11	Germany	9,613	9,302	−3.2
12	Brazil	8,972	8,388	−6.5
13	United Kingdom	8,414	8,326	−1
14	Pakistan	8,644	8,123	−6
15	Hong Kong	7,757	8,076	4.1
16	Kenya	7,097	7,862	10.8
17	Colombia	8,068	7,771	−3.7
18	France	7,401	7,223	−2.4
19	Malaysia	7,395	6,595	−10.8
20	Russia	6,643	6,238	−6.1

Source: Institute of International Education (IIE), *Open Doors*, 2003.

enrollment—with significant decreases coming from Indonesia (down 10.2 percent to 10,432), Thailand (down 14 percent to 9,982), and Malaysia (down 10.8 percent to 6,595). Students from the Middle East were down 10 percent from the previous year, with decreases of 25 percent each from Saudi Arabia (4,175) and Kuwait (2,212) and 15 percent from the United Arab Emirates (1,792). The combined total number of students coming from all countries in the Middle East is just 34,803, down from 38,545 in the prior year. Even of the five leading senders examined in this book, Taiwan and Japan experienced a decrease in enrollment. Students from Taiwan and Japan were down 3.2 percent and 1.8 percent from the previous year, respectively.

QUANTITATIVE COMPARISON

As we live in an interdependent world, events that occur in one region invariably affect other areas. Having examined the mass expansion of education at all levels in these five Asian economies in the past half-century, we see that they are becoming less dependent on U.S. higher education for advanced training. These five Asian economies have already surpassed the United States in the combined number enrolled in undergraduate education. The United States retains an advantage in graduate enrollment but is receding in advantage with each passing year. In quantitative terms, the United States will face a severe challenge.

• Although the United States has traditionally been the world leader in providing broad access to higher education, other nations have recently expanded their higher education systems, and the United States is now only one of ten nations providing a college education to approximately one-third or more of its college-age population. Two of these five Asian economies examined—Japan and Korea—are among these ten nations. Most important is that, in 1999 and in 2000, the absolute number of higher education students enrolled in Taiwan and Korea surpassed both the numbers enrolled in the middle and high schools.

• Though the gross enrollment ratio of the college-age cohort at the tertiary level in China was 15 percent in 2002, much lower than that in the United States, China has, for the first time in history, approached the United States in terms of absolute number: In 2002 China had 15.13 million students enrolled in different types of higher education institutions[4] while the United States had 15.31 million students enrolled in higher education institutions in 2000.[5] Moreover, the higher education graduates in China in 2002 outnumbered those in the 2000–2001 academic year in the United States: 2,593,000 to 2,416,645.

• In 2002, the five Asian economies examined had over 30 million students enrolled in tertiary education institutions while the figure in the United States in 2000–2001 was 15.31 million. There was close to a 15 million student difference between the five Asian economies examined and the United States. Moreover, at least 30 percent of these 30 million Asian students were enrolled in engineering.

• These five Asian economies awarded more doctoral degrees in 1999 than in the United States: 42,291 to 41,140 as shown in table 8.3. There was no great difference in the number of doctoral degrees awarded in natural sciences between the five Asian economies examined and the United States, but there was a great difference in engineering: these five Asian economies awarded 9,022 engineering doctoral degrees, 1.7 times as many as the figure in the United States.

• China alone may surpass the United States in the quantity of graduate degree production within the next 20 years, as predicted in chapter 6. The combined number of graduate degrees produced by these five Asian economies will likely outnumber that in the United States in fewer than 10 years.

Table 8.3. Earned Doctoral Degrees in Five Asian Economies and the United States, 1999 or latest available year

				Field				
	All doctoral degrees	All S&E doctoral degrees	Natural sciences	Math and computer science	Agriculture	Social and behavioral sciences	Engineering	Non-S&E
Total	83,431	47,446	17,628	2,680	3,727	9,052	14,359	35,985
5 Asian economies	42,291	21,493	7,639	745	2,762	1,325	9,022	20,798
United States	41,140	25,953	9,989	1,935	965	7,727	5,337	15,187

Note: The U.S. doctoral degrees here exclude first professional degrees such as M.D., D.D.S., etc.
Source: Computed and compiled by the author from: National Science Board (NSB), Science and Engineering Indicators 2002, Vol. 2, p. A2-75.

- Because of the growing capacity of China, Korea, and Taiwan to provide advanced S&E education, the proportion of doctoral degrees earned by their citizens in the United States has decreased. In 1988, for the first time, Chinese students earned more doctoral degrees at domestic universities than at universities in the United States. Korea and Taiwan then followed suit: in 1991 and 1998, their students earned more doctoral degrees at domestic universities than at universities in the United States, respectively.[6]

- In recent years, a growing number of international students have been traveling to these five Asian nations and economies for overseas study. According to incomplete statistics, in 2001, over 200,000 international students enrolled at the universities of these five Asian nations and economies, less than half the figure (547,867) enrolled at universities in the United States in the same year.

Therefore, in the future these five Asian nations and economies will not only send fewer foreign students to the United States but will also compete with the United States for international students and professionals. As questioned previously: If more and more foreign students are attracted by other nations, who will replace the foreign students to fill the positions in the United States' universities, industries, and research institutes? It will be suggested that we turn to our home youth to train more domestic talents. A second question must be raised: Can the U.S. education system train adequate high-quality students to meet the growing needs?

QUALITATIVE COMPARISON

In the past two decades since the report "A Nation at Risk" was issued by the U.S. Department of Education in 1983, Americans have been debating how to reform American schools. Commissions and committees have churned out countless reports, books, and other documents on the quality of American children's academic achievements. Especially in mathematics and science, American children trail their counterparts in Europe and Asia, and they are losing ground.[7]

For a long time, many people, including this author, have been haunted by the question of why the quality of U.S. elementary and secondary education is so poor in mathematics and science in comparison with education in many other major countries while the high quality of its higher education, especially at the graduate level, is recognized worldwide. In 1983 I was surprised by the fact revealed by "A Nation at Risk" that on 19 international academic tests U.S. students never ranked first or second and, in a field comprised of industrialized nations, ranked last seven times.

It is a pity that, in the twenty years since 1983, not much progress has been made in the quality of U.S. elementary and secondary education. In many subsequent international achievement tests, U.S. students still performed very poorly. In the period 1983 to 1986, the International Association for the Evaluation of Educational Achievement (IEA) found these results in a study of science achievement in twenty-four nations at three levels in each school system:

- At the 10-year-old level (typically Grade 4 or 5) the United States scored below the international mean;
- At the 14-year-old level (typically Grade 8 or 9) the Unites States was third-to-last;
- In the final year of secondary school (typically Grade 12) the United States was also among the lowest scoring countries, with the lowest position in biology, third-to-last in chemistry, and fifth-to-last in physics.

In 1991, the Educational Testing Service initiated the International Assessment of Educational Progress, and an international study was made of science and mathematics proficiency. Fourteen industrialized nations and economies assessed nationally representative samples of their 13-year-olds, while 10 assessed nationally representative samples of 9-year-olds. Comparing the overall averages for mathematics, U.S. students ranked at or near the bottom, with scores significantly lower than those of students from Korea, Hungary, Taiwan, the former Soviet Union, and Israel. The U.S. 9-year-olds correctly answered about 58 percent of the questions, in contrast with Korean youth, who correctly answered 73 percent. The U.S. 13-year-olds correctly answered about 55 percent of the mathematics questions, in contrast with Koreans and Taiwanese who correctly answered 73 percent and Swiss, former Soviets, and Hungarians who correctly answered about 70 percent. The U.S. 13-year-old students scored significantly lower than students from all nations except Slovenia, Spain, Ireland, and Scotland.

By the end of the last century, the situation had declined even more. According to the report from the Third International Mathematics and Science Study (TIMSS) on February 24, 1998, U.S. high school seniors, even those in advanced classes, were clinging to the bottom rungs in performance in three sciences (biology, chemistry, and physics) and in math in a recent international math and science survey of 21 nations excluding Asian nations, having scores significantly lower than those of most of their international peers.[8]

The latest report made by the United Nations Children's Fund in November 2002 revealed the findings of its recent surveys of students of 24 OECD countries and presented a broad picture of how well each country's education system is performing when measured by (a) what proportion of students fall below given benchmarks of educational achievement, and (b) how far behind the national average the lowest-achieving pupils are being allowed to fall. The report shows that two Asian developed nations—Korea and Japan—sit firmly at the head of the class with average league table ranks of 1.4 and 2.2 respectively while the United States, with an average rank of 16.2, languishes near the bottom of the class—the 19th of the 24 countries.[9]

IMPLICATIONS

Obviously, this situation does not match the status of a technologically advanced nation and will affect and even threaten the future competition of the United States in the global market in science and technology. Blame for this poor quality can be placed on less instruction time, deemphasis on math and science courses, light homework, no national standard curriculum, and no unified tests in U.S. schools. I would like to conclude my research with the implications for the United States of the educational experience and practices in these five Asian economies examined.

• One of the most distinguished features of these five Asian economies is the role played by their respective central governments in educational administration and finance. As I mentioned in the previous analyses, the advantages are at least three if the central government assumes the responsibility for national education:

(1) First, the central government can set nationwide academic standards for all students and nationwide guidelines for the operation of schools. Centralized guidelines can pertain to education policy, the curriculum, the selection of textbooks, the selection of teachers' handbooks, and the minimum acceptable level of learning. Inherent in academic standards is the concept that all children can learn, given access to excellent and equal learning opportunities. I suggest that the United States adopt a rigorous high school core curriculum in which all students take the same academic courses and in which goals are set that all students are expected to meet.

Adopting national guidelines and standards does not necessarily mean relinquishing local control. School districts could still decide the manner in which they would follow the guidelines and attempt to meet these standards. In sum, while education should remain a state and local responsibility in the United States, a federal role in education can be not only legitimate but also vital at a time when state and local efforts are incomplete.

(2) Another advantage is egalitarian resource allocation. The central government can greatly reduce inequalities in educational resource distribution including finance, teacher placement, class space, and equipment among public schools, regardless of whether each school is located in a metropolitan or a rural area. As we saw in Japan, at the compulsory level there is virtually no variation between prefectures in annual operating expenditures per student. Remarkable equality in distribution has been established with respect to the essentials.

(3) The central government can formulate a nationwide education policy, working out the national short-term, medium-term, and long-term plans of national human resource development, to respond to the needs of the nation's economic development as well as the real economic needs of students. These efforts can include providing incentives to universities to expand and improve the size and the quality of their S&E programs in areas in which student enrollment nationwide is insufficient, and inducing more people to be engaged in S&E programs or to switch from non-S&E programs to S&E programs, by providing financial support and securing their careers. Korea and China have set up special education committees

led by the president or first premier, powerful enough to enforce education policy implementation throughout the country.

• The United States might draw on the practices of the Asian non-formal education system. The mission of the Asian supplementary non-formal education system is to help both quick learners and slow learners engage in individualized learning based on their respective learning pace. This supplementary education can be either in-depth study or remedial study. In Asian countries, particularly Japan, students participate in extra-curricular mathematics and science activities in after-school clubs or in formal tutoring activities. Due to non-formal and extracurricular education, Asian students spend more time on instructional activities than their American peers.

• Improving the general education system is not enough. An economy cannot upgrade rapidly unless enough students gain the specialized skills needed in particular industries. A system for vocational, technical, and specialized industry training is a central priority in any advanced economy (Porter, 1999). Technical universities and vocational schools are respected alternatives to university and regular high school training in a number of nations and economies such as Germany, Mainland China, Korea, and Taiwan. In some fields, German technical universities are more prestigious than regular universities. In Japan, companies themselves play a significant role in postsecondary education.

Conversely, in the United States, a nation with human resource problems, the greatest value has been attached to studying liberal arts and pure sciences rather than engineering or vocations. I would suggest that U.S. companies assume a greater role in the training and continual upgrading of their workforce. U.S. companies must work more closely with the educational institutions in their regions that have high-quality programs with relevance to their industry. Joint programs and training centers with local schools improve the quality of programs and their relevance to industry.

• English is a compulsory course in the elementary schools of all five Asian nations and economies examined. The starting grade of English learning varies from grade 1 to grade 5 among these nations and economies. Some of these regions even offer a second foreign language at the level of senior high school. These nations and economies firmly believe that, if a nation wants to be more competitive in the ever-changing world of globalization and the knowledge-based economy, its young generation should be encouraged to build and develop an awareness and attitude of being global citizens. To meet this goal, foreign language is an indispensable tool for cross-cultural exchanges and communication. However, in U.S. schools, to my knowledge, there is not one state whose educational authority requires foreign language as a compulsory subject to be taught in elementary and secondary schools. When foreign languages are taught in U.S. schools, they are often placed in the elective curriculum instead of in regular curriculum as in these Asian nations and economies. Consequently, Americans, on average, have little real interest in the study of other nations and cultures. The United States will risk losing its leadership in the world unless it trains a large workforce with an international mind. By the time this book was finalized, a piece of good news had arrived, that the Italian and Chinese governments would help to finance Advanced Placement programs in Italian and Chinese languages and cultures for U.S. high school students. The Italian and Chinese programs would be added to the 34 courses and exams in 19 subject areas covered by AP, which gives high school students the chance to prepare for college academic work and, if they score high enough, earn credit.[10] I strongly recommend that foreign languages be taught in both elementary and secondary schools as a compulsory subject in the regular curriculum.

• If nationwide academic standards are set by the federal government, some professional organizations need to be set up to evaluate and control the quality of education. To ensure quality control over the curriculum, students' scholastic achievement tests, an evaluation of schools and educational institutions, and an evaluation of the organization and implementation of the curriculum need to be conducted regularly at either the national or state level. The school should conduct evaluations of the attainment level of students by grade and subject using various assessment tools and methods, and the results of the evaluation should be used to secure the adequacy and improvement of the curriculum and instruction.

• Historically, the United States has enjoyed an influx of many of the world's best minds in science and engineering. These foreign talents have made a great contribution to advancing the frontiers of knowledge and propelling the United States to a position of global leadership in S&E. As expressed in congressional testimony by Dr. Bruce Alberts, President of the National Academy of Sciences: "International science and technology cooperation is an extremely effective way to leverage one of the defining strengths of the United States. We benefit from an extraordinary set of personal, professional, and cultural relationships due to the many people from other countries who are working in the U.S. science and technology enterprise, and due to the large number of science and technology leaders in other countries who have been trained in the United States."[11] My suggestion is that, in the global competitiveness of the international S&E workforce, the United States should, just as it did in the past, strengthen and maintain the ability to attract internationally competitive researchers, faculty, and students and encourage and support U.S. researchers and students to be integrated into the international community of science.

Perhaps of equal importance is to send more U.S. students to other countries for study. Sending more U.S. students abroad can not only help increase mutual understanding, foster friendship, and expand multilateral relations between the United States and other countries, but also help train citizens with international minds. The current situation is not satisfactory. In the 2002–2003 academic year, 586,323 foreigners studied in the United States; by contrast, only 160,920 U.S. citizens studied abroad in the 2001–2002 academic year. During the same period, there were 332,298 Asian students in the United States but only 10,901 U.S. students studying in Asia. Figure 8.4 shows the disproportionate ratio of foreign students from the five major Asian economies examined in the United States to U.S. students studying in these economies. The ratio between these figures is 31:1 (264,856 to 8,510). What a sharp contrast!

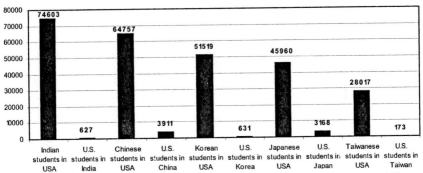

Figure 8.4.   Foreign Students of Five Asian Economies in the United States vs. U.S. Students in These Five Asian Economies

Note: The figures on five Asian economies are for the 2002–2003 academic year while the figures on the USA are for the 2001–2002 academic year.
Source: Compiled by the author from: International Institute of Education (IIE), *Open Doors*, 2003.

• Aside from centralized control of the school system and measures such as increased expenditures on education, allowing choice of schools, creating smaller classes, setting higher standards, and instituting merit pay, another critical factor affects the Asian experience of education: internal motivation and high expectations. When Asian children from China, Japan, Korea, Taiwan, and India are placed in the troubled U.S. education system, they still do well and, more often than not, rise to the top of their class in most subject areas. Four recent examples support this claim. The first example draws on the Siemens Westinghouse Math, Science, and Technology Competition—the nation's leading research-based science and mathematics competition for high school students. Of the 16 national finalists in its 2002 competition held on December 9, 2002, 6 were Chinese Americans, accounting for 37.5 percent.[12] Moreover, of the 19 national finalists in its 2003 competition held on December 9, 2003, 2 were Chinese Americans and the grand prize, for the first time, was taken by a Chinese American, a senior at Stuyvesant High School in Manhattan, New York City.[13]

The second example observes the Dupont Challenge Essay Award Program, one of the foremost student science and technology prize programs in the United States and Canada. Sponsored by DuPont in cooperation with General Learning Communications and the National Science Teachers' Association (NSTA), the Science Essay Awards Program is a widely recognized and respected student science and technology essay competition. Over 10,000 junior and senior high school students from all the parts of the United States and Canada participated in its 2003 program. Among the 48 honorable mentions awarded in Senior Division (grades 10, 11, and 12), one-sixth went to Chinese Americans. Further, the first-place, second-place, and third-place winners were all Chinese Americans.[14]

The third example looks at the United States Presidential Scholars Program, established in 1964 by executive order of the President to recognize and honor some of the nation's most distinguished graduating high school seniors. In 1979 the program was extended to recognize students who demonstrate exceptional talent in the visual, creative, and performing arts. Each year up to 141 students are named as Presidential Scholars, one of the nation's highest honors for high school students. The scholars represent excellence in education and the promise of greatness in young people. In recent years, the proportion of Chinese Americans winning the

Presidential Scholars medallions has notably increased. In 2000, 9 Chinese Americans were named as Presidential Scholars. In 2001 and 2002, their numbers increased to 14 and 17, respectively. In 2003, their number greatly increased to 32, accounting for 23 percent of the total 137 awarded Presidential Scholars medallions. This percentage is very high considering the fact that Chinese Americans accounted for less than 1 percent of the United States' population![15]

The College Board has provided us with the fourth example, shown in figure 8.5. According to a recent report of the College Board, Asian American students have always had the highest level in math scores in the ten-year period between 1993 and 2003. Of particular notice is that overall verbal scores were aided by a strong showing from Asian American SAT takers, whose mean verbal scores were in 2003, for the first time, higher than the national mean. Asian American SAT takers improved their average scores on the verbal section by seven points from 2002.

Such success derives from internal motivation on the part of schoolchildren and their parents and relatives. Unfortunately, this motivation is absent from the sociological and psychological makeup of most American children and families. Asian students usually demonstrate a stronger belief in the value of efforts over innate ability in school performance while their U.S. counterparts believe more in innate ability as the driving force behind achievement. That is one of the main reasons why Asian students outperform American students.

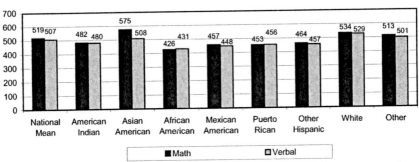

Figure 8.5.   SAT Scores Vary by Race/Ethnicity (Data for SAT Takers in the Class of 2003)

Source: "SAT® Verbal and Math Scores Up Significantly as a Record-breaking Number of Students Take the Test Average Math Score at Highest Level in More than 35 Years," the College Board, August 26, 2003. http://www.collegeboard.com/press/article/0,3183,26858,00.html (3 Dec. 2003).

- Students' beliefs about learning are not developed in a vacuum. They are very much influenced by the beliefs of their parents, peers, and teachers, as well as the social and cultural environment in which they are growing up.[16] The tradition of respecting teachers and honoring education derived from historical Confuciandom has played a great role in forming a society devoted to learning in Asian nations. In such learning environments, the government and individuals usually grant education first priority. Bearing this tradition, a nation with lower per capita GNP can enroll more students in schools than other nations with higher per capita GNP; families sacrifice their own standard of living to educate their children, and parents sell even their only ox to pay for school fees. This argument is also supported by the recent study made by the OECD and UNESCO. On July 1, 2003, the OECD and UNESCO jointly announced in their published survey of 15-year-olds in 43 countries held in 2000 that higher average spending per student tends to be associated with higher average performance of students, but does not guarantee it. For example, Italy spends about twice as much per student as Korea, but whereas Korea is among the best performing countries in all of the three literacy areas (reading, mathematics, and science) assessed, Italy performs significantly below the OECD average.[17]

Many similar exceptions to the overall relationship between spending per student and student performance suggest that, as much as spending on educational institutions is a necessary prerequisite for the provision of high-quality education, spending alone is not sufficient to achieve high levels of outcomes. This becomes most apparent in the United States, which spends much more per student than any of the five nations and economies examined, but whose students' performance lags behind those of these nations and economies. Factors underlying the relationship between money spent per student and students' performance include the effectiveness with which resources are used.

Although I cite many examples from the education systems in Asian nations and economies, I don't expect Americans simply to import Asian culture. Instead, I hope that Americans will draw on some Asian practices and build up a society devoted to learning, in which everyone manifests a love for education. Only in this way can the nation and individuals solve the educational quality problem.

- Discerning educational vitality requires a comparative judgment. To understand better the strengths and weaknesses of the American educational process, we must look beyond the United States to other societies that are also attempting to realize quality schooling. By studying education in other regions, alternative approaches to teaching and learning may be discovered. There already exist research agencies in these Asian nations and economies that watch and trace the education and science and technology reforms and developmental trends in developed countries including the United States. Such research will be an important strategy for keeping the U.S. competitive in science and technology. I would recommend that the U.S. create permanent research agencies or positions affiliated either with the Department of Education, the National Science Foundation (NSF), the National Academy of Sciences, the Council on Competitiveness, or Building Engineering and Science Talent (BEST) so as to provide up-to-date information on the changes and trends of other nations and economies to Congress and the executive branch, which, based on the information collected, can make corresponding policy adjustments in a timely manner. Aside from K–12 education, higher education, and international education in these five Asian nations and economies examined, we can extend our research to other areas such as the comparison of the S&T workforce and S&T and R&D progress. I hope to contribute to such research in the future.

NOTES

1. The employment-based preferences consist of five categories: priority workers; professionals with advanced degrees or aliens with exceptional ability; skilled workers, professionals (without advanced degrees), and needed unskilled workers; special immigrants (e.g., ministers, religious workers, and employees of the U.S. government abroad; and employment creation immigrants or "investors.")

2. U.S. Immigration and Naturalization Services (INS), *2000 Statistical Yearbook* (Washington, DC: 2000).

3. Jean M., Johnson, "Human Resource Contributions to U.S. Science and Engineering from China," *Issue Brief,* NSF 01-311 (Arlington, VA: NSF, January 12, 2001).

4. Zhili Chen, (Minister of Education, China), *Speech* at Annual Working Conference of MOE (Beijing, China: December 26, 2002) <www.china.org.cn/chinese/OP-c/252999.htm> (30 Dec. 2002), and MOE, China, *Educational Sta-*

tistical Report, Vol. 26, No. 1, February 27, 2003 <http://www.moe.edu.cn/stat/tjgongbao/report_2002.doc> (18 Nov. 2003).

5. U.S. Department of Education, *Digest of Education Statistics 2002*.

6. National Science Board (NSB), *Science and Engineering Indicators—2002*, Vol. 1 (Arlington, VA: National Science Foundation, 2002), 2–41.

7. Harold W. Stevenson and James W. Stigler, *The Learning Gap* (New York, NY: Summit Books, 1992), 13.

8. Carol Innerst, "High School Seniors Land in Math, Science Cellar," *Washington Times*, 25 February 1998, A1.

9. United Nations Children's Fund (UNICEF), "A League Table of Educational Disadvantage in Rich Nations," *Innocenti Report Card No. 4*, November 2002, UNICEF Innocenti Research, Florence.

10. Jay Mathews, "China to Help Create Classes for U.S. Schools," *the Washington Post*, 6 December 2003, p. A3.

11. Bruce Alberts, *International Science: What's In It For The United States*, Statement of the President, National Academy of Sciences before the Committee on Science, U.S. House of Representatives, March 25, 1998.

12. Siemens Foundation, Web: available at <http://www.siemens-foundation.org/science/default.html> (28 Dec. 2002).

13. Ellen Yan, "Memorable Prize: Queens science whiz wins $100G scholarship," *New York Newsday*, December 9, 2003, (9 Dec. 2003).

14. Chinese World Journal, available at <http://www.chineseworld.com/publish/today/11_0900.4w/a/4was(030426)04_tb.htm> (26 April 2003).

15. Xinmu Tan, "Chinese Ambassador to the USA Encouraging Chinese Americans Winning the Presidential Scholars Medallions to Study the Chinese Culture," *Xinhua News Agenc*, 26 June 2003, available at <http://www5.chinesenewsnet.com/MainNews/NorthAmerica/062620031813L:400165499.htm> (8 July 2003).

16. Andrew C. Porter and Adam Gamoran, "Introduction," in *Methodological Advances in Cross-National Surveys of Educational Achievement*, ed. Porter, Andrew C. and Gamoran, Adam (Washington, DC: the National Academies Press, 2002), 122.

17. OECD/UNESCO, *Study Identifies Regional Disparities in Student Performance*, available at <http://www.oecd.org/EN/document/0,,EN-document-4-nodirectorate-no-12-42475-4,00.html> (1 July 2003).

Selected Bibliography

Academic Degrees Committee under the State Council. China, June 2002. http://www.moe.edu.cn/moe-dept/xueweiban/2 (accessed Dec. 22, 2002).

Adams, Don and Esther E. Gottlieb. *Education and Social Change in Korea.* New York, NY: Garland, 1993.

Alberts, Bruce. "International Science: What's in It for the United States." Statement of the President, National Academy of Sciences before the Committee on Science, U.S. House of Representatives, Washington, DC, March 25, 1998.

Arnove, Robert F. "A Comparison of the Chinese and Indian Education Systems," *Comparative Education Review* 28 no. 3, (1984): 378–401.

Cao, Xiaonan. "Debating 'Brain Drain' in the Context of Globalization," *Compare* 26 no. 3, (1996): 269–85.

The Center for Institutional Data Analysis and Exchange (C-IDEA). *SMET Retention Report, 1999–2000.* Norman: University of Oklahoma.

Chabbott, Colette and Emerson J. Elliott, eds. *Understanding Others, Educating Ourselves.* Washington, DC: National Academies Press, 2003.

Council of Chief State School Officers (CCSSO). *Key State Education Policies on K–12 Education: 2000.* Washington, DC. http://www.ccsso.org/pdfs/Key State2000.pdf (accessed Jan. 21, 2003).

Chen, Guoliang. "Analysis of China's Educational Finance during the Ninth Five-Year National Economic Development," *China Education and Research Network.* http://www.edu.cn/20021111/3071941_1.shtml (accessed Nov. 16, 2002).

Chen, Shun-fen. "Taiwan." In *International Higher Education: An Encyclopedia,* ed. Philip G. Altbach, 550–51. New York, NY: Garland 1991.

———. "Taiwan." In *Asian Higher Education: An International Handbook and Reference Guide,* ed. Gerard A. Postiglione and Grace C. L. Mak, 345–58. Westport, CT: Greenwood Press, 1997.

Chen, Zhili, (minister of education of China). "Historical Achievements in Chinese Education." Speech made at the Chinese central government conference, Beijing, China: September 24, 2002. http://edu.enorth.com.cn/system/2002/09/25/000425433.shtml (accessed Sept. 27, 2002).

———. "Seven Progresses in Reform and Development in Chinese Education." Speech at Annual Working Conference of MOE, Beijing, China: (December 26, 2002). www.china.org.cn/chinese/OP-c/252999.htm (accessed Dec. 27, 2002).

China.com. http://edu.china.com/zh_cn/1055/20020103/10184476.html (accessed Jan. 3, 2002).

China.org.cn. *China: Facts and Figures 2002*, http://www.china.org.cn/english/shuzi-en/en-shuzi/index.htm (accessed Dec. 25, 2002).

china.org.cn. www.china.org.cn (accessed Oct. 12, 2002).

China Scholars Abroad. June 5, 1998. www.chisa.edu.cn (accessed July 2,1998).

China Scholars Abroad. October 7, 2002. www.chisa.edu.cn (accessed Nov. 12, 2002).

China Scholars Abroad. June 12, 2003. http://www.chisa.edu.cn/newchisa/web/2/2003-06-12/news_2233.asp (accessed June 12, 2003).

China Scholars Abroad. vol. 513, November 25, 2002. http://www.chisa.edu.cn/week/513/513_30_7419.asp (accessed Dec. 14, 2002).

Chinese World Journal. April 14, 2002. www.chineseworld.com/publish/today/11_0900.4w/m/4wms(020415)13_tb.htm (accessed April 15, 2002).

Chinese World Journal. April 26, 2003. http://www.chineseworld.com/publish/today/11_0900.4w/a/4was(030426)04_tb.htm (accessed April 26, 2003).

Clark, Burton R., ed. *The Research Foundations of Graduate Education: Germany, Britain, France, United States, Japan*. Berkeley: University of California Press, 1993.

Clark, Burton R. *Places of Inquiry: Research and Advanced Education in Modern Universities*. Berkeley: University of California Press, 1995.

Cultural Division of Taipei Economic and Cultural Representative Office in the United States. *Cultural and Educational Digest*, June 1998.

Cummings, William K. *Education and Equality in Japan*. Princeton, NJ: Princeton University Press, 1980.

Dunson, Marlies A., "From Research to Practice and Back Again: TIMSS as a Tool for Educational Improvement." *Policy Briefs*. Graduate School of Education, University of Pennsylvania. RB-30-April 2000.

Greenspan, A. "Remarks of the Chairman." Board of Governors of the Federal Reserve System to the National Governors' Association 92nd Annual Meeting. Washington, DC, July 11, 2000.

Hood, Christopher P. *Japanese Education Reform: Nakasone's Legacy.* New York, NY: Routledge, 2001.

Innerst, Carol, "High School Seniors Land in Math, Science Cellar." *Washington Times,* February 25, 1998: A1.

Institute of International Education (IIE), *Open Doors,* 2001, 2002, and 2003.

International Mathematics Olympiad (IMO). http://imo.math.ca/results/TCBY .html (accessed Dec. 14, 2002).

Jackson, Shirley Ann. "The Quiet Crisis: Falling Short in Producing American Scientific and Technical Talent." *Building Engineering and Science Talent.* http://www.bestworkforce.org/publications.htm (accessed Sept. 10, 2002).

Jiangnan Times, "Reform Curriculum for Senior High Schools Will be Finalized: Increase Proportion of Selective Courses and Adopt Credit System." February 13, 2003. http://www.china.org.cn/chinese/EDU-c/275934.htm (accessed Feb. 15, 2003).

Johnson, Jean M. "Collaboration in S&T Information Exchange between the United States and China." Paper presented at CIES 2000 Conference, San Antonio, Texas. March 7–11, 2000.

Johnson, Jean M. "Human Resource Contributions to U.S. Science and Engineering from China." *Issue Brief,* NSF, Jan. 12, 2001.

Khadria, Binod "Case-Study of the Indian Scientific Diaspora," in *Scientific Diasporas: How Can Developing Countries Benefit from Their Expatriates and Engineers?* vol. 2, ed. Institut de Recherche Pour le Developpement. Paris, France: IRD Editions, 2003.

Khadria, Binod. "Divides of Development-Underdevelopment Relationship in Higher Education and the Policy for Brain Drain." In *Education, Development, and Underdevelopment,* ed. Sureshchandra Shukla and Rekha Kaul, 175–98. New Delhi, India: Sage Publications, 1998.

Kitamura, Kazuyuki. "Japan." In *International Higher Education: An Encyclopedia,* vol. 1, ed. Philip G. Altbach. New York, NY: Garland, 1991.

Law, Wing-wah. "Fortress State, Cultural Continuities, and Economic Change: Higher Education in Mainland China and Taiwan." *Comparative Education* 32 no. 3 (1996): 377–93.

———. "The Role of the State in Higher Education Reform: Mainland China and Taiwan." *Comparative Education Review* 39, no. 3 (1995): 322–55.

Li, Chen-ching. "Returning Home after Studying in the USA: Reverse Brain Drain in Taiwan." *Cultural & Educational Digest* (1995a): 20–24.

Lin, Jing. *Social Transformation and Private Education in China.* Westport, CT: Praeger, 1999.

Lu, Mu-lin, (vice minister of education of ROC), "Higher Education Reform in the Republic of China." Speech delivered during his visit to Latvia in 2001. http://140.111.1.22/english/index.htm (accessed Oct. 23, 2002).

McGinn, Noel F., Donald R Snodgrass, Yung Bong Kim, Shin-bok Kim, and Quee-young Kim. *Education and Development in Korea*. Council on East Asian Studies, Harvard University. Cambridge, MA: Harvard University Press, 1980.

Ministry of Education and Human Resources Development (MOEHRD), Korea. *Education in Korea: 2001–2002*. (2002). http://www.moe.go.kr/English/ (accessed Nov. 16, 2002).

Ministry of Education and Human Resources Development (MOEHRD), Korea. *Education in Korea: 2002–2003*. (2003).

Ministry of Education and Human Resources Development (MOEHRD), Korea. *2001 Brief Statistics of Korean Education*, 2002. http://www.moe.go.kr/ English/ (accessed Dec. 12, 2002).

Ministry of Education (MOE) (PRC). *A Brief Account of Education in the People's Republic of China*. November 2000.

Ministry of Education (MOE) (PRC). *Basic Education in China*, 1996.

Ministry of Education (MOE) (PRC). *Education in China*, July 2002.

Ministry of Education (MOE) (PRC). *Educational Statistical Report* 26 no. 1, February 27, 2003 http://www.moe.edu.cn/stat/tjgongbao/report_2002.doc (accessed Nov. 18, 2003).

Ministry of Education (MOE) (PRC). *Educational Statistics Yearbook of China 1994 and 2000*, Beijing, China: People's Education Press, 1994 and 2001.

Ministry of Education (MOE) (PRC). *Statistical Report of National Education Development in 1998, 1999, 2000 and 2001*. 2002.

Ministry of Education (MOE) (ROC). *Education Statistical Indicators, Republic of China (ROC)*, 2001 and 2002.

Ministry of Education (MOE) (ROC). *2001 Education in the Republic of China (ROC)*, 2001.

Ministry of Education (MOE) (ROC). *Educational Statistics of the Republic of China (ROC)*, 2000 and 2003.

Ministry of Education (MOE) (ROC). *2001 Education in the Republic of China (ROC)*, 2002.

Ministry of Education, Culture, Sports, Science, and Technology (MEXT), Japan. *Japanese Government Policies in Education, Culture, Sports, Science, and Technology 2001: Educational Reform for the 21st Century*, 2002.

Ministry of Education, Culture, Sports, Science, and Technology (MEXT), Japan. *The Role of the Ministry of Education, Culture, Sports, Science, and Technology*, 2002.

Ministry of Education, Culture, Sports, Science, and Technology (MEXT), Japan. *Statistics*, 2001. Tokyo. http://www.mext.go.jp/english/statist/xls/168-169-1.xls (accessed Oct. 10, 2002).

Morris, Paul. "Asia's Four Little Tigers: A Comparison of the Role of Education in Their Development." *Comparative Education* 32 no. 1 (1996): 95–109.

National Center for Education Statistics. *Digest of Education Statistics 2000*. (NCES 2001-034). Washington, DC: U.S. Department of Education, Office of Educational Research and Improvement, 2001.

National Science Board (NSB). *Science and Engineering Indicators 1998, 2000, and 2002*. Arlington, VA: National Science Foundation, 2002.

National Research Council. *Everybody Counts: A Report to the Nation on the Future of Mathematics Education*. Washington, DC: National Academies Press, 1989.

Newsweekly, July 31, 2000. http://www.china.org.cn/chinese/9837.htm (accessed Aug. 5, 2000).

OECD/UNESCO. *Study Identifies Regional Disparities in Student Performance*. July 1, 2003. http://www.oecd.org/EN/document/0,,EN-document-4-nodirect-orate-no-12-42475-4,00.html (accessed July 5, 2003).

Okano, Kaori and Motonori Tsuchiya. *Education in Contemporary Japan: Inequality and Diversity*. Cambridge, UK: Cambridge University Press, 1999.

Paige, Rod (secretary, U.S. Dept. of Education). Address given in Washington, DC, April 2002.

Person Jr., Willie and Daryl E. Chubin. "Scientists and Engineers for the New Millennium: Renewing the Human Resource." *Commissions in Science and Technology*, 2001.

Porter, Andrew C. and Gamoran, Adam. Introduction to *Methodological Advances in Cross-National Surveys of Educational Achievement*, ed. Andrew C. Porter and Adam Gamoran, 3–23. Washington, DC: National Academies Press, 2002.

Porter, Michael E. *The Competitive Advantage of Nations*. New York, NY: Free Press, 1990.

Presidential Scholars Program. 2003. http://www.ed.gov/offices/OIIA/Recognition/PSP/about.html (accessed July 16, 2003).

Public Agenda Online. *Reality Check 2001*. New York, 2001. http://www.public agenda.org/specials/rc2001/reality6.htm (accessed Nov. 5, 2002).

Rausch, Lawrence M. *Asia's New High Tech Competitors*, U.S. National Science Foundation, NSF 95-309. http://www.nsf.gov/sbe/srs/s4495/report.htm (accessed Nov. 14, 2002).

Research, Reference and Training Division (RRTD). *India 2000: A Reference Annual*. Ministry of Information and Broadcasting Government of India, 2000.

Schmidt, W. H., C. C. McKnight, and S. A. Raizen. *A Splintered Vision: An Investigation of U.S. Science and Mathematics Education.* Boston: Kluwer, 1997.

Shukla, Sureshchandra. "India." In *International Higher Education: An Encyclopedia*, vol. 1, ed. Philip G. Altbach, 467–77. New York, NY: Garland, 1991.

Siemens Foundation. http://www.siemens-foundation.org/science/default.html (accessed Dec. 15, 2002).

Smith, Douglas C. *Middle Education in the Middle Kingdom: The Chinese Junior High School in Modern Taiwan.* Westport, CT: Praeger, 1997.

State Statistical Bureau, China. *China Statistical Yearbook 1995.* Beijing, China: China Statistical Publishing House, 1995.

State Statistical Bureau, China. *China Statistical Yearbook 2002.* Beijing, China: China Statistical Publishing House, 2002.

Stevenson, Harold W. and James W. Stigler. *The Learning Gap.* New York, NY: Summit Books, 1992.

Stigler, J., and J. Hiebert. *The Teaching Gap.* New York, NY: Free Press, 1999.

Stigler, J. W., P. Gonzales, T. Kanaka, S. Knoll, and A. Serrano. *The TIMSS Videotape Classroom Study: Methods and Findings from an Exploratory Research Project on Eighth-Grade Mathematics Instruction in Germany, Japan, and the United States.* NCES 1999-074. National Center for Education Statistics, Office of Educational Research and Improvement, 1999. Washington, DC: U.S. Department of Education http://nces.ed.gov/pubs99/timssvid/index.html (accessed Feb. 2, 2003).

Tilak, Jandhyala B. G. "Financing Higher Education in India." In *Higher Education Reform in India: Experience and Perspectives*, ed. Philip G Altbach and Suma Chitnis, 41–83. New Delhi, India: Sage, 1993.

Tsuneyoshi, Ryoko. *The Japanese Model of Schooling: Comparisons with the United States.* New York, NY: Routledge, 2001.

United Nations Children's Fund (UNICEF). "A League Table of Educational Disadvantage in Rich Nations." *Innocenti Report Card No. 4*, November 2002. Florence: UNICEF Innocenti Research.

U.S. Department of Education, *Digest of Education Statistics 1996, 1997, and 2001.*

U.S. Department of Education, *A Nation at Risk*, 1983.

U.S. Department of Education, National Center for Education Statistics. *Pursuing Excellence*, by Lois Peak. Washington, DC: U.S. Government Printing Office, 1996.

U.S. Immigration and Naturalization Services (INS), *1998, 1999, and 2000 Statistical Yearbook.*

Valent, Jasper J. and Gerald L. Gutek. *Education and Society in India and Thailand*. Washington, DC: University Press of America, 1977.

Wang, Pichang. "The Study of the Latest Trends of Overseas Chinese Students." *China Scholars Abroad* 132 no. 2 (2001).

Weidman, John C. and Namgi Park. *Higher Education in Korea: Tradition and Adaptation*. New York, NY: Falmer Press, 2000.

Wenxuecity.com, 2002. www.wenxuecity.com/BBSview.asp?SubID = newsdirect&MsgID = 9040 (accessed Feb. 5, 2002).

———. www.wenxuecity.com/BBSview.asp?SubID = newsdirect&MsgID = 10375 (accessed April 15, 2002).

World Bank. *Primary Education in India*. The International Bank for Reconstruction and Development/The World Bank, 1997.

World Bank, *Statistics*, 2002.

Wray, Harry. *Japanese and American Education: Attitudes and Practice*. Westport, CT: Bergin & Garvey, 1999.

Xinhua News Agency. 2003. http://www5.chinesenewsnet.com/MainNews/NorthAmerica/062620031813L:400165499.htm (accessed June 26, 2003).

Xinhua News Agency. *China to Expand Senior High School Education*. May 20, 2003. http://www.china.org.cn/english/2003/May/65039.htm (accessed May 22, 2003).

Yamamoto, Shinichi. "Graduate Education Reform and International Mobility of Scientists in Japan and Related Information for Korea." In *Graduate Education Reform in Europe, Asia, and the Americas and International Mobility of Scientists and Engineers: Proceedings of an NSF Workshop*. Arlington, VA: U.S. National Science Foundation, April 2000.

Zhou, Ji, (vice minister of education of China). "Speech." *Xiaoxiang Morning News*, Changsha, China: October 12, 2002.

Index

About the Author

Yugui Guo received his Ph.D. in International and Comparative Education from the State University of New York, Buffalo. He is currently an independent scholar and a consultant to Community of Science, Inc.